An Eclectic Guide to
TREES
East of the Rockies

An Eclectic Guide to

TREES

East of the Rockies

GLEN BLOUIN

The BOSTON
MILLS PRESS

Cataloguing in Publication Data

Blouin, Glen
   An eclectic guide to trees east of the Rockies

Includes bibliographical references and index.
ISBN 1-55046-351-9

1. Trees – Canada. 2. Trees – United States. I. Title

QK110.B56 2001   582.16'0971
2001-930108-1

Copyright © 2001 Glen Blouin

05 04 03 02 01   1 2 3 4 5

Published in 2001 by
Boston Mills Press
132 Main Street
Erin, Ontario N0B 1T0
Tel 519-833-2407
Fax 519-833-2195
e-mail books@bostonmillspress.com
www.bostonmillspress.com

An affiliate of
Stoddart Publishing Co. Limited
895 Don Mills Road
400 2 Park Centre
Toronto, Ontario
Canada M3C 1W3
Tel 416-445-3333
Fax 416-445-5967
e-mail gdsinc@genpub.com

Distributed in Canada by
General Distribution Services Limited
325 Humber College Boulevard
Toronto, Canada M9W 7C3
Orders 1-800-387-0141 Ontario & Quebec
Orders 1-800-387-0172 NW Ontario
   && other provinces
e-mail customer.service@genpub.com

Distributed in the United States by
General Distribution Services Inc.
PMB 128, 4500 Witmer Industrial Estates
Niagara Falls, New York 14305-1386
Toll-free 1-800-805-1083
Toll-free fax 1-800-481-6207
e-mail gdsinc@genpub.com
www.genpub.com

Design by Mary Firth
Cover design by Gillian Stead
Photographs by Glen Blouin
Printed in Canada

THE CANADA COUNCIL | LE CONSEIL DES ARTS
FOR THE ARTS | DU CANADA
SINCE 1957 | DEPUIS 1957

We acknowledge for their financial support of our publishing program the Canada Council, the Ontario Arts Council, and the Government of Canada through the Book Publishing Industry Development Program (BPIDP).

Contents

To my wife Michelle, for her support and patience, to Stephanie, my environmentalist, and Phillip, my wanderer, and to my mother, Agnes, still going strong at eighty-six, who was always there for me, and still is.

In memory of my close friend, a friend to all who knew him, Hugues Roy — I have planted a tree for you, Hugues.

Acknowledgments

I would like to thank the following people for providing information or direction during the course of my research: Les Benedict, Harry Bombay, Roxanne Comeau, Ken Cox, Mary Firth, Kathy Fraser, Ralph Getson, Don Gordon, Girvan Harrison, Dave Holmes, Brigitte Lafond, Doug Larson, Richard Lipman, Lisa Ludford, Rick Mah, Ellen Nollman, Paul Peddle, Laura Poppy, Doug Stokke, Bill Tikkela, Dale Wilson, and Wayne Young. Thanks as well to the librarians at the following institutions: Agriculture Canada, Ottawa, ON; Canadian Museum of Civilization, Hull, QC; Environment Canada, Hull, QC; Natural Resources Canada, Ottawa, ON; New Brunswick Museum Library and Archives, Saint John, NB; University of New Brunswick Science Library, Fredericton, NB; and National Agriculture Library, Washington, DC.

Special thanks to my wife, Michelle, for reviewing drafts and screening photographs; my daughter, Stephanie, for reviewing drafts, screening photographs, coaching me in my hopeless computer illiteracy, and compiling the two bibliographies; Michael DePencier, fellow tree lover and conservationist, for his support and encouragement; Gary Satenstein, Janice Payne, and Ernest Rivet (you each know what you have done); John Denison at Boston Mills Press, for his kind cooperation; and two of the most respected foresters in Canada — Jim Cayford, for scrutinizing and critiquing drafts of nineteen chapters, and John Torunski, for reviewing two difficult chapters, and providing his usual clear and concise insights.

No government, private industry, or foundation funding was received for the research, writing, or photography of this book.

Foreword

I enroled in forestry at university because I love trees. And I mean everything about trees, including their color, shape, form, history, ecology, biology, uses, and cultural significance.

Now, no matter where I travel in the world, I have "friends" everywhere in the form of trees — some of them analogous to Canadian species, some completely different. While everyone else is taking in other aspects of the landscape, I find myself gazing at the trees, individually and collectively, reflecting on the forces that brought them into being, and speculating about how a particular forest will change in the future. Sometimes I wonder who is gazing at whom. Because just as we humans watch trees "come and go," so also do they witness our brief time on this earth, often outliving us as individuals and even as generations.

This thoughtful book by Glen Blouin nicely explores the broader significance of tree species found east of the Rockies in Canada and the United States. It expands on all that interesting information that is only touched upon through a sentence or two in standard field guides and identification texts. So we learn about how each species relates to landscaping and planting, insects and disease, wildlife and native people, home workshop and industrial uses. The history of exploitation, which accounts for the current status and distribution of each species, is particularly interesting to me as a forest conservationist. And Glen's "relevant digressions" use species characteristics to illuminate larger ecological lessons. Every forest is a treasure house of such knowledge, if we only have a companion such as this book to help us gain access.

Read and enjoy *An Eclectic Guide to Trees East of the Rockies,* then take a walk in the woods.

Monte Hummel,
President,
World Wildlife Fund Canada

Introduction

The landscape, and the forests, are at the centre of not only our culture, but our self-image.

Robert Fulford, 1991

Trees are our living legacy. They tell the story of our past, reflect our present, and may indeed augur our future. We have inherited them from previous generations — a gift — but we in no sense own them. We are their custodians, their stewards, their caretakers. Yet they would survive just as well, perhaps better, without us. If we are wise, we will allow them to pass to future generations, so that they too may reap the benefits, the treasures, they have provided us.

Our history in North America is inextricably interwoven with trees and forests — what we have done with them, and what they have done for us. Since the migration of our Native people south of the treeline, our relationship with trees, with the forest, has defined who we are as people. It is reflected in the works of countless poets, artists, novelists, and musicians.

The chronicles of the earliest European explorers, to a one, express their awe of the natural wealth and beauty of this newly discovered land. Soon, with the help of the Native people who had migrated here long before, they learned of the bounty the forest held.

* * * * *

This book is about the trees that grow naturally east of the Rocky Mountains. Why not the whole continent? Because the Rockies are the dividing line between two very distinct forest ecosystems. West of the mountains, the mix of tree species changes dramatically.

The scope of this investigation is biological rather than geopolitical. It is neither a "Native Trees of Canada," nor a "Native Trees of the United States." Trees are apolitical characters — they do not recognize international boundaries. They grow where they are comfortable, where the climate and soils suit them. The entire range of each tree is considered, covering most of northern Canada, southern Canada east of the Rockies, and the north central and northeastern states. For some species, the range extends as far afield as Florida and Texas and Alaska.

In these pages, each species is first examined by its components, as a field guide to identification. You can explore a little of its history, and gain some insights into its niche in the forest ecosystem. Learn its value as habitat — food and shelter — for a variety of wildlife. Enter into the bug world and look at some of the common critters that feed on each species. See how we use living trees — as ornamentals and shade trees, as windbreaks and shelterbelts, as sources of food and medicine — and delve into some of the myriad uses we make of them when harvested, many of which we take for granted. And then look at the wood itself, to see whether it is suitable for your bookshelf project or for carving a duck decoy.

In the course of your explorations, you may find you have detoured off the beaten path on what I call relevant digressions, to more deeply probe some topic — from Christmas trees to clearcutting, maple syrup to prairie shelterbelts, alien species to aerial spraying, and from forest succession to old-growth forests.

the identification page

At the top of each identification page, the most widely accepted English name is featured center stage. Below it, in parentheses, is the universally recognized scientific or Latin name. At the risk of giving purists anxiety attacks, author citations — abbreviated versions of the names of the botanists who officially named the species — have been omitted, as they are not relevant to the average reader.

The left column lists the other common English names, and the right the common French names. The variances are mostly regional. For example, balsam fir is called "balsam" in northern Ontario, "fir" in New Brunswick, and "var" on Prince Edward Island. Similarly, in French, spruce is "épinette" in most of Quebec, and "prusse" in Acadian areas of the Maritimes. These regionalisms underscore the value of the Latin names, which transcend not only regional terms, but language as well. Out of respect for the people who had named all the trees long before European botanists set foot on the North American continent, a Native name is listed for each species, from Beothuk to Shawnee.

Each species or group of species is described by its leaf, needle, or scale; male, female, or perfect flower; winter twig and buds; fruit, cone, nut, berry, or seeds; young and old bark; and wood characteristics including heartwood, sapwood, and annual growth rings. With the added help of the photographs, the reader should be reasonably comfortable with field identification.

Wherever possible, I have avoided technical botanical terms, but without, I hope, sacrificing scientific accuracy. For example, a petiole is called a leaf stalk, and a cordate leaf base is simply described as heart-shaped. For the technical terms that were unavoidable, a glossary appears on page 270.

At the bottom of the identification page, tree heights, diameters, and life expectancies are listed, averaged across the species range. In addition to inherited good genes, differences in site, elevation, and climate are major factors that influence tree size. Sugar maple in the Maritimes and Manitoba maple on the prairies and plains tend to be shorter than specimens in southern Quebec, Ontario, or Michigan.

Many deciduous species reach their optimum size in the Ohio Valley, but white spruce and jack pine grow tallest in the northern prairie provinces. Similarly, age ranges cited are occasionally exceeded by individual trees or groups of trees, especially when they grow in unusual environments. White cedars on the Niagara Escarpment may live three to four times the "normal" age for the species.

ornamental and shade trees

Also examined is each tree's potential as an ornamental or shade tree, its strengths and weaknesses, and the sites and soils where it performs best.

The benefits of urban trees are many. Aside from their obvious aesthetic contribution to properties and communities in general, and the enhanced quality of life for urban and near-urban residents, they reduce noise and sight pollution, ensure privacy, absorb carbon dioxide and pollutants, filter the air we breathe, release oxygen, lower energy costs, moderate the climate, abate or deflect wind, reduce storm runoff, and provide habitat for wildlife. It has been suggested that trees raise the resale value of a home or a property by 5 to 20 percent.

Use of our native species in landscaping is not a new concept. But for the past several centuries it has been overshadowed by an emphasis on imported or exotic species and on horticultural varieties. Twenty years ago, you would have been hard pressed to find a garden center that carried a varied line of native species. Fortunately this is changing, as more people today are recognizing the value of encouraging our native trees and shrubs around the home and urban environment.

There are essentially three options for planting trees and shrubs: purchase young trees from a reputable garden center or nursery, transplant young trees from the wild, or plant from seed. The emphasis in this book is on the latter. This is a matter of personal preference — many people may wish to get speedier results by planting nursery stock or wildlings that have a few years' head start.

The advantage of planting from seed, aside from cost saving, is the family educational value and satisfaction in finding parent trees, gathering the seeds, sowing them, and watching them germinate and grow into healthy young trees. The emphasis here is also on fall sowing, more or less the way nature does it, eliminating the need for cold storage or stratification of seed over winter before spring planting.

The third alternative, transplanting young wildlings, combines low cost with faster results. However, if the tree is not growing on your own property, it is absolutely imperative to ask the owner's permission digging it up. Otherwise, it is considered theft.

common insects and diseases

Insects and diseases, if not introduced from abroad, are a natural part of the functioning of our forest ecosystem. Insects prey upon leaves or cones or shoots, and they in turn become prey to parasites, other insects, birds, and so on up the line. But this may be of little consolation if one's lovely mountain ash on the front lawn turns leafless in mid-summer, or if the 100-year-old elm that provides the charm and character to one's property suddenly withers and dies. I've looked at some of the more common insects and diseases, how they go about their business, and what we can do to minimize their damage. My own bias against chemical pesticides — although I admit to having used them as a last resort — will likely show through.

The insects and diseases described are by no means a complete list. The books bibliography at the back of this book cites a number of excellent publications that are far more thorough and comprehensive.

wildlife habitat

The interaction of trees and wildlife is fascinating. Trees and shrubs of all species provide food and homes for nature's critters, and they return the favor by pollinating flowers, spreading seeds, consuming insects, fertilizing the soil, and by the countless other activities we have only begun to understand. I've looked at birds and their nesting and food preferences, rodents from bats to beavers, and the larger mammals that rely upon tree-browsing for summer and winter sustenance.

trees and Native people

Native people were custodians of the forest long before Europeans arrived. They generally lived in harmony with nature, taking what they needed and leaving the rest.

Many tribes were simply hunters, fishers, and gatherers. Some were nomadic. Others had seasonal settlements — often at the oceanside in summer and in the forest in winter. Those who practiced agriculture had more permanent roots, clearing forests for their settlements, gathering firewood for cooking and heat, and cultivating the subsistence farms that fed their families. The Native people who had the greatest impact were those who burned extensive tracts of forests or underbrush for hunting, travel, or defense.

Because their populations were small, however, the scale of that influence on the forest was negligible. In 1535, Jacques Cartier estimated the population of Hochelaga, one of the larger Iroquois villages in the St. Lawrence region, at 3,600 people. We will never know the exact size of the Native population when the first explorers arrived, but we do know that it was minuscule relative to the total North American population today.

When the Europeans arrived, most but certainly not all of the forests were primeval, untouched by humans, from the Atlantic coast to the prairies and plains, and from the

Arctic tundra to the Florida peninsula. Amid the sea of forests were villages, farms, lakes, rivers, wetlands, burns, barrens, and savannas, but essentially eastern North America was wall-to-wall forest.

Native use of the forest and trees for food, shelter, canoes, implements, dyes, weapons, and firewood was what might be expected of an Aboriginal people. But the medicinal use of trees, shrubs, and other plants was unprecedented. In the sixteenth century, they were as advanced — in some cases more advanced — as the post-medieval medical practices of Europe. Native medicine was a blend of scientific experimentation, superstition, ritual, and religion. But it was by no means hocus-pocus magic. Through trial and error they had discovered that certain parts of certain plants had an effect on the body. All reports of the early explorers and adventurers, and, to a lesser extent, those of the missionaries, testified that Native medicines worked.

The traditional uses of trees, indeed all plants, were handed down by word of mouth from one generation to the next. Nothing was written down. With the upheaval to their civilization caused by the encroachment of Europeans, the decimation of their population from wars and foreign diseases, and the consequent disruption of their homelands and lifestyles, the knowledge of many of the traditions was in danger of imminent loss.

Society owes a debt of gratitude to the ethnobotanists who had the foresight to live with and interview elders, shamans, medicine people, and ordinary folk to record on paper their use of plants in their everyday lives. People such as Huron Smith, Frank Speck, Frances Densmore, Gladys Tantaquidgeon, William Waugh, and Melvin Gilmore — not exactly household names in either Native or non-Native cultures — wisely foresaw that these cures and remedies might be lost forever unless they were documented. Others followed — Nancy Turner, Anna Leighton, James Herrick, Virgil Vogel, Charlotte Erichsen-Brown, Meredith Jean Black, and Daniel Moerman — continuing the research or consolidating what had been uncovered and publishing it.

The traditional cures and remedies cited in this text are presented for historical purposes only. None of the medicines are recommended for use without first consulting a medical doctor or professional homeopathic practitioner. There are plants in the wild that can nourish, cure, drug, or poison humans.

The terms First Nations, Native Americans, Native people, Aboriginal people, Indians, Indigenous people, and Natives have been used throughout this book. Similarly, the word "tribe" has been used to describe people of the same culture or language, although to some Native people today this has a negative connotation. None of these terms is intended to show disrespect.

As Native people rediscover their roots, some tribe names are reverting to what is thought to be their origins. To select a name that is current, universally accepted, most familiarly known, or is the oldest recorded (at least by non-Native people) presents a dilemma. For example, *The Handbook of Indians of Canada,* published by the Geographic Board in 1913, cites 175 different names for the Ojibwe people, the most recognizable of which are Ojibway (first used in 1843), Chippewa (1754), and Ojibwe (1861). The oldest recorded name was Baouichtigouin, found in *The Jesuit Relations* of 1640. A sincere effort has been made to use names in common use today by Native people themselves.

in the workshop

Those who like to work with wood can discover each species' potential in the workshop, its qualities and shortcomings, and its best applications. To the serious woodworker or professional cabinetmaker, there may be little new here, other than perhaps a refresher on the basics. For other bumbling handypersons — like me — there are some good tips on which wood is best suited to which project.

the wood and paper industry

Part of the history and reality of the forest is that people have cut down trees and used their wood. From prehistoric times, wood was the sole source of heat for cooking and warmth. Later, our Native people harvested firewood — they knew from experience which trees burned hottest and longest — and used trees to construct their tipis, lodges, longhouses, canoes, implements, and weapons.

European settlers took it one step further. They not only cleared the forest for fuel, farmland, fencing, barns, houses, villages, and roads, but they began harvesting trees for market — the genesis of a forest industry in North America. Pines were cut for ships' masts and spars, oaks for sailing vessels and barrels, hemlocks and chestnuts for tannin in the leather industry, other hardwoods for potash, and pitch pine for charcoal, to name but a few.

Some people adamantly believe that we should not cut down trees for commercial purposes. The fact remains that trees do not live forever. Like people, they are born, live, and die. When sustainably managed, trees are a renewable resource, unlike cement and concrete, steel and aluminum, plastics, and oil and natural gas — all non-renewable.

Nothing has the warmth of wood. Without harvesting trees, you could not sit comfortably in front of the fire in a log cabin, put your feet up on the coffee table, set aside the newspaper or magazine, and sit back and relax reading this book or any other.

The reality is that, whether we like it or not, we need wood, paper, and panel products, and wood comes only from trees that have been cut down. It is comforting to know that the wood comes from a continent where more trees are planted or naturally regenerated than are harvested. If those who manage the forest resource are prudent, professional, and environmentally sensitive, if those who process it are not wasteful and control their pollution output, and if those of us who consume it are moderate in its use and recycle whatever we can, future generations will continue to reap the same rewards nature has provided us.

The economic importance of our forests, in these days when we all seem to be preoccupied with the booming high-tech industry, seems to be lost on some folks. Here are a few Canadian statistics often quoted by government officials and forest industry representatives. The forest industry employs, directly and indirectly, 900,000 people, or one in 17 jobs. Among university students, spending part of a summer vacation planting trees is as common as Kraft Dinner.

Silviculture, including forest harvesting, supports 250 Canadian communities, large and small. It contributes as much to our net balance of payments as agriculture, fisheries, mining, and energy combined. In a sense, we are still hewers of wood — albeit with very high-tech equipment and technology, and with a more enlightened approach to the environmental impacts of our activities.

relevant digressions

At times I like to detour away from the beaten path to explore some topic in a little more depth — think of getting off the Interstate or the Trans Canada Highway to investigate some small road. Some species naturally lead to digression.

Pin cherry and gray birch touch upon the role of pioneer species in the ecological concept of succession. Black walnut and jack pine provide a glimpse of the unseen interaction among forest plants. Tamarack and black spruce afford the opportunity to step into the complex world of wetlands ecology. Sugar maple explores the uniquely North American tradition of maple sugar making, and balsam fir invites a mention of the Christmas tree industry. Jack pine opens the door to the controversial topic of clearcutting. Willow underscores the seriousness of soil erosion and suggests ways to prevent this tragedy. White spruce generates a brief discussion of the pulp and paper industry. Manitoba maple and red ash are the springboard for the history and benefits of prairie shelterbelts. Red spruce touches upon the concept of release, and hemlock the phenomenon known as old-growth forests. And white elm raises the issue of alien plants, insects, and diseases.

These digressions merely scratch the surface of these topics, and readers who wish to delve more deeply are encouraged to let the bibliographies serve as a guide for further study.

* * * * *

As with any legacy, we have a responsibility to safeguard the welfare of our trees and forests, and all the living creatures that inhabit them. We must not repeat the mistakes of the past — nor should we judge them on the basis of the standards of today. We must build upon the foundations of respect, harmony, and stewardship handed down from generation to generation of our Native people, and nurture the land ethic later espoused in the writings of Aldo Leopold and others.

We have inherited something special, something unique on this planet. We are fortunate that we have not inherited the history of forest manipulation and destruction of Europe, which will likely never recover in any grand sense. And our diverse and established economy allows us to avoid the pitfalls experienced by developing Third World, especially tropical, countries as they exploit their forests in an effort to catch up with those of us who are fortunate to have more.

The grandeur of our legacy allows us the option of preserving those areas of special value or interest, leaving them untouched and allowing nature to take its course. It allows the option of managing some of our forests for multiple use — recreation, tourism, scenic values, Christmas trees, and maple products, as well as wood and paper. And it includes the option of intensively managing other forests for fiber production, without sacrificing the environmental integrity of the land or its wildlife.

We have a responsibility to maintain the legacy we have received, and, wherever possible, to improve it as our gift to future generations.

Balsam Fir
(*Abies balsamea*)

balsam
fir
var (in PEI)

sapin baumier
sapin blanc
sapin rouge
baumier du Canada

Maliseet: *sta'kwun*

Leaf
- needles soft, flexible; fragrant when crushed; 2–3 cm (about 1") long;
- upper side shiny dark green; underside paler, with 2 silvery lines;
- twisted at the base; spirally arranged on twig, but appear as 2 flat horizontal ranks;
- flat, will not roll easily between thumb and index finger;
- persist on tree 7–10 years.

Flower
- inconspicuous; males yellow; females greenish yellow;
- on same tree; females near top, males lower.

Fruit
- cones upright on upper branches, 5–9 cm (2–3½") long, barrel-shaped, purple until ripe;
- ooze white sticky resin; take 1 season to ripen; turn brown at maturity in late summer;
- disintegrate on the tree, leaving central stalk or "candle," which persists 1–2 years;
- purple seeds winged, dispersed by wind;
- begin bearing cones at age 15–20; good seed crop every 2–4 years.

Twig
- mostly opposite, greenish gray, smooth, hairy;
- smooth round scars after needles are shed;
- on branches in annual whorls of 2–7 around main stem;
- buds round, chocolate-brown, resinous.

Bark
- on younger trees, smooth, gray, with prominent oval resin blisters;
- on older trees, red-brown, cracking into scaly plates.

Wood
- soft, light, weak, brittle; straight-grained; odorless; not rot resistant;
- heartwood and sapwood both whitish to creamy brown;
- annual growth rings distinct.

Height	Diameter	Longevity
15–20 m (50–65')	30–50 cm (12–20")	100–125 years

Branches grow in distinct annual whorls of two to seven — occasionally more — a quick way to count the age of a fir.

a catalyst for change

Balsam fir has contributed to our environment, our economy, and our culture in countless ways — food and shelter for wildlife, medicines, oils and resins, wood for lumber, wood fiber for pulp and paper, the aesthetics of the countryside, and the aroma and spirit it fills homes with at Christmas.

But fir's most noteworthy contribution has been its role as the unwilling victim of the eastern spruce budworm, and the profound changes in society's attitudes it has generated.

Rachel Carson's *Silent Spring* may have kindled concerns over pesticides, but the annual spraying of balsam fir and spruce forests fanned the flames. It took environmental concern to a new level, from the voices of a vocal few to an unprecedented awareness that permeated the population in general. In the 1970s and 1980s the spray controversy reigned throughout the areas under budworm attack, concerns often based more on gut feelings than on science, exaggerated and unsubstantiated claims on all sides, sometimes alarmist, sometimes not, sensationalism in the media, and half-truths that proved to be half true.

No, no children suffered or died from Reye's Syndrome, as headlines suggested, as a result of aerial spraying of chemical insecticides. But countless non-targeted insects, songbirds, and aquatic wildlife fell victim. Chemical spraying was having a direct impact on the forest ecosystem.

The public outcry changed the way governments and the forest industry did business. They re-evaluated their techniques, strategies, and indeed their philosophy, in dealing with the budworm. It spawned new and innovative research into alternative methods for managing this insect and others, reduced the scale and changed the contents of spray programs, fueled the demand for greater public participation in forest decision-making, and moved society as a whole a step forward in its level of environmental awareness. In retrospect, these were all positive outcomes, and balsam fir was the catalyst.

the rise and fall of Canada balsam

Almost 400 years ago, chronicler Marc Lescarbot wrote: *Firs, and pines, can generate good profit, for they render a strong and abundant resin. The resin is as good as Venice turpentine currently in vogue at the time and has great potential as a pharmaceutical.*

Sixty years later, historian John Josselyn extolled its virtues: *The Firr-tree bark is smooth with knobs or blisters in which lyeth clear liquid turpentine very good to put into salves and ointments . . . the resin is altogether as good as frankincense.*

By the eighteenth century, Canada balsam was listed in the *New Universal English Dispensatory* for "cleansing and deterging abscesses." Its astringent and antiseptic properties were part of the traditional knowledge of Native people, who had been using it as a wound dressing for centuries.

Resin was used not only medicinally, but also in the perfumery and optometry trades. Canada balsam's high refractive index, roughly the same as glass, produced the most superior optical cement for prisms, lenses, eyepieces, and microscope slides. For 200 years, the resin extracted from balsam fir bark blisters supported a sizable cottage industry.

The process of tapping blisters for resin was simple, but slow and labor-intensive. In summer, Natives and settlers alike supplemented their meager incomes by collecting fir resin using a sharpened tube soldered to a metal cup. Each blister was punctured, and its resin drained into the cup. Tapping half a gallon a day was considered a good day's work. Resin collecting was often a family affair, children happily climbing trees to tap the higher blisters.

At the beginning of the twentieth century, production of Canada balsam, mostly from Quebec, peaked at twenty tons a year. In the 1960s, resin fetched about three dollars a pound. No resin collector ever got rich.

After World War II, cheaper and more uniform plastics largely replaced Canada balsam as an optical cement. Its use continues today in alternative medicines, in perfumery, and in the flavoring industries.

O Tannenbaum

The tradition of decorating evergreens for Christmas is rooted in the Rhine region of Germany. Some suggest it was begun by Martin Luther in the fifteenth century, and introduced to America by Hessian mercenaries in 1778. In eastern North America, balsam fir became the Christmas tree of choice, for several reasons: its symmetrical shape, fresh

Tapping the clear resin from the bark blisters is a centuries-old cottage industry.

forest fragrance, ability to retain its needles throughout the holiday season, and its stiff boughs capable of holding ornaments. Further south in the Carolinas, its close cousin, Fraser fir, has the same attributes.

The largest Christmas-tree producing region in Canada is southern Quebec, in particular the Eastern Townships and Beauce areas just north of the U.S. border. Thousands of hectares of former farmland are under cultivation. Ontario, where more Scotch pine is grown, is next, followed by Nova Scotia and New Brunswick. Since 1982, the giant Christmas tree that adorns the Boston Common has annually been harvested in New Brunswick, where balsam fir is the provincial tree, as a gift to the children of Boston.

Each year over four million trees are harvested — and replanted — on private land in Canada, with a value of 60 million dollars. Over half are exported, primarily to cities along the Atlantic seaboard, with smaller quantities shipped elsewhere within Canada, and as far away as the Caribbean and Central and South America.

While a few larger Christmas tree growers operate as full-time businesses, most supplement their family incomes with their seasonal work, some leaving the marketing of their trees to their associations and co-ops. A marketing variation is the U-pick, or Choose 'n' Cut, where families have an outing to a tree farm, select and cut their tree, and are often treated to hot chocolate and other goodies by the tree farmer.

There are two basic options for growing balsam fir: plantations and cultivated wild stands. In the former, seedlings or larger transplants are planted in rows in prepared farm fields. In some regions, Nova Scotia, for instance, wild stands are more common. Growers take advantage of natural regeneration of fir after a clearcut by thinning and weeding the young trees to reduce competition and allow sunlight to reach each tree. From that point, the cultivation techniques are essentially the same for both plantations and wild stands. Producing a quality balsam fir with full dark green foliage requires mechanical or chemical control of competition from grass, weeds, shrubs, and other tree species. A few growers use sheep. Fertilizing, application of insecticides when required, pruning, and shearing, are the other essentials for a top-grade tree.

Major insects that attack fir are the spruce budworm, balsam twig aphid, and balsam gall midge. When infestation levels are high, trees are sprayed to maintain their quality. Where moose are plentiful, they present a problem by munching on the nutritious branch tips, which fertilizer has made particularly tasty. Late spring frosts can pose another difficulty, killing tender new shoots and turning them unsightly brown.

By-products of the industry include wreaths, garlands, floral roping, and grave blankets, all using fir tips or branches. At one time, pillows were commonly stuffed with soft and fragrant fir needles. Today souvenir balsam needle cushions are still available in shops in the Adirondacks.

a cure for the common cold?

In 1861, John Gunn reported the properties of fir in his book on home remedies: *Internally it is good in coughs, gonorrhea, gleet, whites, affectations of the urinary organs, and ulcerations of the bowels.*

From Nova Scotia to Minnesota, medicinal uses of fir by Native people were remarkably similar. Blister resin was taken orally to allay the symptoms of colds, cough, lung congestion, and other pulmonary problems. Pure, or mixed with other herbal ingredients to produce salves, Canada balsam was the most common dressing to heal wounds and sores. Northern Saultaux applied the resin directly on the wound and allowed it to dry. The Ojibway poured it on hot stones or coals, and inhaled the fumes for convulsions, colds, and other breathing problems.

The Menominee steeped the inner bark and drank the tea to relieve pains in the chest. The Penobscot in Maine included fir twigs as one of the seven herbs taken as a sudorific before entering the sweat lodge; the Montagnais of Labrador and Ontario's Hurons steeped the twigs to brew a laxative tea.

The medical profession eventually recognized the medicinal qualities of balsam fir. *The Canadian Pharmaceutical Journal* included it in its 1868 list of medicinal plants, and Canada balsam was listed as an official medicine in the *United States Pharmacopoeia* from its first edition in 1820 until 1916. In the mid-nineteenth century it was available in drugstores, whence one might be tempted to speculate came the expression: "Take two blisters and call me in the morning."

fir and its fauna

A large number of forest fauna rely on balsam fir for food and shelter. The twigs, needles, and buds can comprise one quarter of the winter diet of moose. In fall and winter, white-tailed deer browse the branch tips, and when the snows deepen and their small hooves no longer allow them to travel freely, they herd under the evergreen boughs in "deer yards."

Fir needles are a consistent part of the vegetarian menu of both sharp-tailed and spruce grouse. The large and striking pileated woodpecker forages deep into the heart of a standing dead fir for a feast of carpenter ants, and the eastern flying squirrel quickly invades the cavity to set up her nest. Fir's dense foliage provides an inconspicuous nest site for robins, mourning doves, jays, grosbeaks, purple finches, nuthatches, and warblers. Nuthatches, often seen standing upside down on tree trunks, gather balsam resin to cement their nests of shredded bark and grasses. Most of these birds dine on the treetop seeds as well, as do chickadees, crossbills, and kinglets — if they can get to the cones before the squirrels.

the woes and foes of fir

Non-introduced insects that attack our native trees are part of the natural functioning of the ecosystem. Bugs eat trees, birds eat bugs, and birds are preyed upon by the next species up the food chain. Nature replaces dead trees with seedlings, and the cycle starts anew. However, when insect populations reach epidemic levels and become a major threat to the species, to the mills that process the wood, to their employees and families, and to the economic survival of forest-dependent communities, there are some difficult decisions to be made by society. Chemical aerial spraying has been reduced dramatically in the past decades; long gone are the days of spraying forests with deadly

Green female flowers evolve into upright woody cones by autumn.

DDT, and some of the less harmful but still toxic chemicals that replaced it.

More target-specific alternatives such as the bacterial insecticide Bt (*Bacillus thuringensis*) have been adopted, and are being applied at greatly reduced scales. Meanwhile, research into more benign alternatives and amended silvicultural practices is ongoing.

Fir is host to a wide variety of insects, some of which can be life threatening. The eastern spruce budworm (which, ironically, prefers fir to spruce) has, since the early 1700s, reached epidemic proportions in cycles of from ten to forty years. It has ravished huge tracts of fir in the boreal and Acadian forests, as well as smaller pockets further south. In the mid-1970s, infestations covered 55 million hectares (135 million acres) of our eastern forests. When a cycle is peaking, the caterpillar larvae of the grayish brown moths can annihilate healthy firs in three years or less, by devouring all the needles, buds, and unfolding shoots.

Newfoundland is reported to have been the original home of another voracious fir foliage consumer, the hemlock looper, which now ranges as far west as Alberta and south

to Georgia. In Newfoundland, it is still the most serious threat to balsam fir.

fir as fiber

Balsam fir wood is whitish, with no difference in color between the heartwood (the central core of non-living tissue) and the sapwood (the outer ring of living tissue). Its whorls of small branches result in an uncommon number of small knots. Fir lumber is not as hard, heavy or strong as spruce, and requires almost twice the drying time. It is used in light construction, framing, scaffolding, studs, concrete forms and the like. Being odorless and tasteless, it was formerly used to fabricate food barrels, cheese boxes, and butter crates.

It is in the pulp and paper industry that balsam fir rises to the fore. Often mixed with spruce, its long fibers give strength to pulp, newsprint, cardboard, and other paper products. In the mid-1990s, for example, Canadian mills annually produced 24 million tons of pulp and 9 million tons of newsprint; 60 percent of the newsprint was exported to the United States to feed the newspaper and advertising industries. In 1996, Canada produced 26 percent of the world's newsprint. In central and eastern Canada, balsam fir was a primary source of that paper. In the United States, Wisconsin is the leading paper-producing state, processing almost 6 million tons a year, and employing over 50,000 people, nearly 10 percent of the state's manufacturing workforce.

landscaping with fir

And up on the hills against the sky,
A fir tree rocking its lullaby,
Swings, swings,
Its emerald wings
Swelling the song that my paddle sings.

E. Pauline Johnson,
"The Song My Paddle Sings"

Lustrous dark green foliage, a compact spire-like crown, fast growth, and adaptability to a variety of soils make balsam fir an ideal candidate as an ornamental. It is particularly attractive when poised against a backdrop of autumn hardwoods.

Like all evergreens, firs on the south side of the home provide summer shade, lowering home temperatures and air-conditioning costs, and saving energy. In winter, however, they block the warming sun. The north side is the appropriate place for firs, the south side for hardwood shade trees.

Once permission is obtained, young fir wildlings along roadsides and forest edges can be easily dug up and transplanted, as soon as the frost is out of the ground. Care should be taken to get all the shallow roots, including the fibrous root tips. A local Christmas tree grower might be willing to sell a few four-to-five-year-old transplants, or your nearest nursery or garden center may stock native balsam fir, as well as the fertilizer required for best growth and color.

Facing page: The compact spires of balsam fir are natural icons of the north country. In winter, the boughs intercept and hold snow, providing shelter for white-tailed deer, who congregate below in "deer yards" to conserve energy.

Manitoba Maple
(*Acer negundo*)

boxelder
ash-leaved maple

érable à feuilles composées
érable à Giguère
érable du Manitoba
aune-bois
érable à feuilles de frêne

Winnebago: *nahosh*

Leaf
- compound, opposite; composed of 3–7 pointed leaflets in opposite pairs;
- leaflets 3-lobed, or with uneven teeth; 5–7 cm (2–3") long;
- upper side light green; lower side paler green; musky odor when crushed;
- new leaves grow all summer, until first frost;
- turn yellow or green-brown in autumn.

Flower
- yellowish green male flowers in clusters on slender stalk; 1–4 cm (½–1½") long;
- pale green females in hanging clusters on central stalk;
- flowers appear in early spring, with or before leaves;
- males and females on separate trees.

Fruit
- samaras (winged keys), 3–4 cm (1–1½") long, in 45° V-formation; hanging in dense clusters;
- seed wings membranous; wrinkled seed cases contain narrow pointed nutlets;
- yellowish green in summer, maturing to brown in fall; remain on tree all winter; good seed crop every year.

Twig
- round, somewhat stout; olive green to chocolate brown to purplish;
- coated with light gray film which can be rubbed off;
- dotted with thin horizontal lenticels;
- opposite buds green or purple, covered with gray down; positioned on leaf scars; pairs of leaf scars meet, almost encircling the twig; pith large, white, solid;
- terminal bud often killed by fall frost.

Bark
- on younger trees, smooth, light gray-brown;
- on older trees, darker brown, furrowed into narrow ridges.

Wood
- moderately light, soft, weak, fine-textured, close-grained;
- heartwood and sapwood both creamy white.

Height	Diameter	Longevity
12–18 m (40–60')	30–60 cm (12–24")	50–70 years

Female Manitoba maples are usually prolific seeders.

maple or ash?

Although boxelder has always officially been considered a member of the *Acer*, or maple family, at one time there was popular confusion as to whether it was a maple or an ash. Was it an ash with seed keys like the maples, or was it a maple with compound leaves like the ashes? The uncertainty led to localized names such as sugar ash, ash-leaved maple, black ash, cut-leaved maple, maple ash, and water ash. Another of its colloquial, less flattering names was stinking ash, undoubtedly due to the foul smell of its leaves when crushed. Today both boxelder and Manitoba maple are the widely accepted common names.

where it grows

Manitoba maple is a tree of bottomlands, river valleys, stream banks, and floodplains. Here it fulfills its natural conservation role. Its roots bind the soil to prevent erosion and siltation of waterways, and its shade cools the waters for freshwater fish such as trout.

It attains its best size and form in the river valleys of Indiana and Kentucky. On the prairies it is one of the few tree species lining the banks of streams and rivers in an otherwise semi-arid landscape. It prefers moist soils and can withstand spring flooding, but is also very resistant to drought.

While its natural range in Canada is southern Manitoba, Saskatchewan, and the river valleys of southeastern Alberta, it has been planted and spread extensively in urban and rural areas throughout the east as far as Nova Scotia. Females are prolific seeders, and wherever seeds find anything that faintly resembles soil, they germinate.

Manitoba maple is among the widest-ranging trees in North America — from the Maritimes and New England to the foothills of the Rockies, and south to Florida and Texas. There is even a variety native to California. While its range is remarkable, in most regions it is not abundant.

between a brick building and a paved parking lot

Female trees are actually ugly because fruits hang like dirty brown socks through fall and winter.

Michael Dirr,
Manual of Woody Landscape Plants

Poor old Manitoba maple — the abuse it has suffered over the years! Horticulturist Michael Dirr calls it an "alley cat tree," a "noxious weed," and "spectral pollution." Others concur. It has been labeled "a dirty tree," "ragged," "cheap and ugly," "scraggy," and "a weedy, short-lived, insect- and disease-prone seed machine with weak wood." A Kansas Department of Agriculture bulletin summed it up succinctly: "There is no excuse for planting this tree."

Manitoba maple has four virtues as a shade tree: it grows fast, it is very hardy, it is drought resistant, and it prospers just about anywhere. One can find it downtown amid a postage-stamp patch of weedy grass, wedged between a paved parking lot and a brick building, in derelict backyards littered with discarded tires and car parts, and even pushing through cracks in weathered asphalt and cement.

In the countryside, stumble upon the stone foundation of some long-abandoned farm house, and it's likely there will be a Manitoba maple nearby. Walk a rural railroad line, and there it will be, growing in the gravel alongside the tracks.

In the open, the trunk usually forks near the ground into several large crooked stems, forming an irregular crown. It would be an ideal climbing tree for kids, were it not for its brittle branches. The compound leaves and seed clusters are a nuisance to clean up, and it is susceptible to a host of insects and diseases. Although many box-elder leaves turn a pleasant golden yellow in autumn, just as many suddenly turn brown, dry up, and remain shriveled on the tree for weeks.

If one needs a shade tree to fill an otherwise barren and treeless landscape quickly, Manitoba maple fills the bill. Two suggestions: plant a male, and plant several longer-lived, shade-tolerant, and more attractive trees around it. When the other trees are big enough, you can cut down the Manitoba. Or, if you have become attached to it, you can keep it. The conclusion, in a nutshell, is: despite its numerous shortcomings as an ornamental, Manitoba maple is better than no tree at all.

They took all the trees,
Put 'em in a tree museum
And they charged the people
A dollar and a half just to see 'em
Don't it always seem to go
That you don't know what you've got
Till it's gone
They paved paradise
And put up a parking lot.

Joni Mitchell
"Big Yellow Taxi," 1969
from *Ladies of the Canyon,*
Siquomb Publishing Co. BMI

where it shines

On the prairies, Manitoba maple was one of the first trees planted in farm windbreaks and shelterbelts. Settlers from the east and from Europe had difficulty adapting to the treeless landscape and the harsh winter winds, and were given hardy trees such as Manitoba maple, cottonwood, and green ash to ease their discomfort. Since 1901, the federal Shelterbelt Centre nursery at Indian Head, Saskatchewan, has distributed over 600 million free tree seedlings to prairie farmers, enough to create a shelterbelt that would encircle the Earth.

Settlers planted these seedlings around the farmhouse, and alongside fields and roads. Around the farmstead, shelterbelt trees and shrubs beautify the landscape, provide summer shade, conserve energy, and reduce winter heating costs. In the field, they control drifting snow, prevent soil erosion, increase crop yields, and provide wildlife food and shelter. Along roadsides, the belts reduce snow removal costs and increase safety in blizzards.

Manitoba maples are still one of the key species in prairie shelterbelt plantings, where their branches provide nesting sites for robins, kingbirds, orioles, flycatchers, yellow warblers, and mourning doves.

a symbiotic relationship

Manitoba maple is not heavily used by wildlife, with one striking exception — the evening grosbeak. The winged seeds that hang on the tree all winter are the favorite food of the *gros-bec errant,* the wandering grosbeak. Originally a bird of Alberta when first discovered by settlers 150 years ago, its range has expanded as far east as Nova Scotia. Might it be just a coincidence that Manitoba maple has spread in the same pattern and in the same period of time?

In winter, grosbeaks are attracted to feeders filled with sunflower seeds, and, in turn, homeowners are rewarded with the sight of a flock of these large colorful creatures, adding a splash of splendor to the winter landscape. But the benefit of grosbeaks is more than ornamental. They are voracious consumers of spruce budworm larvae in the spring, and help control populations of this extremely damaging insect, especially when they are at epidemic levels. The symbiotic relationship of Manitoba maple, evening grosbeaks, spruce, and balsam fir — and man — is intriguing, and worth exploring further.

baseboards and breadboards

Early in the nineteenth century, cabinetmakers used small amounts of boxelder's white wood as inlay, to contrast with darker woods such as black walnut, mahogany, and black cherry. That was likely the most valuable use it has ever had. It has been turned into broom handles, woodenware, breadboards, and interior finish such as baseboards and stair rails, where the clear color is its major asset. It has also been sawn into rough lumber, and used in the disposable box business. As firewood, boxelder ranks rather low in heat value, on a par with red pine and black spruce, and a little better than the aspens.

For many years in Manitoba and Saskatchewan, small quantities of Manitoba maple syrup have been produced locally, with a taste very much like that of sugar maple. However, sap yields per tree, as well as sugar content, are lower than sugar maple. Strong potential exists for producing and marketing this untapped resource on a larger scale, a concept that is being explored and promoted at this time.

tapping and tattooing

Native dwellers of the prairies introduced white settlers to the art of tapping Manitoba maple for its sweet sap. When tapping wounds failed to heal properly and decay set in, Dakota women harvested the tender young elm cap mushrooms that fruited around tapholes, for a delicious addition to their menus.

The Meskakwi, Pillager Ojibway, and Cree peeled the inner bark of boxelder, steeped it in boiling water, and drank the tea as an emetic. Cree also drank the decoction for liver and spleen disorders, and as a mild tranquilizer.

Boxelder wood was used not only as fuel by the Omaha and the Dakota, but was burned by these tribes to produce charcoal for ceremonial body painting and tattooing.

Trees typically fork near the ground into a profusion of crooked stems and branches.

cecropia moth — a Hollywood sci-fi natural

Manitoba maple is accosted by more than its fair share of bugs of every size and description. Some are life threatening; others cause only cosmetic damage. Caterpillars, loopers, leafrollers, leaf tiers, gall midges, mites, aphids, and skeletonizers eat the leaves. Beetles and borers tunnel into the wood. Midges consume the buds, and scales suck the sap out of twigs and branches.

The cecropia moth evolves from one of the ugliest caterpillars around — it looks like an alien slimy green blob with eyes and legs — into one of the largest and most attractive moths in North America. It once plagued prairie shelterbelt trees, but its populations are now naturally controlled by parasites, insects, birds, and rodents. At the other end of the size spectrum are minute mites that feed inside boxelder leaves, creating tiny red and yellow galls on the surface.

Most of these bugs are kept in check naturally, but occasionally some populations reach threatening levels that may necessitate manual control, or perhaps bacterial or chemical spraying.

Striped Maple
(*Acer pensylvanicum*)

moosewood
moose maple
goosefoot maple
whistlewood
green striped maple
snake bark maple

érable de Pennsylvanie
bois barré
bois d'orignal
érable barré
bourdaine
bois noir

Penobscot: *adoki'mus*

Leaf
- simple, opposite; large, thin, soft-textured; 10–20 cm (4–8") long and wide;
- 3 lobes in upper half; long tapering tips sharply pointed, toothed;
- upper side bright green; underside paler, with 3 raised main veins leading to lobe tips;
- edges with sharp teeth of variable shapes and sizes;
- base rounded or heart-shaped; occasionally with 2 smaller lobes near base;
- stalk 3–8 cm (1–3") long, round, grooved on top; reddish green;
- turn pale to bright yellow in autumn.

Flower
- males tiny, greenish yellow, in drooping clusters; on slender stalks;
- females canary yellow, bell-shaped; in dangling clusters 8–14 cm (3–5") long;
- males and females usually on same tree, occasionally in same flower; before leaves fully grown.

Fruit
- pairs of green winged seeds (samaras), hanging in bunches; reddish brown at maturity;
- seeds indented on one side; angle between wings 90° or greater;
- released in early fall; borne by wind;
- good seed crop most years.

Twig
- slightly stout; glossy red on one side, often beige-green on the other;
- smooth, hairless, with no lenticels; on striped branches;
- large glossy red buds in pairs; terminal bud larger, stalked, pointed; covered by 2 scales.

Bark
- on younger trees, thin, smooth, dark green; with white, black or multicolored stripes;
- on older trees, gray and rough near base.

Wood
- moderately light, soft, weak, close-grained;
- heartwood pinkish brown; thick sapwood paler.

Height	Diameter	Longevity
5–10 m (15–30')	15–25 cm (6–10")	50–70 years

Pairs of seeds hang in attractive clusters, turn reddish brown when ripe.

beauty in the shade

Striped maple is one of the prettiest little trees in the forest. It flourishes on moist, well-drained soils, in the shade of taller trees such as yellow birch, hemlock, and sugar maple. From Nova Scotia west to Manitoba, and as far south as North Carolina, striped maple shares the forest understory with iron-woods, hobblebush, alternate-leaf dogwoods, and a host of forest ferns and wildflowers.

landscaping au naturel

Striped maple is out of its element as an exposed lawn tree. Its landscaping preference is au naturel, in borders and groupings in the cool shade and shelter of overstory trees that replicate its forest habitat.

It may be one of the smallest maples in North America, but its leaves are the largest east of the Rockies. In autumn, they turn a pleasant pale, or occasionally vibrant, yellow.

In spring, the dangling strings of delicate yellow, bell-shaped little flowers are unique among the maple family. Year-round, the smooth dark green bark is its outstanding decorative feature, with long vertical stripes that run the gamut of the artist's palette.

Striped maples are most easily propagated by transplanting seedlings from the wild. Carefully conserve all the wide-spreading roots and as much soil, humus, and litter as possible, to minimize the shock in adjusting to their new environment.

Planting from seed is another option. Pick when reddish brown in autumn, and sow 2–3 centimeters (1") deep, wings and all, in a sand and peat moss bed. Mulch for the winter. In spring, remove the mulch, and partially shade the seedbed. Covering with a snow fence or branches works nicely. Ensure that the soil is kept moist, but not wet. Germination rates are typically low, so don't despair. Seedlings should be ready to transplant to their permanent home in partial shade, in two to three years.

Once established, striped maple is relatively free of insects and diseases — it is often one of the few trees whose leaves remain unblemished throughout the summer.

inner bark medicinals

> There are many Medicinal Herbs which are not in Europe, whose Effects are infallible, according to the Experience of the Savages: They cure with them all sorts of Wounds, the Tertian and Quartan Agues; some of them purge well, and allay the Pains in the Reins, and such like Maladies.
> Father Louis Hennepin, Recollet missionary, A New Discovery, 1698

First Nations people employed striped maple inner bark as both internal and external medicine. The Ojibway and Iroquois scraped the inner bark from the tree, boiled it, and drank it as an emetic. Emetics were herbal concoctions that were so vile that drinking them would cause the patient to vomit, purging the intestines of whatever was causing the illness. Maine's Penobscot and New Brunswick's Maliseet applied compresses of the boiled inner bark to soothe swollen limbs, and the leaves themselves were applied to inflamed breasts.

eater of branches

In several Algonquian dialects, *mousou* meant "eater of branches," from which the settlers derived the English name "moose" for the undisputed heavyweight of the forest. Moose are serious winter browsers. To remain healthy, an average adult moose must consume 15 kilograms (35 lbs.) of twigs, buds, and needles every day.

Throughout its range, striped maple is the moose's favorite browse; hence its more popular names, moosewood and moose maple. A smaller, and also very pretty, shrub of the *Viburnum* genus, the hobblebush, has earned the nickname moosewood for the same reason.

Moose are not alone. They are joined by their fellow twig browsers, white-tailed deer. At fall harvest time, chipmunks and squirrels gather the seeds for instant consumption, or to put in cold storage. Ruffed grouse join in; when they have duly disposed of the seeds, they move on to the big red buds.

Bees, attracted to the nectar of the male flowers, are responsible for pollination of the females in the spring.

a delicate subject

Around the evening campfire, forestry folk, fishermen, and hunters have long debated which moosewood — striped maple or hobblebush — provides the softest and strongest woods toilet paper. Both have large, thin, finely textured, tear-resistant leaves.

Red Maple
(*Acer rubrum*)

soft maple
swamp maple
scarlet maple
white maple

érable rouge
plaine
plaine rouge

Forest Potawatomi: *cigime'wic*

Leaf
- simple, opposite; 3–5 lobes; margins coarsely toothed; 10–15 cm (4–6") long and wide;
- upper side mid-green; underside paler;
- on red stalk 6–12 cm (2–5") long;
- in autumn, turn wide range of shades of red.

Flower
- males small, red; females with tiny red petals;
- appear well before the leaves, in clusters encircling twigs;
- males and females on separate trees, or on different branches of same tree.

Fruit
- samaras, twin winged red seeds, in V-formation;
- hang on slender stalks emanating from central point on twig;
- ripen, fall, and germinate in early summer;
- begin bearing seed at age 4–10; good crop every year.

Twig
- slender, wine red, smooth, shiny, with tiny white lenticels;
- dark red buds in pairs; smooth, roundish; terminal bud flanked by 2 side buds;
- flower buds slightly larger, on thicker twigs.

Bark
- on younger trees, smooth, ash-gray;
- on older trees, gray brown, rough, with scaly vertical ridges loose at both ends.

Wood
- moderately heavy and strong; close-grained; not decay-resistant;
- heartwood gray to pale reddish brown, with brown streaks; thick sapwood much paler;
- occasionally with flecked or curly grain;
- annual growth rings not very distinct.

Height	Diameter	Longevity
20–30 m (65–100')	40–90 cm (16–36")	100–150 years

from Newfoundland to Florida

The range of red maple from north to south is remarkable. No other tree flourishes from the valley bottoms of rugged Newfoundland down to the tropical swamps of southern Florida. Its tolerance to the extremes of temperature, soil, precipitation, daylight hours, and particularly length of growing season is testimony to red maple's adaptability. Its east-west range is not nearly as impressive; the westward limit is Lake Nipigon at the Ontario-Manitoba border, beyond which the dryness of the soil and air is the limiting factor.

The American Forests record red maple stands in the Great Smoky Mountains National Park in Tennessee. It is a giant: 43 meters (141') tall.

red the year 'round

There is not a more exhilarating tree to behold in the autumn than red maple. Its foliage turns every shade of red imaginable — sometimes so brilliant it affects the eyes like dayglow. These colors, blended with the subtler fall tones of sugar maple, ash, and oak, and contrasted with the deep greens of the conifers, annually lure thousands of folks from the Atlantic Seaboard to the countryside of New England and the Maritimes. It's called the "color season," when one should not be so foolhardy as to make the pilgrimage without making inn reservations well in advance.

One can experience a touch of this splendor on the home landscape. Red maple grows on such a wide range of soils and sites that it is hard to imagine a planting failure — except perhaps where the soil is not acidic enough. In the wild, it grows from the edges of bogs to rocky hillsides; it even flourishes on floating logs in swamps in the most southern part of its range.

Seeds should be sown as soon as they flutter to the ground in early summer, and covered with 2–3 centimeters (1") of soil. If possible, select a slightly wet site on the property, or a spot near a ditch or hollow where the maple's shallow but wide-spreading roots can find the moisture they prefer. If you do not wish to plant from seed, commercial nurseries carry both our native red maple and scores of cultivated varieties.

Open-grown red maples have a short trunk, which forks into a number of erect branches, forming a dense crown that is usually taller than it is wide. Some branches may stretch beyond the crown outline, creating a tufted appearance.

In early spring, thousands of tiny red flowers are a welcome bonus; its leafless crown casts a wine-red glow against a blue sky, while other hardwoods still stand gray and lifeless. The species is most aptly named. There is something red about red maple all year long — its flowers in spring, its seeds and leaf stalks in summer, its dazzling foliage in autumn, and its twigs and buds all winter.

the maple leaf forever

It is the blood-hued maple straight and strong,
Voicing abroad its patriotic song.

E. Pauline Johnson,
"Autumn's Orchestra"

Since Confederation, there have been a number of unofficial symbols of Canada — the beaver, the Mountie, and the loon, to name a few — but none has held such prominence or widespread acceptance as the maple leaf. Oddly enough, maple was not declared Canada's official arboreal emblem until 1996. Since none of the ten species of native maples grows throughout this vast country, the maple genus *Acer* was chosen, comprising the red, sugar, mountain, Manitoba, striped, silver, and black species east of the Rockies, and the bigleaf, vine, and Douglas maples of British Columbia.

Red maple flowers appear long before the leaves in spring.

The red maple leaf on the Canadian flag, officially unveiled in 1965, depicts no specific maple species, but is a stylized leaf representing all native maples, and perhaps most closely resembles sugar maple.

Red maple also has the distinction of being the state tree of Rhode Island.

untapped potential

Red maple has been traditionally underutilized. It was at one time considered a weed, with little or no commercial value; likely because it stood in the shadow of its big brother, the sugar maple. Red maple wood is not as heavy, hard, or strong as sugar maple, but it is often substituted for sugar where these qualities are not critical. It produces fine furniture, cabinets, turnings, wooden-ware, scrollwork, molding, and handsome rifle stocks. In colonial days, red maple was the preferred wood of crafters of shoe pegs, who whittled them by hand.

In the lumber yard today it is marketed as soft maple, a category that includes both red and silver maple, even though there are some differences in the characteristics of the two woods. Red maple wood is close-grained, and moderately heavy, and its heartwood usually has a slight rosy tinge. Like sugar maple, the thick sapwood is more valuable than the heartwood. It is easier to work with tools than is sugar maple, it bends well when steamed, and takes stains and finishes nicely.

Perhaps its moment of glory came during World War II, when red maple veneer was molded into skins of fighter aircraft. Its

Ablaze in autumn...there is something red about red maple in all seasons.

most common use today is in crates, pallets, panel products, and pulpwood.

As firewood it ranks above average, on a par with white birch, with less heat value than oaks, hickories, and sugar maple, but more than poplars, basswood, and most of the eastern softwoods.

Like all maples, its sap is tapped to produce maple syrup, but the fact that it has a lower sugar content than sugar maple means that almost double the sap has to be boiled to produce the same quantity of syrup, and the syrup is generally darker.

just browsing

When cut down or destroyed by fire, red maple stumps have a tremendous capacity to sprout new stems. With the root system of the parent tree to supply nutrients, the red sprouts grow rapidly in their early years. This succulent growth, high in fiber and protein, is one of the most important winter foods of white-tailed deer. Deer browse (chew off the twigs and buds) the sprouts, and the sprouts respond by growing more stems. Browsing poses a problem to red maple regeneration only when deer populations exceed the carrying capacity of the forest. Much of the red maple today is in clumps, a result of sprouting after some disturbance years ago.

Moose, rabbits, and hares eat the twigs as well. Porcupines and beavers gnaw on the bark, and chipmunks and gray squirrels consume the seeds. Young clumps of red maple sprouts are one of the favorite nesting sites of prairie warblers, and larger clumps conceal the nests of black ducks. Higher up, warbling vireos construct their nests on red maple branch forks. Roving flocks of evening grosbeaks feast on the buds, seeds, and spring flowers; Carolina chickadees confine themselves to the seeds.

Seeds ripen in early summer, flutter to the ground, and germinate immediately.

early Americana

Native people and the colonists who followed them found an assortment of uses for red maple. French and German settlers observed the Indians' practice of boiling the inner bark to produce dyes, and added copperas (iron sulfate) to create dark blue and black dyes, also used as ink. Many First Nations people relieved eye soreness, often caused by smoke in confined areas, by washing their eyes in a solution of boiled inner bark. Potawatomi trappers deodorized and disguised their traps by boiling them in water with red maple bark. The Iroquois crafted ceremonial bowls, spoons, and ladles from red maple burls. They also pounded the inner bark into flour to make bread, particularly in times of food shortage. Native people generally were not fond of salt, and seasoned much of their cooking with red or sugar maple syrup.

red maple marauders

Red maple is prey to a host of insects that chew, skeletonize, tie, and roll the leaves, burrow into the buds, bore into the shoots, mine the stems and branches, and tunnel into the bark. These come in an assortment of caterpillars, aphids, sawflies, scales, midges, mites, and miners. Fortunately none of these pests poses a serious threat to the hardy red maple, and they provide food for insect-eating birds and other forest critters.

Should one of these bugs attack your prized red maple, have it identified by a specialist, and, if warranted, take the steps necessary to control or eliminate its damage. The remedy may be as simple as manually picking off rolled leaves with larvae inside, or it may require more drastic measures.

Silver Maple
(*Acer saccharinum*)

soft maple
river maple
swamp maple
water maple
white maple

érable argenté
plaine blanche
plaine de France
érable blanc

Dakota: *tahado*

Leaf
- simple, opposite; thin, 10–16 cm (4–6") long; with 5 narrow, deeply notched, pointed lobes;
- upper side bright light green; underside silvery; teeth coarse, irregular, sharp;
- base even or heart-shaped;
- on slender, drooping red stalk 8–12 cm (3–5") long.

Flower
- in late winter, early spring; long before leaves unfold;
- males small, greenish yellow; females small, reddish yellow, clustered;
- males and females in separate clusters on same or separate trees;
- occasionally male and female parts in same flower (perfect).

Fruit
- samaras, pairs of large winged seeds, 4–7 cm (1½–3") long; widely angled; often of uneven lengths;
- suspended in clusters; seed case wrinkled;
- begin bearing seed at age 10–15; good seed crops irregular, almost annually.

Twig
- greenish or reddish brown; rank odor when broken;
- paired buds conical, red;
- on gray branches that rise, then dip, and angle upward at tip.

Bark
- on younger trees, thin, smooth, and silvery gray;
- on older trees, darker reddish brown; fissured, shaggy;
- scales loose at top and bottom.

Wood
- relatively heavy, hard, strong, and stiff; straight-grained, fine textured;
- heartwood light brown; thick sapwood nearly white;
- annual growth rings faint.

Height	Diameter	Longevity
20–30 m (65–100')	60–100 cm (24–40")	100–130 years

Silver maple is one of the earliest trees to flower in spring, long before the leaves unfold.

a waterside delight

Silver maple thrives on rich, moist soils bordering rivers, lakes, and swamps, and on islands and other bottomlands. Like its common associates, red ash, white elm, and willow, it withstands spring flooding. The shallow widespread roots bind fragile soils to prevent erosion.

Silver maple ranges from the lower St. John River valley in New Brunswick, west through southern Quebec and Ontario to Minnesota, south to the northwestern tip of Florida, and back up northeast to Maine. It is rare along the Atlantic seaboard.

In forested stands it grows straight and tall, often without a limb for 10–12 meters (30–40'). In the open, it is a different tree. It divides near the base into thick upright stems with long branches which sweep downward, then curve up at the tips, to form a large impressive crown.

In urban areas, silver maple has been planted extensively as a shade tree on lawns, in parks, and along streets and boulevards. It is beautiful, but it has its drawbacks. The brittle branches snap in heavy snows, winds, and ice storms. Its pervasive and thirsty roots can strangle sewer and water lines, and heave sidewalks and driveways. It is not recommended for planting around the home unless one's property is extensive. But it can contribute a touch of elegance to parks, cemeteries, golf courses, and suburban office sites, and is perfect for lining the borders of ponds.

Seeds should be gathered as soon as they mature in late spring, sown in a nursery bed, covered with 1–2 centimeters (½–1") of soil, and partially shaded. Some may germinate immediately; others may wait until the following spring. They are usually ready for transplanting after two years.

ducks call it home

Large old silver maples are frequently hollow, and provide ideal nesting cavities for black ducks, goldeneyes, wood ducks, and mergansers. When ready to follow mom, ducklings simply slip out of the nest and plop into the water. Raccoons, owls, and flying squirrels also set up home inside hollow maples, as do opossums, North America's only marsupials, who have recently expanded their range northward into Canada.

In late spring, long before the seeds of most trees mature, grosbeaks, cardinals, red squirrels, and chipmunks get an early treat.

boat floors and ballot boxes

At the lumber yard, no distinction is made between silver maple and red maple — they are both sold as soft maple. Not as strong — or expensive — as sugar maple, the soft maples are less widely used in furniture, flooring, and cabinetry. They are usually relegated to unseen components, as well as crates, boxes, and pallets.

At one time silver maple was employed as a light inlay to contrast with darker woods, such as mahogany, cherry, and walnut; however, with age the wood darkens and loses its effect. While silver maple has been crafted into numerous sundry items including boat floors, stairways, ice boxes, farm grain hoppers, children's cribs, ironing boards, coat hangers, barbed-wire reels, and ballot boxes, it has generally been used, not because of any special attribute, but rather because of its local availability and low cost.

With exposure to air, the wood often takes on a slight bluish tinge. It takes stain, polishes and other finishes beautifully. Silver

maple seasons without major shrinking or warping, is easy to work with, glues well, and holds nails firmly. Like red maple, it has endless possibilities that have not yet been explored.

dye and diarrhea

When times were tough, the Iroquois dried the inner bark of the silver maple, ground it into flour, and baked it into bread. The Omaha and Winnebago boiled the twigs and inner bark and mixed the water with iron-rich clay and tallow, to produce a brown or black dye in which they soaked their hides. The Mide'win Society of the Ojibway prepared a decoction of the inner bark to treat diarrhea.

As with all maples, its sap was boiled down into sugar, a popular food flavoring for most Native people. The sugar content of silver maple sap, however, is only half that of sugar maple; twice as much sap is needed to yield the same amount of sugar.

ants love aphids

A few species of midges and mites form galls on silver maple leaves, detracting from their appearance but not posing a threat of any kind. Another nuisance is the cottony maple scale, which deposits small white egg sacs on the branchlets. Fortunately, various beetles and flies find them appetizing, and they keep their numbers in check.

An interesting character is the woolly alder aphid. Colonies extrude masses of white waxy filaments on the leaves. Then in midsummer, they fly off to a nearby alder, reproduce without sex, and deposit more of the waxy stuff on the alder leaves. In fall, they head back to the silver maple to lay eggs on the bark. In spring the eggs hatch, and the cycle repeats itself. Aphids secrete a honeydew liquid that ants love — where you find aphids, you usually find ants.

Sugar Maple
(*Acer saccharum*)

hard maple
rock maple

Mohawk: *wahtha*

érable à sucre
érable franc

Leaf
- simple, opposite; usually 5-lobed, with 5 veins; tips round pointed; with few wavy teeth;
- sides of end lobe nearly parallel; base heart-shaped; on stalks 4–8 cm (2–3½") long;
- upper side dark yellowish green; underside paler;
- turn yellow, orange, or scarlet in autumn.

Flower
- males yellow, hanging from stalks; before and with emerging leaves;
- females greenish yellow; usually mixed with short sterile male stamens;
- in clusters, hanging from thin pale yellow stalks with white hairs; 3–7 cm (1–3") long;
- males and females on same tree, combined or in separate clusters;
- pollination by bees and other insects.

Fruit
- seeds plump, reddish brown, winged; in keys (samaras) 2.5–3 cm (1–1¼") long;
- hanging in U-shaped pairs, on slender stalks; mature in autumn; wind-disseminated;
- begin bearing seed at age 30–40; good seed crop every 2–5 years; occasional bumper crops.

Twig
- somewhat slender; tan or light reddish brown, smooth, slightly glossy, with tiny lenticels;
- terminal bud cone-shaped, pointed, dark reddish brown; flanked by 2 smaller lateral buds;
- opposite pairs of lateral buds spiral around twig, each pair 90° from that below.

Bark
- on younger trees, smooth, silver gray;
- on older trees, variable, deeply furrowed, irregularly ridged, sometimes scaly.

Wood
- heavy, hard, strong, stiff; straight-grained;
- narrow heartwood pale grayish brown to reddish tan;
- wide sapwood ivory white, with very slight reddish tinge;
- annual growth rings fairly distinct.

Height
18–30 m (60–100')

Diameter
60–90 cm (24–36")

Longevity
150–300 years

In spring, flowers emerge before or with unfolding leaves.

the maple leaf — the untold story

In Canada, sugar maples range from the Acadian forest of the Maritimes, through southern Quebec and Ontario, to just inside Manitoba. Below the border, they extend from Maine to Minnesota, down to northern Texas and Louisiana, and back east along the Appalachians to New England.

The American range of sugar maple is roughly double that of Canada. Yet somehow over the past two centuries, Canada has claimed sugar maple for its own. Conspiracy or coincidence? Let the record speak for itself.

Some say it began in the early 1800s, when the St. Jean Baptiste Society of Lower Canada adopted the maple leaf as its symbol. At the time of Confederation in 1867, both Quebec and Ontario had incorporated the leaf into their coats of arms. Less than a decade later, it was popularized when Alexander Muir wrote "The Maple Leaf Forever," the poem that, when later put to music, nearly became the national anthem.

In World War I the military joined the movement — the troops in the trenches bore maple leaf badges emblazoned on their uniforms, and they were entertained at Maple Leaf Clubs throughout England. Then the world of sport followed, with the renaming of the Toronto NHL franchise to the Maple Leafs. Shortly thereafter, the Canadian mint coined the first King George VI cent with two maple leaves on the reverse. Not to be outdone, private enterprise stepped in — by the late 1950s, 63 different Canadian products touted the Maple Leaf brand.

The coup de grâce came in 1965, when Canada, after considerable controversy, unveiled its new flag, with a red maple leaf depicted front and center. The icing on the cake came in 1996, when Parliament finally proclaimed the maple genus Canada's arboreal emblem.

Was it a 200-year conspiracy, or merely a long string of innocent coincidences? Without bilateral negotiations, international treaties, United Nations sanctions, or armed warfare, Canada had wrested the maple leaf away from its powerful neighbors, the United States of America.

There has been, however, some consolation for the Americans. The states of Vermont, New York, West Virginia, and Wisconsin all declared maple their state tree. And America can lay claim to the largest recorded sugar maple on the planet, in Kitzmiller, Maryland, a stone's throw from the nation's capital. The diameter of its trunk measures a whopping 2.2 meters — over 7 feet.

maples in the forest

Sugar maple is extremely tolerant of shade. Under the forest canopy, seeds germinate with as little as 2 percent sunlight, frequently carpeting the forest floor with seedlings. Some die because they have landed on a poor microsite; others are nibbled by mice, rabbits, and deer; but many survive, growing very slowly but otherwise healthy, patiently waiting for a clearing above so they can take advantage of the sunlight. When an older tree dies or is cut down, young maples seize the opportunity to fill the void.

In pure stands or in close company with other hardwoods and conifers, maples grow into tall straight trees, branchless for over half their height — a lumberjack's and a sawmiller's delight.

Sugar maple leaves are rich in minerals. They are slow to decompose, but when they do, they enrich the soil and reduce its acidity. Thick mats of moist maple leaves inhibit germination of other hardwood seeds, giving maples a competitive advantage from the start. They are, however, excellent sites for wildflowers, including early spring trilliums.

maple syrup

Technology in the maple bush may have changed a wee bit in the last 500 years or so, but the principle — and the product — remain the same.

Gone are the elm and birchbark vessels in which Native people collected sap. They were replaced first by oak buckets, then galvanized pails, and now by elaborate labor-saving networks of plastic tubing plugged into every taphole of every tappable tree. Pipelines may flow downhill to collecting tanks, or vacuum pumps can give gravity a helping hand.

Battery-powered portable drills have replaced the brace and bit of the pioneer. Cast iron cauldrons hung over open fires have given way to complex and efficient chrome evaporators that would fill a large living room. To speed the process along, many maple producers have installed reverse osmosis machines — like those used to desalinate sea water — to reduce the water content of the sap before boiling.

High-tech may have invaded the maple camp, but the basic principles remain the same as those the Natives taught us centuries ago. Each spring, frosty nights and warmer days trigger the sap flow within the tree. Tap a hole in the tree, collect the watery sap, which contains 2–4 percent sugar, boil it down until two-thirds of the water has evaporated in steam, and voilà — you have maple syrup with a sugar (vanillin glucoside) content of 66 percent. It is not only sweet and delicious, it has a higher calcium content than milk.

Further finishing produces maple sugar, creams, butters, candies, chocolates, and even cotton candy, as well as maple wines and liqueurs.

Quebec, which produces 70 percent of

Sugar maple — what the autumn color season is all about.

the maple in the world, is famous for its hundreds of *cabanes à sucre*, where families, students, senior citizens, and tourists visit a maple bush, have a sleigh ride, watch the evaporation process, eat taffy on the snow, and sit down for a meal of québecois fare — sausages, bacon, and ham, baked beans, and, of course, heaps of pancakes smothered in fresh maple syrup.

Just across the U.S. border, Vermont, synonymous with maple syrup, thrives on its reputation for maple sugar, with dozens of spin-off industries, including the maple museum in St. Johnsbury, founded on the sap of the sugar maple tree.

The one-time cottage industry has become big business — about half a billion dollars a year — but it has not lost its charm, its sense of tradition, and its raison d'être — quality maple syrup that just can't be found outside eastern North America.

a breath of fresh air

Sugar maple is the stuff of poetry and art. It is without doubt the most photographed autumn tree anywhere. In the open, the trunk divides into several large limbs within a few meters from the ground, developing a dense billowy crown that casts a deep summer shade.

In spring, hanging clusters of tiny yellow flowers adorn the branch tips. In autumn, sugar maples take on a beauty all their own, painting the landscape yellow, orange, scarlet, and every shade in between.

Sugar maple is not a downtown tree. The wide-spreading roots require plenty of room to stretch out. It struggles to survive where exhaust fumes, smoke, and other pollutants abound. Soil compaction, drought, and road salt are its enemies. Give it deep, moist, fertile, well-drained soil — pH neutral to slightly alkaline — in the clean air of the suburbs or countryside, and it will flourish.

child's play

Planting maples from seed is not exactly a horticultural challenge. If there is a sugar maple around the home, after a good seed year, seedlings will volunteer on the lawn, alongside the foundation, among the perennials, in shade or in full sun. If they are not where you would like them, resist the temptation to mow them down. Wait a year or two, dig them up, and transplant them. Potted, they make great gifts for new homeowners that will last a lifetime, and more.

If nature hasn't complied, simply gather seeds from the ground in the fall, bury them in 1 centimeter (½") of soil, and mulch for the winter. Remove the mulch in the spring. Leave them in the bed for two growing seasons, and transplant the seedlings the following spring while they're dormant. Considering the ease and success rate, it is a fun and educational activity to do with the kids.

the asheries

Following the explorers, soldiers, and missionaries to North America, settlers flocked here in search of fertile farm sites. The best soils were blanketed with predominantly maple hardwood forests that had to be cleared. It is estimated that 6,000 maple trees were cut down to clear the average farm.

Hardwood logs, too heavy to float in river drives, were virtually impossible to transport to seaports, and local markets were still in their infancy. Some timber was used for house and barn construction, a dozen or two cords for firewood and cooking, and a little for tools and implements. But the majority was waste, and was burned. This was the genesis of the potash industry in the new homeland.

Pioneers added water to wooden barrels of maple ashes, drained off the leached liquid into large iron pots, and boiled it down. The residue was pot ash. After the mid-eighteenth century, potash exports to Europe were a major source of income for settlers in their first years of farming. At the industry's peak in 1865, 44,000 barrels of potash were shipped to England, half of which was destined for soap for the Royal Navy. Potash represented 13 percent of total forest products exports. Sugar maples comprised 80 percent of it, mostly from land clearing in Quebec and New England.

The discovery of mineral salts in Germany late in the century provided a cheaper and less labor-intensive source of potash, and by 1900 the North American industry had all but ended. Millions of maples had been converted to potash over the 150-year period. In addition to soap, it was used as bleach in the textile industry, in glassmaking, and as a pottery glaze. Today, of course, it is one of the three basic elements in commercial chemical fertilizers — the K in N-P-K.

wears like marble

A comprehensive list of wood products from sugar maple would fill this page and several more. Here is a sampling, spanning the last several centuries: sled runners, gunpowder, spinning wheels, canoe paddles, wipple trees, shoe lasts, barrel staves, rifle stocks, whip handles, drum hoops, meat mauls, bicycle rims, factory floors, iceboxes, lawn rollers, croquet balls, railway ties, rolling pins, butcher blocks, bushel baskets, bowling pins, violin backs, golf club shafts, gym rings, photographic paper, anti-freeze, and pool cues. The men who harvested the trees relied on strong and sturdy peaveys, cant hooks, and pickaroons — the tools of the trade — all made of maple.

But still the most popular uses of maple are furniture, flooring, and woodenware. Maple wears as well as marble — some say better. It is the preferred wood for gymnasium floors, bowling lanes, and dance floors. A number of major league baseball players have switched to maple bats in recent years. They are reported to stand up to impact better than traditional ash bats. Maple is the top-selling hardwood in North America.

birdseye

The unique grain figure of birdseye maple has been treasured for luxurious furniture for at least 2,000 years — ancient birdseye table tops have been found amid Roman ruins. It is equally valuable today. Birdseye is scarce. Less than 5 percent, in many areas only 1 percent, of sugar maple trees contain commercial birdseye wood. Because of its scarcity and beauty, veneer-quality birdseye garners up to 40 times the price of ordinary sugar maple. In some areas, birdseye rustling has become a problem; tree DNA evidence has been used to track down the culprits.

Birdseye occurs throughout the range of sugar maple in North America. Since 1893, scientists have been researching the cause of the abnormality. Theories have abounded — adventitious buds, sapsucker pecking, boring insects, and fungi — but none have proved conclusive. Investigations into the influence of site, inherited genes, and long-term suppression by taller trees have been similarly pursued, but without success. Some suggest that the presence of hemlock in a stand is linked to birdseye, a relationship worth exploring. While most common with sugar maple, the grain figure also appears occasionally in red maple, white ash, and yellow birch. When all is said and done, no one really knows why birdseye is birdseye.

Birdseye can often be detected with a keen eye. A slightly coke-bottle shaped lower trunk, small dark dots on the outer bark, and cone-shaped indentations on the inner bark are clues that the wood inside may be birdseye. While not foolproof, they can help woodlot owners determine which trees are valuable, without resorting to cutting them down.

in the workshop

Unlike most hardwoods, maple's thick pale sapwood is preferred to its grayish heartwood, and is more expensive. Maple's strength, hardness, resistance to abrasion and impact, and uniform texture, color, and grain are all qualities essential for tongue-and-groove flooring. In the kitchen, its close texture and lack of taste or odor make it ideal for salad bowls, steak boards, bread boxes, canister sets, cutting boards, and butcher blocks.

Cabinetmakers consider hard maple a delight to work with, but it does have a few minor drawbacks — although it holds nails and screws securely, it tends to split, and may require pre-drilling. And its naturally smooth surface can be tricky to glue.

Maple is moderately easy on tools, does not splinter or sliver, turns well on a lathe, bends without breaking, and finishes to a pleasing color and grain with a minimum of preparation. Little wonder it is one of the most popular hardwoods in North America.

mostly for the birds

Sugar maples are not extraordinary wildlife trees, but they are the favorite haunt of a few critters, both feathered and furry. Evening grosbeaks savor maple seeds as much as the sunflower seeds in our feeders. Rich in protein and fat, and low in carbohydrates, they are also prime pickings for cardinals, pine grosbeaks, and rose-breasted grosbeaks. Chipmunks and squirrels, including flying squirrels, harvest the seed crop for in-tree dining and take-home for future consumption. In spring, maple buds are a dietary staple of gray squirrels; they build their nests of leaves high up in maple crowns.

City and country robins prefer the dense crowns of sugar maples for nesting, as do vireos, scarlet tanagers, grosbeaks, orioles and goldfinches.

In Vermont, where sugar maples are vital to both farming and tourism operations, bark-eating porcupines have been a problem, especially in spring when the sap is running.

bowls and arrows

Native people drank maple sap fresh from the tree as a cold refreshing beverage. Some Iroquois bands considered the sap a spring tonic, with diuretic or laxative properties, to flush the body of its ills after a long winter. They held ceremonies to honor the maple and revered it among hardwoods as the spring awakener of the forest. They carved elaborate ceremonial bowls, spoons, and pipes from birdseye maple and burls.

The Mi'kmaq crafted their bows, and the Ojibway their arrow shafts, from sugar maple. The Potawatomi fermented maple sap into vinegar, which they used as what we would call today a marinade, for venison. As was the custom with many tribes, the Meskwaki seasoned much of their food with maple syrup or sugar, in the same way we use salt.

Ojibway boiled the inner bark into a decoction for diarrhea, while the Seneca brewed a leaf tea as a mild astringent to help contract the womb during childbirth.

maple dieback

In the early 1980s, there was growing concern over the health of sugar maples. Trees were dying back from the top at rates not previously observed. The suspected culprit was acid rain. An international monitoring program was set up in 1988, with study plots strategically scattered across maple's range, to assess the condition of sugar maple. The good news is that results to date indicate no overall decline in their state of health, with mortality registering within the normal 1–2 percent range. Locally, maples on sensitive soils are susceptible to acid deposition, particularly an increase in soil aluminum, which hinders nutrient uptake by the tree.

The bad news is that it is premature at this time to assess the long-term impacts of the 1998 ice storm, which caused heavy damage to maple branches throughout southeastern Ontario, southern Quebec, and northern New York and New England, a region where sugar maple is the dominant species.

black maple

Black maple is a close cousin of sugar maple. Various authorities have labeled it a separate species, a subspecies, or a variety of sugar maple. There are some notable differences. Black maple leaves are usually three-lobed, covered with brown velvet on the underside and stalk, and appear somewhat wilted. The winter twigs are dull and faintly hairy, as are the seed stalks. The bark is blacker.

Black maple does not grow as far south, east, or north as sugar maple. While found in and around Montreal, north of Lake Ontario, and in the Carolinian forest, black maple's range is more westward — from the extreme west of New England to Minnesota, Iowa, and Missouri, dipping down to Tennessee and North Carolina.

Where the ranges of sugar and black maple overlap, they often hybridize naturally, the offspring displaying a blend of both parents' characteristics.

Black maple is also tapped for maple syrup. Its lumber, like that of sugar maple, is sold as hard maple.

The Serviceberries
(*Amelanchier* genus)

Saskatoon berry
shadbush
Juneberry
Indian pear
bilberry
sugar plum
sugar pear
shadblow

amélanchier
petite poire
bois de flèche
poirier

Dogrib Dene: *K'eàjie*

Of the dozen or so species of *Amelanchier* native to eastern North America, only two or three attain the height of a small tree; the rest are shrubs. Saskatoons, the most common serviceberry on the prairies, are usually shrubs, but can reach 4 meters (15') in height. These are the characteristics common to the tree species of *Amelanchier*.

Leaf
- simple, alternate; small, 3–8 cm (1–1½"), oval to roundish, symmetrical; tip pointed;
- finely toothed; twice as many teeth as veins; veins ending before teeth;
- on slender stalks 1–3 cm (approx. 1") long;
- turn yellow, orange, or red in autumn.

Flower
- white, with 5 showy petals; in erect or nodding clusters at branch tips;
- in early spring, with folded or unfolding leaves; insect-pollinated;
- flowers contain both male and female parts (perfect).

Fruit
- berry-like pomes, round, like miniature apples; dried flower parts on top; on long stems;
- dark purple at maturity, from June to August;
- juicy or dry; containing 5–10 hard dark brown seeds.

Twig
- slender, ridged; pith green, 5-pointed;
- buds brown, pointed, usually pressed against twig.

Bark
- smooth, gray; often with long thin vertical lines.

Wood
- hard, heavy, tough; close-grained;
- heartwood dark reddish brown; thick sapwood paler.

Height	Diameter	Longevity
up to 12 m (40')	up to 20 cm (8")	varies with species

Early spring beauty.

the Amelanchier maze

The range of the *Amelanchier* genus is vast — from Newfoundland to Alaska to Florida. There is at least one species of serviceberry native to every province and state except Hawaii.

When you venture into the botanical maze searching for the specific identity of a serviceberry, you may never return. What may be a 10-meter (35') tall tree in one locale could be a shrub in another. The small, nondescript leaves exhibit tremen-

dous variation in shape, often on the same tree. Furthermore, the various species hybridize extensively, spawning progeny with traits of both parents. Serviceberry has even been reported to interbreed with mountain ash, its distant cousin in the rose family. Taxonomists themselves, the authorities who classify and name species, do not agree on the division of the *Amelanchier* genus into species. In the nineteenth century, they considered them all one species.

By process of elimination, one can usually identify a tree or shrub as one of the *Amelanchiers.*

The lay person would be well advised to leave it at that. The botanist is welcome to pursue it further, but frustration and confusion may well be the result. If you refer to ten different tree manuals, you will likely find nine different treatments of the genus. The tenth author would no doubt be a student of one of the other nine.

a few clues

Look for serviceberries in early spring along roadsides, in fencerows, on the edges of old fields, and occasionally in the understory of hardwood stands. The display of white flower clusters, before the leaves have fully unfurled, is the best clue. In midsummer, the presence of dark purple berries on long slender stems is another. Once the wildlife have made off with all the fruit, serviceberries become inconspicuous again until autumn, when the foliage turns yellow, orange, or red. In winter, most *Amelanchier* buds look a little like smaller versions of beech buds — long, narrow, and pointed.

transplanting or seeding

If you intend to transplant a serviceberry from the wild to the home landscape, identify the young tree the previous spring when it is in flower, and flag it. Otherwise serviceberries are not easy to spot while dormant in late winter or early spring. And at flowering time, they don't take kindly to being transplanted.

To plant from seed, gather the berries as soon as they mature — June to August, depending on the species — before the birds strip the twigs bare. Plant immediately, fruit and all, cover with 1 centimeter (½") of soil, and mulch until next spring. Some species may not germinate until the second spring. Western Saskatoons should be half-shaded for the first growing season. Leave in the nursery bed for two to three years before outplanting.

Serviceberry trees or shrubs are attractive native ornamentals. The clusters of elegant white blossoms are among the first to welcome the arrival of spring, and the midsummer berries are an open invitation to a host of songbirds.

not just another pretty face

Serviceberries are not just another pretty face in the forest. They are one of our most important wildlife groups. Two-thirds of Canadian wildlife depend on the forest for habitat, and the little serviceberries contribute more than their share. Over 40 species of birds get a carbohydrate boost from the berries — among them, Bohemian waxwings and hairy woodpeckers, wood thrushes and brown thrashers, robins and rufous-sided towhees, scarlet tanagers and wild turkeys. Ruffed grouse consume the fruit in the summer and the phosphorus-rich buds in winter.

The forest's furry set get in on the action as well. Skunks, black bears, martens, chipmunks, and eastern flying squirrels all include serviceberries in their summer diet. Red foxes save their energy by filling up on the fruits, relieving some of the pressure on their prey, the bird population. White-tailed deer nibble on the berries in summer, and return in spring to browse the twigs. The largest consumer, in size, is the grizzly of the northwest, who may dine on a salmon for dinner and a pawful of Saskatoons for dessert.

All of this wildlife activity ensures that serviceberry seeds are dispersed far and wide.

deep-fried pemmican

Although details are sketchy, there was a pattern among medicine people from a number of nations of prescribing the inner or root bark for female and birth-related ailments. The bark was steeped into a tea that patients drank to prevent miscarriage, control excessive menstrual flow, and as a strengthening tonic during pregnancy or after giving birth.

Native people across the continent ate serviceberries fresh, a practice continued today by prairie residents. Serviceberries were a routine ingredient in Native cookery, and were the fruit commonly used in their food staple, pemmican. They dried and pulverized moose, deer, or buffalo meat, mixed in the fruit, and deep-fried the two in fat. When it was cooled, they shaped it into small loaves for the winter larder and carried it with them whenever they traveled or hunted away from home. It was the granola bar of the times. The Lewis and Clark expedition to the Pacific Ocean relied on pemmican given them by the Indians when their food supplies were exhausted.

In the days of Cartier and Champlain, the taste of serviceberries reminded the explorers of pears, and they dubbed them petites poires or "little pears," a name still in common usage today in Quebec. In the Maritimes, Acadiens call them *poiriers*.

When the voyageurs traveling among the Cree saw them fashioning their arrow shafts from hard and tough serviceberry wood, they called the tree *bois de flêche*, the other common French name still heard over 300 years later.

Yellow Birch
(*Betula alleghaniensis*)

silver birch
curly birch
swamp birch
hard birch
black birch

bouleau jaune
merisier
bouleau des Alleghanys
bouleau frisé

Ojibway: *wiinizik*

Leaf
- simple, alternate; oval; tapered to a toothed, pointed tip; 7–12 cm (3–5") long; base rounded or slightly heart-shaped; somewhat asymmetrical;
- upper side dark green; underside yellowish green, with raised midrib and veins; fuzzy at junctions;
- 9–11 straight parallel veins per side, ending in larger teeth; 2–5 smaller teeth between;
- thin, soft textured; stem round, yellowish green, fuzzy; 2 cm (1") long;
- turn yellow in autumn.

Flower
- male catkins brown, 2–3 cm (1") long, in small clusters on twig tips all winter;
- elongate to 8 cm (3") long at pollination time; hanging;
- female solitary, green, fuzzy, upright, before leaves unfold; wind-pollinated;
- male and female on same tree.

Fruit
- upright, squat, oval green cone, 2–3 cm (1") long; brown, woody at maturity in fall;
- seed a tiny 2-winged nutlet, released gradually throughout late fall and winter;
- good seed crop every 3–4 years; bumper crop every 10 years;
- begin to produce seed at age 30–40, occasionally much earlier.

Twig
- slender, orangey or greenish brown, slightly hairy;
- distinctive mild wintergreen taste;
- buds sharply pointed, fuzzy, 2 shades of brown; no true terminal bud.

Bark
- on younger trees, thin, smooth, glossy, golden or reddish brown, with lenticels;
- on older trees, silvery gold; peeling in thin, horizontal, curly, papery strips;
- on mature trees, rough, thick, dark brown on lower trunk; broken into large plates.

Wood
- heavy, hard, strong; straight-grained (sometimes wavy or curly); fine-textured;
- heartwood brown or reddish brown;
- thin sapwood creamy white, pale yellow, or light reddish brown;
- annual growth rings indistinct.

Height	Diameter	Longevity
20–30m (70–100')	60–90 cm (24–36")	150–300 years

l'emblème arboréale du Québec

Yellow birch is a tree of moderate cool climes. It ranges from Newfoundland and the Maritimes, through southern Quebec and Ontario, north of Lake Superior to the southeast tip of Manitoba, then down as far as the Appalachians in North Carolina and Tennessee, and back up to Maine. The largest and longest-living of the birches in North America, it thrives on moist fertile soils. Where there is yellow birch, hemlock is frequently nearby, as well as sugar maple, beech, and white ash. Yellow birch is also found lining the borders of swamps.

The climate and soils of southern Quebec, Ontario, the Maritimes, New England, and the Lakes states are ideal for yellow birch. A 350-year-old veteran in a park in Stoneham, north of Quebec City, has a diameter of 140 centimeters (over 4½'). Quebec supplies over half the yellow birch lumber in North America. In the 1990s, *la belle province* declared yellow birch its official arboreal emblem.

But huge yellow birches are not confined to Quebec. The American Forests record holder grows on Deer Isle on the coast of Maine, with a diameter measuring over 200 centimeters (6½').

Yellow birch rarely forms pure stands, but comprises a major component of most eastern hardwood stands. For example, one quarter of the hardwoods in Nova Scotia are yellow birch; two out of three birches in the United States are yellow.

maple leaf mat

Yellow birch is not as plentiful as it once was. Land clearing for agriculture and development, harvesting for lumber and firewood, and a widespread birch dieback problem in the 1930s and 1940s — much-researched, but never fully explained — have all taken their toll.

The other culprit is sugar maple. Yellow birch and sugar maple commonly share the same sites. Maple leaves do not decompose readily, and form a thick mat on the forest floor. Tiny yellow birch seeds germinate on the moist maple leaves, but their roots are unable to penetrate the mat to reach the soil below, and seedlings perish over the summer.

something for everyone

Yellow birch hosts a world of wildlife in all seasons. Seedlings, stump sprouts, and winter twigs of young trees are a wintergreen delicacy to mice, rabbits, moose, and especially white-tailed deer. In some areas, yellow birch is the deer's favorite browse. Higher up in the branches, ruffed grouse gobble the nutritious buds and catkins, protein providers to guarantee good health for spring breeding. Porcupines enjoy gnawing on the aromatic bark.

In spring, after vacationing in the Caribbean all winter, yellow-bellied sapsuckers seek out a birch with a decaying core to peck out their nests. Their large handsome cousins, pileated woodpeckers, chisel out hollows in the trunks for nesting and roosting. When the pileated woodpecker moves to a new tree, in comes a female wood duck, after her migration north, to claim the cavity for her nest.

Pairs of rare red-shouldered hawks nesting among yellow birch branches take turns incubating their eggs while the other partner is off hunting rodents. The crow-sized hawks are listed as vulnerable on Canada's endangered species list.

Back at ground level, snowshoe hares, cottontail rabbits, and beavers munch away on the flavorful bark. Larvae of the bronze birch borer provide a high protein meal for woodpeckers.

Yellow birches are prolific seeders, scattering most of their tiny winged nutlets onto the snow over winter. Enter the finch family

Up to eleven veins either side of the midrib lead to large teeth.

of redpolls, goldfinches, and pine siskins, to clean them up. Other avian winter residents, notably blue jays, nuthatches, and chickadees, join in the seed fest. And of course the red squirrel, never one to miss anything edible, takes its share.

Insects, songbirds, woodpeckers, ducks, raptors, and mammals, from the lowly mouse to the majestic moose, all benefit from yellow birch, the granddaddy of the birch family.

oil of wintergreen

The forest has two natural sources of oil of wintergreen: the leaves and red berries of the creeping wintergreen plant, *Gaultheria procumbens,* and the bark and twigs of both yellow and cherry birch, *Betula lenta.* Cherry birch, also known as black or sweet birch, grows in only one location in Canada, near Port Dalhousie on the south shore of Lake Ontario. In the United States, it ranges from southwestern Maine to northern Georgia.

The chemical compound that provides the wintergreen taste is identical in both plants. It is methyl salicylate, a sweeter relative of aspirin. At one time most of the commercial oil of wintergreen used to flavor gum, candy, and toothpaste was extracted from cherry birch. Today it is produced synthetically. In mild preparations, such as birch wintergreen tea steeped from the twigs, it is a pleasant beverage. In concentrated doses it can be toxic and even fatal.

The Ojibway scraped the inner bark from yellow birch, mixed it with maple bark, and brewed a tea to stimulate urination. In the spirit of "a spoonful of sugar helps the medicine go down," the Potawatomi extracted wintergreen from the twigs to flavor less appetizing medicines.

In spring, male catkins at the end of the twigs elongate, then release their pollen.

a cabinetmaker's delight

The island of Cape Breton is principally forest land. Here grow the greatest quantity of a species of timber called by us Black Birch [yellow birch]. The wood of this Tree is firm, close-grained, in color resembling the Mahogany but stronger and more substantial. It is used here in shipbuilding and has been found to be more durable than Oak, especially for those parts of vessels as lie under water.

Charles Morris, 1774
Surveyor General of Nova Scotia

Shipbuilding and, of course, firewood were among the first uses of large old-growth yellow birch in the virgin hardwood forests of the northeast. By 1800, furniture makers recognized the merits of the hard, reddish-toned heartwood, and elevated its use from mundane items such as wagon wheel hubs, broom handles, sled frames, tubs, and pails to fine furniture and cabinetry. The heartwood was employed for exposed surfaces, while the whiter sapwood was concealed in components such as drawer interiors.

Yellow birch was transformed into ice boxes, butcher blocks, toys, radio and phonograph cabinets, flooring, doors, and kitchenware. It was second only to white birch for turning of spools, bobbins, and spindles for the textile industry. Its good bending ability was capitalized on in crafting baby cradles and chair backs.

Yellow birch is a cabinetmaker's delight. The heartwood, often marketed as red birch, planes, drills, and shapes better than most hardwoods, and despite its hardness, it doesn't blunt tools. It produces the smoothest of mortise and tenon joints. It does not splinter or sliver, but takes nails and screws without splitting, and holds them firmly. The close grain and uniformly smooth surface yield a satiny finish when stained or polished, and it stands up to heavy wear and tear. When the price gap between black cherry and yellow birch lumber periodically widens, it is often substituted for cherry.

Over half the yellow birch harvested today is sliced into veneer for paneling, door skins, and plywood products such as kitchen cabinets.

a stately shade tree

With the right climate and soil, yellow birch develops slowly into a stately shade tree. Open-grown birches have massive spreading limbs and a full crown of graceful foliage. In spring, dangling catkins adorn the boughs, the foliage fades to a pleasant yellow in autumn, and the lustrous bronze bark is resplendent in all seasons.

Yellow birch roots are shallow and wide-spreading. On thin or wet soils they may not anchor a large tree firmly, rendering it susceptible to strong winds. Like white birch, its roots are very sensitive to soil temperature changes caused by landscaping.

Fall planting is the simplest approach. Gather the cones before they disintegrate, and sow the seeds immediately in a prepared seedbed. Cover very lightly with a few millimeters (¼") of soil. In spring, build a raised platform over the seedbed with snow fence or branches, to provide partial sunlight. Leave the seedlings in the seedbed for two growing seasons before transplanting them to a site that is moist and fertile.

attacks from within

In the fall, larvae of the bronze birch borer excavate meandering tunnels between the wood and the bark. When their numbers are high or they persist for several years, they can fatally girdle the tree. Parent beetles usually start laying their eggs in the upper branches, so the first sign of borer presence is a yellowing or browning of leaves near the top. They prey upon weakened and stressed trees, so maintaining good health and vigor is the key to controlling them.

Heart rot is a common yellow birch malady in many regions caused by fungi that enter the tree through wounds. Since tree heartwood is not living tissue, afflicted trees can survive for many years with the condition, providing homes for those mammals and birds who nest or den in cavity trees. The trees, once structurally weakened, are susceptible to breakage, and, of course, their value as lumber is nil.

White Birch
(*Betula papyrifera*)

paper birch
canoe birch

bouleau à papier
bouleau blanc
bouleau à canot

Woods Cree: *waskway*

Leaf
- simple, alternate; oval; tapering to sharp pointed, toothed tip; 5–10 cm (2–4") long;
- base toothless, flat, slightly rounded or heart-shaped; stalk yellowish green, curved; up to 9 veins each side of midrib, each leading to a large tooth, with several smaller teeth between;
- in pairs, emanating from same twig bud;
- upper side dark green, somewhat lustrous;
- underside paler, yellowish green; raised midrib and veins fuzzy at junctions;
- turn yellow in autumn.

Flower
- male catkins brown, at end of twigs all winter;
- in spring, elongate into hanging clusters of 1–3; shiny dark brown and yellow at pollination, 7–9 cm (3–4") long;
- female catkins greenish, 2 cm (1") long, erect or leaning, on short shoots;
- both male and female catkins on same tree.

Fruit
- catkins cone-like, cylindrical, yellowish green; 4–5 cm (2") long;
- hanging from short shoots;
- at maturity in summer, fall apart, disperse seeds, leaving only thin central stalk;
- tiny oval seeds with 2 filmy wings; cone scales fleur-de-lys shaped; wind-disseminated;
- begin bearing seed at age 15; good seed crop most years.

Twig
- slender, reddish brown, slightly rough;
- buds slender, tapering to blunt point; gummy; brown and green.

Bark
- on saplings, reddish brown, somewhat shiny, with prominent lenticels;
- on trees, white, composed of many thin papery layers; inner layers pink, with horizontal lenticels up to 5 cm (2") wide;
- on mature trees, charcoal black and rough, starting at the base;
- inner bark orange.

Wood
- hard, strong, tough, straight-grained, uniform-textured; odorless; not decay-resistant;
- heartwood light brown to reddish brown;
- thick sapwood creamy white, with yellow or reddish brown tinge;
- annual growth rings faint.

Height
18–22 m (60–70')

Diameter
45–60 cm (18–24")

Longevity
100–120 years

the Lady of the Forest

White birch truly ranks as one of the most distinguished — and easily distinguishable — of our native trees. Its striking white bark shines among the browns and grays of its fellow forest inhabitants. White birch is at its best amid a grove of evergreens.

About 40 species of birch permeate the northern regions of America, Asia, and Europe. Coleridge described European white birch as the most beautiful of forest trees, dubbing it "the Lady of the Forest" in tribute to the grace and charm of its bark.

Our white birch is one of the few trees that grows in all provinces and territories. It has officially been designated the arboreal emblem of Saskatchewan, where it is a major component of the province's northern forest. It is also a popular ornamental in the south. Primarily a tree of the north, birch ranges down to the northeastern and Lakes states, and as far west as Montana and Idaho. In eastern North America, the birch family includes the diminutive hornbeams and hop hornbeams, as well as hazelnut and alder shrubs.

Other closely related birches are mountain paper birch in the east, water birch in the west, and Alaska and Kenai birch in the northwest.

from seed to senility

White birch needs full sunlight, so it finds a home on former forest fire sites, clearcuts, idle farmland, roadsides, and forest fringes. Its intolerance of shade, its light, windborne winged seeds, and its readiness to germinate on exposed mineral soils make it an ideal pioneer to re-establish a new forest after a disturbance. Home gardeners know that if there is a birch nearby as a source of seed, seedlings will pop up wherever they expose bare soil.

A bumper crop of birch seed will reduce a tree's annual growth and production of buds, as the tree's energy is redirected from growth to reproduction. It is not uncommon for a birch in its final years to produce a bumper crop of seeds, perhaps nature's way of ensuring the proliferation of the species.

In its southern range, birch serves as a nurse crop for shade-tolerant hardwoods such as beech and sugar maple, as well as for conifers such as white pine and red spruce, which settle in as seedlings beneath its shade and shelter. Young birches generate a great amount of nitrogen and phosphorus-rich litter — leaves, catkins, and twigs — which decomposes rapidly to fertilize the soil. With a short lifespan, a little longer than that of the average person, they are eventually replaced by longer-living trees, having fulfilled their ecological mission in the natural succession toward a climax forest.

In northern boreal forests, where forest fires, usually caused by lightning, recur every forty to eighty years, birch maintains its position as a dominant tree until succumbing to the inevitable flames. Birch's papery bark is an open invitation to even a moderate fire. But it is prepared. When the organic layer of soil is burned off, millions of birch seeds are ready to take root — a cycle that has been repeated for over 7,000 years, since the retreat of the glaciers. Trees in the boreal forest seldom live longer than 100 years.

As white birch grows rapidly out of its sapling stage, it loses its characteristic dark red, pin-cherry-like bark. The resemblance is so pronounced that the word for pin cherry in many Algonquian languages, including Mi'kmaq and Potawatoni, means "birch with berries." On occasion, birch evolves into an intermediate stage, with pink bark. For the majority of its life, its unique white papery covering is the key to its easy identification. Those trees that reach old age develop a coarse, charcoal black bark, particularly near the base. Birches die of old age from the top down — first the twigs, then branchlets, then large branches, until all that remains standing is a pole. Finally they topple, but not before they have played host to fungi, insects, and assorted woodpeckers.

New leaves are somewhat glossy in spring, gradually growing duller until the second set of leaves unfold.

Birch wood is not at all resistant to decay when in contact with the soil. But its bark is. It is not unusual to find on the forest floor an intact hollow cylinder of bark, whose wood contents have long since rotted away.

its bark and its bite

White birch was instrumental in the lives of First Nations people. As Samuel de Champlain explained in 1603, *With the canoes of the Savages a man may travel freely and readily into all countries, as well in the small as in the great Rivers.* Transportation depended on lightweight birchbark canoes to allow them to move settlements, to trade, to fish, to hunt, and gather, and when necessary, to portage.

Canoe construction was not only ingenious, but it reflected Native people's intimate knowledge of the gifts the forest offered. Birch bark was peeled off in long sheets, fitted around a framework of cedar ribs that had been steamed and bent to shape, sewn together with pliant and strong spruce roots, and the holes and seams sealed with balsam fir resin.

White birch bark provided Native people materials for crafting bowls and dishes, fans, vats and baskets, chests and granaries, buckets to collect the spring run of maple sap, candles and torches, weatherproof maps and posters on which they communicated their whereabouts to others, and for fashioning a host of curios, trinkets, and ornaments — and ultimately their coffins. It was said that anything perishable, when wrapped in birch bark, would be preserved.

In the Lake Superior region, Ojibway women created artistic designs, called transparencies, by biting on folded layers of paper-thin birch bark. Sometimes the bark was folded up to twelve times; when unfolded, it created elaborate symmetrical patterns. The art form continues today in a few Native communities.

from firewood to syrup to beer to toothpicks

Where people have the good fortune to choose their firewood from beech, maple, oak, and even hickory, white birch is not highly prized for firewood, except perhaps for

The bark is composed of many thin papery layers; the inner layers are pink.

kindling, or its aesthetic contribution to the family hearth. It generates only two-thirds the heat value of sugar maple. But in the northern boreal forest, where hardwood firewood choices are limited to poplar, willow, or birch, white birch firewood was, and still is, in great demand. Once cut down, it has to be bucked up, split, and dried fairly quickly, as it rots faster than most hardwoods.

The bark will ignite readily even when wet, providing warmth to many a camper or woodland voyageur unable to reach home at night. Wherever possible, bark for such emergencies should be torn off dead trees, as live birches may be permanently damaged by bark removal.

In Maine and the Maritime provinces, nineteenth-century settlers capitalized on the decay-resistant and waterproof qualities of birch bark by applying sheets of bark to the walls and roofs of their homes, between the rough boards and the exterior cedar shingles or siding, as insulation against the cold and bitter winter winds. Unfortunately, it was also highly inflammable.

In northern areas of Canada, beyond the natural range of sugar maple, birch syrup makes a fine substitute for maple syrup. Since the sugar content of its sap is less than that of maple, much more sap needs to be boiled to produce an equal quantity of syrup. For those with more of a thirst than a sweet tooth, fermentation of the sap produces a fine birch beer. Many Native tribes aged birch sap to produce vinegar.

White birch wood is straight-grained, fine-textured, and uniform, but is not as hard, heavy, or strong as yellow birch. It dries well, but shrinks considerably in the process. It is still the wood of choice for wood turning, and has supported generations of New England mills that produce "spoolwood."

For home flooring, cabinetry, and furniture, white birch wood takes a variety of oil and water-based stains well. It is easy to glue, but may split when nailed. It does not dull tools such as chisels and planes. The ultimate consumer products of white birch are furniture, dowels, and wooden toys. It is sliced into a creamy white veneer and plywood, for kitchen cabinets and the like. It is broken down into wood pulp, usually in a mixture with other species. Among its more unusual end products are clothes pins, ice cream sticks, tongue depressors, and toothpicks — the wood is smooth, odorless, and tasteless.

landscaping with the Lady

Within the natural range of white birch, its lightly filtered shade provides one of the most beautiful additions to home landscaping with native species. Birches are a little particular — they require full sunlight and moist soils. Their shallow wide-spreading roots are very susceptible to disturbances such as grading, soil compaction, or changes in elevation or depth of the soil — anything that alters soil temperature. Many a new homeowner who has cleared all trees from the building lot except the birches has been bitterly disappointed to find the birches dead within a year or two.

Where summers are dry, in the prairies for example, weekly watering may be required from May to August, with a good soaking just prior to frost setting in. If the tree is under stress, fertilizer may be applied in May. Branch pruning should be done in late spring, after leaves reach full size; earlier pruning may result in excessive sap bleeding. As with all trees, prune at the edge of the branch collar, and not flush with the trunk.

Planted or transplanted under the right conditions and on the appropriate site, white birch will provide a relatively maintenance-free ornamental. There are, however, some insects, diseases, and weather conditions that may pose a problem. Early spring pollen may trigger allergies in some people.

the oppressors

White birch are host to an unusually large variety of insects, which feed on the leaves, bark, catkins, and shoots. Two of the most important are the bronze birch borer and the birch leaf miner.

The larvae of the bronze birch borer feed on the sap-conducting tissue in the trunk and branches. In early summer, beetles lay their eggs in the bark, and the emerging worm-like larvae tunnel inside. The long galleries they create girdle the trunk or branch, cutting off the sap flow, and causing dieback. The borers overwinter as grubs, pupate the next spring, and emerge as adult beetles to start all over.

The birch leaf miner was introduced into North America in Connecticut in 1923, and has become a problem with all birch, especially those near the bottom of its natural range. In May, the adult female sawfly lays her eggs in slits on the upper surface of the leaves. Tiny flat larvae feed on the tissues between the two surfaces of the leaf. Initially the damage appears as light green blotches; these eventually turn brown and spread and merge with other blotches, until the whole leaf is discolored. In early June the larvae emerge from the leaf, drop to the ground, and pupate; two weeks later they emerge as adults. This life cycle may be repeated two to four times a summer. Unfortunately for male leaf miners, who are rare, mating is not required for this reproduction.

Chickadees and warblers feed on the larvae as they emerge; they rarely destroy the whole population, but help keep the numbers in control. If the problem is life-threatening, arboriculturists recommend a soil-drenching with undiluted dimethoate, a systemic insecticide that is effective and relatively safe. Dig shallow holes inside the drip line and pour in the chemical at the dosage recommended on the label for the size of the tree. The insecticide is absorbed by the roots, and takes a week to move up to the leaves and reach the larvae.

Leaf miner damage distracts from the beauty of the tree and causes premature leaf shedding. But it is rarely lethal. Therefore

avoiding chemicals and relying on the insect's natural predators is suggested.

Insects are not the only threat. Birch canker is a fungal disease that causes a swelling near poor pruning or broken branches. The swelling cuts off water supply and kills the branch.

In New Brunswick's Fundy National Park, scientists have for decades been studying the causes of a phenomenon called birch decline. While the trees have been stressed by other factors, it is now believed that acid fog from pollution may be the underlying cause of leaf browning.

Ice storms, such as the catastrophic event of January 1998 in the northeastern states, southeastern Ontario and southern Quebec, can cause massive and permanent damage to white birch. The weight of the ice encircling limbs and twigs can add up to 40 times the normal weight to the crown, resulting in large branches being torn off the trunk, hundreds of small twigs — the last season's growth — being snapped off, and even sizable trees bowing over until their tops are encrusted in the snow. Some trees never regain their original straight form, and all trees are stressed, rendering them more susceptible to insects and disease.

for aches and agues

The medicinal properties of many parts of white birch were well recognized by Native people across North America and the settlers who learned from them. The Ojibway suffering from headaches would wrap a thin layer of bark around the head. Birch, like willow, contains small amounts of methyl salicylate. The Ojibway also used the boiled roots of

Facing page: The bark evolves from deep red as very young trees, to the familiar white above. Occasionally there is an intermediate pink stage. Bark on mature trees becomes black and crusty at the base.

birch to flavor unpleasant medicines. Saskatchewan's Woods Cree boiled the inner bark into a lotion for skin rashes and sores.

In 1674, John Josselyn reported in the findings of his trips to New England: *the bark of the birch is used by the Indians for bruised wounds and cuts, — boyled very tender, and stamped betwixt two stones to a plaister, and the decoction thereof poured into the wound.* In 1900, Auguste Mockle noted that Natives in Quebec drank birch leaf tea for rheumatism and dropsy. In Maine, birch leaf tea was a popular drink with both the Natives and colonists.

white birch as habitat

White birch provides both food and shelter for a variety of mammals, insects, and birds. Mice gnaw at the bark of young trees, often girdling them and causing premature mortality. Porcupines and beavers eat both the bark and the wood. White birch buds are a staple in the diet of purple finches. Their common partners in flight, redpolls and pine siskins, savor the seeds and return the favor by distributing them far and wide. Philadelphia vireos and American redstarts decorate their nests with pieces of the papery bark.

Catkins, seeds, and buds are a favorite of the red squirrel, as they are with the three species of grouse who inhabit white birch territory — ruffed (commonly called partridge), spruce, and sharp-tailed grouse. In winter, the twigs and buds are browsed by white-tailed deer, moose, and snowshoe hares. The latter, also called varying hare, turn as white as birch bark in winter.

Downy and hairy woodpeckers, yellow-bellied sapsuckers, and vireos find cavities in white birch a convenient and safe nesting site to rear their young. Robins perch on birches, seeking out a succulent worm below, while dead and leafless branches provide hummingbirds the opportunity to rest and survey the available sources of nectar from the colorful flowers below.

Gray Birch
(*Betula populifolia*)

wire birch
fire birch
water birch
swamp birch
old field birch
poverty birch

bouleau gris
bouleau à feuille de peuplier
bouleau rouge

Maliseet: *sak'-pa-kwetsk'*

Leaf
- simple, alternate; dark glossy green on upper side, paler green below;
- arrowhead-shaped, with toothed edges; almost flat base and long tapering tip;
- stalks slender, causing leaves to flutter in a breeze;
- turn buff yellow in autumn.

Flower
- males and females on same twig;
- male, usually solitary, visible in winter as 5 cm (2") brown catkin at end of twig;
- male elongates to 10 cm (4") in spring, turns yellow, hangs, and releases pollen;
- green female appears with unfolding of leaves.

Fruit
- cylindrical cone 2–3 cm (1") long; brown and woody at maturity in fall;
- opens and releases very light seeds with heart-shaped wings.

Twig
- wiry, slender, dark reddish brown; warty, rough to the touch;
- buds pointed, resinous, chestnut brown, 6 mm (¼") long;
- on proliferation of dark branches, branchlets, and twigs;
- branches often contorted.

Bark
- on younger trees, reddish brown with white lenticels;
- on older trees, white; wrapped tightly around trunk; does not peel;
- triangular black patches below point where limbs join trunk;
- base of older trees dark gray and rough; inner bark orange.

Wood
- soft, light, not strong; decays quickly;
- heartwood light reddish brown; thick sapwood creamy white;
- annual growth rings inconspicuous.

Height	Diameter	Longevity
8–10 m (25–30')	20–30cm (8–12")	30–50 years

Leaves are arrow-shaped, with long tapering tips.

reclaiming the forest

Man may pattern it and change its variety and shape, but leave it for even a short time and off it goes on its own . . . swallowing man's puny intentions.

Emily Carr

Each species was designed as a strand in the web of nature we call an ecosystem — even the mosquito, poison ivy, and the human. The humble gray birch is no exception. It plays the role of a healer. It colonizes disturbed sites and begins the long process of nursing them back to the healthy forests they once were. A prolific producer of winged windborne seeds, as well as a vigorous stump sprouter, gray birch blankets burnt areas, cutovers, and abandoned farm fields with young trees. In pure stands or in association with other pioneers, such as pin cherry, trembling aspen, alder, sweet fern, or white birch, it lays the groundwork for the forest of the future.

Gray birch supplies shade and protection for seedlings of longer-lived and more tolerant trees. Its fallen leaves, catkins, and twigs decompose rapidly and add organic matter and vital nutrients to the soil. Its shallow roots stabilize the soil, preventing erosion and nutrient loss. Within its short lifespan of 30 to 50 years, it takes barren, burnt, sterile or exhausted land and rehabilitates it into a forest. In its later stages it may temporarily retard the growth of more valuable trees, but it soon dies off naturally, or can be harvested for firewood.

onward and westward

They also serve who only stand and wait.
John Milton, 1608–1674
"On His Blindness"

Gray birch will grow just about anywhere there is full sunlight and no competition. It is at home at the forest edge, along roadsides, in farm fencerows, and lining waterways. It appears to stand patiently awaiting an opportunity for its seeds to fulfill its pioneer role. It is equally comfortable on sandy or gravelly soils, on barren ground, at the edges of wetlands, and on sites too sterile to support other tree species.

In a 1960s experiment, 16 species of trees and shrubs were planted on Pennsylvania coal strip mine spoils, very acidic sites and certainly not ideal conditions for growing trees. After 11 years, gray birch had the highest level of survival and were the best-growing trees.

Gray birch has a rather small range, along the Atlantic Seaboard up to Prince Edward Island, west to Lake Ontario, and down to Delaware. With the increase in human activity, abandoned farmland, and clearcuts, the species is slowly expanding its range northward and westward.

one person's weed is another's wildflower

Gray birch is sometimes looked upon with disfavor by country folk, who may view it as a weed or perhaps a not-too-pleasant reminder of impoverished soils, failed farms, or forest fires. This is likely the reason it is more popular as an ornamental outside its natural range. Alone or in a clump, it can be a handsome little tree around the home, especially where space is limited. With today's trend toward smaller building lots in cities and suburbs, gray birch may add a touch of the woods without monopolizing the green space.

It earned its Latin name *populifolia* — poplar-leafed — not because its leaves resemble those of poplars, but because they flutter in the breeze, as those of trembling aspen do. In autumn they turn a buffy yellow. It is a compact tree, with a profusion of dark branches and twigs that rise from the trunk and then droop at the tips. In winter they contrast with the white bark and snow.

Gray birch is hardy, salt-resistant, and adaptable to almost any soil. If selecting a sapling or clump of saplings from the wild to transplant before the leaves unfold, it is easy to confuse gray birch with white birch or pin cherry. Look for the warty twigs.

barrel hoops, fuelwood, and spoolwood

Anyone who has seen a gray birch bend to the ground in an ice storm recognizes its flexibility. Until the 1950s, coopers capitalized on this trait to create barrel hoops. Saplings 2 or 3 centimeters (1") in diameter were chopped down, split in half, cut and bent to the desired size, and secured around the staves. The barrels were used for shipping apples, potatoes and nails.

Gray birch is a favorite fire starter with many a rural resident. Its size requires a minimum of splitting, but, if necessary, it splits easily, especially when frozen. It burns quick and hot, but not long. Acadians have a yarn about the branchiness of gray birch. They claim: "You chop it down, you limb it, you buck it up, you limb it, you split it, and you limb it again. The only time you don't have to limb it is when you carry out the ashes."

Today, entrepreneurs market gray birch logs as decorative fireplace wood. Others capitalize on its pliability to craft rustic lawn

furniture. Gray birch, like its big sister, the white birch, is excellent for turning on a lathe. Its commercial value is, however, limited by its size.

native medicinals

American Indians lived close to nature. They had an intimate knowledge of animals and plants — where they lived, how they behaved, what use could be made of them, when and how they could be obtained. They had great respect for natural resources. . . Their whole lives were intricately woven into a pattern of plant-animal-man relationships.

Frank G. Speck and Ralph W. Dexter, ethnologists, 1952

Until recently, First Nations' medicinal remedies, like all their traditions, were passed on orally from generation to generation. Nothing was written down, yet their prescriptions persisted. Written documentation on their medicinal use of trees, shrubs, and herbs has come from three sources.

First were the chronicles of early European explorers and pioneers, such as Jacques Cartier, Samuel de Champlain, Marc Lescarbot, John Josselyn, Christien Leclercq, Nicolas Denys, Alexander Mackenzie, and others.

These were supplemented by the 73-volume *Jesuit Relations,* written by missionary priests who lived among First Nations people. Their reports were sent back to France, where they were compiled, abridged, and published. For example, one of *The Jesuit Relations,* from 1634, reported that New Brunswick Maliseet commonly drank a decoction of gray birch inner bark as an emetic, to induce vomiting, a common practice among most bands to rid the body of unwanted ills.

A century ago, a handful of far-sighted ethnobotanists began to interview shamans, medicine men and women, and elders to record their sources of medicine. On the basis of interviews conducted in 1910, anthropologist W. H. Mechling reported in a professional journal the following Maliseet cure for infected and inflamed cuts:

Scrapings from outside of inmost layer of bark [of the gray birch] are put in a gill of hot water. The quantity of scrapings is about a handful. A rag is soaked in the mixture, which is brown. The rag is tied tightly above the infection; if on the hand, it is tied around the arm. The swelling is said to go down very rapidly. The rag leaves a brown stain and the swelling will not pass above it. The rag is left on an hour or more until it dries.

It is from these three sources that we are able today to gather some insight into the medicinal practices of North America's native people, whose affinity to the land, whose intimate knowledge of the plant community gleaned over centuries of experimentation, paralleled, and in some cases, surpassed the body of knowledge of the European medical community at the time.

Facing page: Gray birches need full sunlight. These trees have reached their maximum size and age. They will eventually be shaded out by the conifers, and die off. Their ecological role as pioneers will have been fulfilled.

The Hickories
(*Carya genus*)

Caryer
Hicorier

Cayuga: *onenoga*

Leaf
- compound, alternate; 5–11 leaflets on central stalk; 12–35 cm (5–14") long;
- leaflets finely toothed; aromatic; stalkless; base of lateral leaflets uneven;
- terminal leaflet large; lower leaflets smaller.

Flower
- male catkins yellowish green; hanging from 3-branched stems; in spring;
- females inconspicuous, in small erect clusters at tip of new shoots;
- males and females on same tree; when leaves emerging; wind-pollinated.

Fruit
- nut sweet, edible (except bitternut); in thick yellowish green husks; 3–6 cm (1½–3");
- ripen in 1 season; at maturity, turn brown, split in 4;
- begin bearing fruit at age 20–40; good crop every 1–3 years.

Twig
- stout to somewhat slender; flexible; reddish brown; pith solid, star-shaped;
- terminal bud 6–20 mm (¼–¾") long;
- leaf scars conspicuous, raised, 3-lobed.

Bark
- varies with hickory species.

Wood
- very hard, heavy; strong, straight-grained; impact-resistant;
- heartwood pale brown to reddish brown; thick sapwood white, tinged with brown;
- annual growth rings very distinct.

Height
15–25 m (50–80')

Diameter
30–75 cm (12–30")

Longevity
150–250 years

Hickories produce the hottest of fuelwoods in eastern North America.

home of the hickories

The hickories are members of the walnut family, *Juglandaceae*. At least a dozen species are native to the southeast quadrant of our continent, from the Great Lakes down to Florida, and from New England west to Texas.

Only four grow in Canada, all in southern Quebec and Ontario. Shellbark (*Carya laciniosa*) and pignut or red hickories (*C. glabra*) are limited to a few locales within the Carolinian forest. Shagbark (*C. ovata*) and bitternut (*C. cordiformis*) range further north and east, up the St. Lawrence and Ottawa River valleys, as far as Trois-Rivières and Ottawa-Hull.

By far the bulk of the hickory population lies within the central and southern states, where they reach their optimum size.

It is there that the pecan (*C. illinoensis*), the best-known hickory, grows both wild and under cultivation as a plantation crop.

Hickories are renowned for four things: magnificence as shade trees; edible nuts (but, as the name implies, not bitternut hickory); hard, heavy wood; and the flavor of meat cured over hickory smoke.

a task to transplant

Hickories are outstanding shade trees. In addition to being visually impressive, they attract a wealth of wildlife. The delicate hanging flower catkins in spring, the fall tones of yellow and gold, and the bounty of sweet nuts are three attributes worth considering in landscaping plans. In winter, the texture of shagbark hickory, whose bark seems to be perpetually molting, stands out from its neighbors.

Hickory seedlings rapidly develop a long tap root, which makes them particularly difficult to transplant. Plant from seed 2–3 cm (1") deep, and cover with thick mulch. After germination in spring, remove the mulch.

wheel spokes, sledgehammers, and smoked hams

No other North American wood has the combined weight, strength, hardness, and resilience of the hickories.

At the turn of the twentieth century, hickory was prized for wheel spokes of carriages, horseless and otherwise. The world of sports was indebted to hickory, primarily pignut and shagbark, for an assortment of equipment: golf club shafts, skis, one-piece lacrosse sticks, archery bows, baseball bats, gymnastics bars, and horse-racing sulkies. Ladder rungs and drumsticks, two items where strength and resilience are critical, were made from hickory dowels.

At one time, almost all of the hickory harvested in the United States was converted into rugged, shock-resistant tool handles, especially for hammers, picks, axes, and sledgehammers, making them virtually shatterproof even if the wielder's swing was somewhat less than accurate.

Today hickory occupies only a small share of the hardwood lumber market, essentially for two reasons. It is relatively scarce, and it is a pain to work with. If not carefully seasoned, hickory shrinks, checks, and warps more than most hardwoods. It blunts woodworking tools quickly, splits when nailed, and accepts most glues poorly. However, it is straight-grained, has excellent steam-bending properties, and stains and polishes to a nice finish. In recent years, more hickory has been employed in furniture, cabinetry, and hardwood flooring.

Hickory is the best firewood around — it burns hotter than any other wood, and leaves glowing coals for overnight heat in the wood stove, or for roasting hot dogs and marshmallows long after the campfire has died out. Bacon and ham slowly smoked over green hickory have a flavor all their own.

food, medicine, and weaponry

The high-fat nuts of the various hickories, fresh from the tree, roasted, or processed, were a dietary staple for many indigenous peoples. Delaware Indians roasted unshelled nuts in hot ashes, pounded them into powder, boiled it, and skimmed off the oil for cooking and to flavor squash, beans, and pumpkins.

For medicinal purposes, the Meskwaki steeped hickory inner bark into a laxative and diuretic tea. The Cayuga used it both internally and externally for arthritis. They boiled the bark, drank half, and applied the other half in a poultice on the sore joints. The Mohawk blended the bark with that of butternut and balsam poplar, and added sugar to form a syrup that they swallowed, in small doses, for worms. The Ojibway inhaled the vapors of steamed young shoots for convulsions and headaches.

Potawatomi and Ojibway tribesmen meticulously selected prime pieces of hickory to craft their bows, which were essential to their success in both battle and the hunt. The Ojibway also used hard, heavy, virtually indestructible hickory for their war clubs.

nuts about hickory nuts

As might be expected, each fall the squirrel population consume and cache as many hickory nuts as they can muster. Red, gray, and, further south, fox squirrels rely on this concentrated food that is rich in fat, high in protein, and low in carbohydrates. Wherever they grow, hickory nuts represent 5 to 10 percent of the fall and winter diets of chipmunks. Hickory-eating omnivores include gray foxes, red foxes, and black bears.

Migrating yellow rumped warblers and rose breasted grosbeaks pause for a hickory nut nutrition break while heading south for the winter. Year-round resident cardinals and tufted titmice, close cousins of chickadees, enjoy the nuts without straying far from home.

Cerulean warblers are one of 81 forest-dwelling species on Canada's endangered list. At the northern limit of their range, above Lakes Erie and Ontario, the greenish female builds her nest high in the crowns of tall oaks and hickories.

A rather peculiar home builder is the tree-climbing brown creeper, who locates her nest under the loose bark of shagbark hickories, as well as on other trees whose bark shreds in strips, and dead trees whose bark is sloughing off.

Mallards and wood ducks, bobwhite quail and wild turkeys, are hickory-nut nuts as well. Yellow-bellied sapsuckers, whose tree sap preferences vary by region, hammer out their rows of tiny holes in hickory bark. Where they peck too deeply into the wood, they often stain or discolor the sapwood around the holes, reducing the value of the tree as potential furniture material.

Hackberry
(*Celtis occidentalis*)

sugarberry
nettle-tree

micocoulier
bois inconnu
bois connu
orme bâtard

Pawnee: *kaapsit*

Leaf
- simple, alternate; roughly oval, with long tapering pointed tip; 5–12 cm (2–5") long;
- base lopsided, toothless; rest of leaf edge with coarse sharp teeth;
- upper side bluish green, smooth or slightly rough; underside paler and slightly hairy;
- short stalk divided at leaf base into three main veins;
- arranged in 2 horizontal rows along branchlets;
- turn pale yellow in autumn.

Flower
- males small, grayish green, in clusters at base of new shoots;
- females grayish green, solitary, hanging from junctions of leaf stalk and twig;
- males and females on same tree, often on same shoot; as leaves unfolding;
- pollinated by wind.

Fruit
- drupe (like a cherry), 7–9 mm (¼–⅓"); solitary; hanging from long slender stem;
- dark purple when ripe in autumn; skin thick; pulp thin, dry, orange, sweet;
- with taste of dates or raisins; pit large, mottled, with one pale brown hard seed;
- good fruit crop every year; berries remain into winter.

Twig
- slender, slightly zigzag; greenish to reddish brown, with pale lenticels;
- pith white, compartmentalized (chambered);
- beige buds oval, pointed, flattened; pressed against twig; no true terminal bud.

Bark
- on younger trees, yellowish brown and gray; soon becoming warty;
- on older trees, gnarled with narrow warty and corky layered ridges; becoming scaly.

Wood
- somewhat hard, weak, and heavy; coarse-grained;
- heartwood light yellowish gray; thick sapwood pale yellow or greenish gray;
- annual growth rings distinct.

Height
10–20 m (30–65')

Diameter
30–60 cm (12–24")

Longevity
60–150 years

Hackberry leaves have long tapering tips.

home in the heartland

Hackberry is at home in the heartland of the central states. Its range extends west roughly to the Missouri River and its tributaries, south to Oklahoma and Georgia, and as far east as southern New England. In the Mississippi valley, it can tower to nearly 40 meters (130') tall. As it radiates east, north and west, the average height shrinks to 10–20 meters (30–65'). Southern Ontario is its northern limit, with isolated patches at the bottom tip of Lake Manitoba, and in southwestern Quebec. It was at one time common on Montreal's Ile Ste. Hélène, site of Expo '67.

bois inconnu

Hackberry is variable in more than just its size. Its distribution across a broad range of soil, moisture, and temperature regimes is reflected in wide fluctuations in the shape, color, and size of its leaves, fruit color, flowering habit, bark texture, longevity, and general appearance. It is a difficult tree to identify. Early French settlers called it *bois inconnu* — loosely translated as "the unidentifiable tree," or "what the hell kind of tree is this?" — and the name has stuck.

Hackberries are an oddity of the forest. The *Celtis* genus is the only member of the elm family in North America that produces edible fruit. It can be slow growing or fast growing. In the north it is most easily recognized by its gnarled corky bark; yet where it grows best, the bark is smooth. Male and female flowers are separate entities on the same tree, but sometimes they are found combined in one perfect flower. In some locales, hackberry will not tolerate shade; in others, seedlings flourish in the forest understory. Its prime habitat is moist fertile bottomlands, alluvial soils alongside rivers and streams, and on low islands, where it withstands annual spring flooding. But it is also drought-resistant. It prospers on upland rocky sites rich in limestone. In some areas it can live to almost 200 years; in others, 60 to 70 is its limit.

they're the berries

Hackberry fruit are rich in protein, ash, and magnesium. The berries contain 160 times more calcium than the average wild fruit. Juicy they are not — they contain only 20 percent water, compared, for example, to 75 percent for black cherries. But over 25 species of gamebirds and songbirds dine on them almost year round, including wild turkeys, mockingbirds, and cardinals. They are a favorite of the eastern bluebird, whose northern population had, until recently, been on the decline. Thanks to thousands of birdhouses erected by concerned citizens, the trend has turned around. Plant a hackberry and build a birdhouse, and bluebirds return the favor by eating beetles, weevils, sowbugs, caterpillars, and other garden and tree pests.

A host of other birds build their nests amid the cover of hackberries, and deer and rabbits browse the sprouts of small stumps. Raccoons, chipmunks, and squirrels relish the berries. Smaller rodents eat the fruit, and they in turn provide lunch for owls and hawks.

dwarf hackberry

A smaller sibling of hackberry, dwarf hackberry, is a shrubby tree that in Canada grows only in the Windsor area, its northern limit. It is listed as "vulnerable" on Canada's endangered species list. Its leaves are more symmetrical, less pointed, and wider than hackberry, and the fruit is smaller. It makes a rather attractive little ornamental.

it's not an elm, but. . .

A number of municipalities have planted hackberry to replace the loss of its distant cousin, white elm, victim of Dutch elm disease. Its ascending branches resemble those of elm, but are less arching. Hackberry doesn't have the beauty, stature, or majesty of the elm, but it is immune to the disease. It is a good city street tree — limbs usually start high up the tree, out of the way from traffic, vandalism, and wires. While it is not fond of soot and smoke, it tolerates other city pollutants.

Open-grown hackberries are variable in form. If you wish to plant one as an ornamental, search out a parent tree with appealing characteristics. Gather the berries when ripe in the fall, and sow immediately, fruit and all, in a prepared seedbed. Cover with 1–2 centimeters (¾") of soil and tamp. Mulch for the winter with leaves or straw. Leave in the seedbed for two growing seasons. If the soil at its permanent location is acidic, incorporate dolomitic lime as deeply as possible before transplanting. Hackberry is somewhat partial to moderately high pH values, and its roots penetrate deeply into the soil.

witch's broom

The most prevalent problem with hackberry is witch's broom, a conglomeration of deformed twigs caused by a mildew fungus. Gall-forming midges, mites, and jumping plant lice cause cosmetic damage to the leaves, detracting from their aesthetic value, but posing no serious threat to the tree's health.

Several species of butterfly larvae feed on hackberry as well as elm leaves. The mourning cloak butterfly, in its other incarnation, is known as the spiny elm caterpillar.

food and medicine

In hackberry's western range, the Omaha ate hackberries fresh, and the Dakota pounded the fruit, seeds and all, into a sweet seasoning to flavor their meat. In the east, Oneida and Cayuga Iroquois brewed a decoction of the inner bark to regulate menstrual cycles. It has been reported that some tribes used a bark decoction to treat syphilis. French settlers in Illinois produced an extract of the inner bark for jaundice.

Beech
(*Fagus grandifolia*)

American beech
red beech

hêtre
hêtre à grandes feuilles
hêtre rouge

Munsee Delaware: *wasa:wé:mensi*

Leaf
- simple, alternate; long oval; 10–15 cm (4–6") long;
- base wedge-shaped, slightly uneven; tapering to a toothless tip;
- 10–14 pairs of straight parallel veins, ending in incurved, slightly hairy teeth;
- upper side dark glossy green; underside yellowish green, fuzzy at vein junctions;
- stalk short, with a few hairs;
- texture somewhat leathery; like notepad paper to the touch;
- bronze or copper in autumn;
- some leaves persist throughout winter, bleached, thin.

Flower
- males yellowish green, in ball-like clusters on long drooping fuzzy stems;
- females in bunches of 2–4, at junction of leaf stem and twig;
- male and female on same tree; while or just after leaves unfold.

Fruit
- shiny brown edible nuts, 2 cm (⅔") triangular, with concave sides;
- nuts fit perfectly between thumb, forefinger, and index finger;
- usually in twos or threes, within a brown husk with fuzzy, soft, curved, red-tipped prickles, on short stem;
- husk splits in 4 after 1 or 2 frosts; high percentage of empty, shrunken nuts;
- begin bearing nuts at age 40; good seed crop every 2–8 years.

Twig
- slender, shiny, smooth, mahogany brown, slightly zigzag; with tiny lenticels;
- buds golden brown, torpedo-shaped, long, pointed; angling away from twig at 60°.

Bark
- steel gray, smooth, thin on both young and old trees.

Wood
- very heavy, hard, stiff, strong; impact resistant; not decay resistant;
- heartwood reddish brown; sapwood almost white;
- annual growth rings faint but visible.

Height	Diameter	Longevity
18–24 m (60–80')	60–100 cm (24–36")	200–300 years

Al loves Betty

With its linguistic roots in Sanskrit, beech has the distinction of bearing the oldest tree name in the world, even predating the historic cypresses and sycamores of Egypt. Beech wood served as writing material, so many Early European languages equated the words "beech" and "book." Some, like Swedish, still do today.

Beech belongs to the same family as chestnut and oak. There are ten species worldwide, but only one in North America. For centuries, varieties of its overseas cousin, European beech, have been planted here as shade trees.

Our native beech is a tolerant hardwood, a climax species with the ability to thrive in the shade. It germinates, grows, and may spend all its life in the shadow of larger trees such as red oak, sugar maple, white ash, white pine, and hemlock. When the opportunity presents itself, it will also grow in full sunlight, and occurs occasionally in pure stands. Its natural range spreads from Cape Breton and Prince Edward Island to Ontario's Georgian Bay and eastern Wisconsin, all the way south to Florida and Texas.

Beech is a little fussy in its soil preferences. Its shallow wide-spreading roots need moisture near the surface, as well as good drainage. Extremes of flooding or drought are its nemesis. A few weeks of flooding can cause death, and in a very dry late summer beech is the first hardwood to shut down its leaf factory for the season. Instead of slipping into their beautiful fall tones of copper and bronze, its leaves turn abruptly brown and shed prematurely. The tree maintains its health by conserving its precious root reserves to develop leaves and flowers the following year.

Young beech can be transplanted from the wild when dormant or can be purchased balled and burlapped from a nursery. Their growth rate is slow, however, and the benefits of planting beech are reaped by future generations. With time it develops into a sturdy handsome tree with a short trunk and long horizontal branches. Little else will grow beneath it, and it frequently re-propagates itself with a colony of clones that sucker from its roots. When winter comes, beech is one of the few hardwoods to retain some of its leaves — bleached and papery, some linger on the branches until spring.

Beech has been the traditional target of amorous, but misguided, young couples who carve their heart-encased initials in its smooth gray bark. A truly romantic gesture, but a definite no-no for the tree! The wounds provide a potential entry point for disease.

the beech niche

Unlike its forest companions the oaks, ashes and maples, beech has never been extensively utilized. For furniture or cabinetry it lacks the beauty of grain of its fellow hardwoods. It tends to crack and warp when drying, and it shrinks considerably in the process. It is difficult to glue, and routinely splits when nailed. When exposed to the elements, it decays quickly. In its favor, tests have shown that beech is one of the best hardwoods for wood turning, boring, mortising, and shaping.

Early settlers discovered that beech wood held up extremely well when submersed in water, and it became the wood of choice for the axles and shafts of water wheels in grist and saw mills.

It was one of the most popular hardwoods to produce charcoal for blacksmith shops, bakeries, and eventually blast furnaces. When charcoal began to be produced through destructive distillation, over one million cords of beech, birch, and maple were consumed annually in the northeastern states alone. By-products of the process were wood alcohol for fuel and solvents, and acetates used to make wood vinegar, acetic acid, ether, and acetone, and ultimately photographic film, rayon, and plastics.

The beautiful coppery tones of beech in autumn.

Both odorless and tasteless when seasoned, beech was employed to construct countless food-related items, including butcher blocks, butter boxes, sugar barrels (hogsheads), lard tubs, iceboxes, and wooden tableware. Beech shavings were used to filter apple cider.

On the farm, where toughness counted more than beauty, it was fashioned into plows, tool handles, wagon wheel hubs, thrashing machines, and grain rollers. In the home, washboards, clothes pins, ironing board frames, and clothes horses were crafted from beech heartwood. Alkali from the ashes of beech made fine soap.

Because of its lackluster appearance, it was rarely used as the exterior of furniture, but its resistance to shrinking and swelling, when seasoned, rendered it ideal for drawers and drawer slides. In factories and warehouses, beech flooring stood up to heavy wear, especially under the wet conditions found in laundries and breweries. Workers in glass factories and steel mills wore shoes with beech soles to protect their feet from burns.

> *Good blocks of beech it was I split*
> *As large around as the chopping block;*
> *And every piece I squarely hit*
> *Fell splinters as a cloven rock*
> Robert Frost, 1874–1963
> "Two Tramps in Mud Time"

All these uses of beech represent what today we would call "niche" markets. By far the primary use of beech over the centuries has been as firewood. It has very high heat value, slightly lower than sugar maple. If splitting beech with an ax, wait until winter when the wood is frozen — otherwise it can be a frustrating experience.

With the advent of wood preservatives, beech has become one of the best sources of strong and sturdy railway ties.

A beech disfigured by beech scale disease.

tag team of destruction

What could possibly be more disastrous for a tree species than an insect accidentally imported from Europe whose prey on this continent has no defense mechanism against it? Consider a biological tag team of insect and disease.

The beech scale, an insect the size of a pinhead, whose piercing and sucking mouth mechanisms are three times larger than its body, sailed into Halifax harbor around 1890. It had hitchhiked across the sea on a European beech destined for the city's Public Gardens. The minute yellow bug, which needs no mate to reproduce, promptly made itself at home and began laying eggs. Borne by the wind, its wingless progeny spread to nearby native beeches, and the invasion was underway. Today, over 100 years later, the scale has migrated throughout the Maritimes, through Quebec and southern Ontario, and below the border as far south as West Virginia.

The problem is compounded by its traveling companion, a Nectria fungus. When the scale pierces the thin bark of the beech to suck out its sap, the Nectria moves in to finish off the job. It kills the inner bark and often the critical cambium layer beyond it, creating craters and unsightly cankers on the normally smooth bark. The scale and fungus tag team has left a path of dead and disfigured beeches in its wake throughout much of its range.

Although entomologists and pathologists have been studying the phenomenon since the 1920s, no cure has been found. Nature itself may provide the answer. Some trees are genetically resistant. In the Maritimes today, a few scattered healthy beeches with smooth steel-gray bark stand out among the majority of gnarled and misshapen victims.

fall food fare

Beech trees are very erratic in their production of nuts. Good seed crops vary from every two to eight years. And in any year, the percentage of viable seeds is low — it is not unusual for half the nuts to be empty and shrunken, perhaps the result of unfertilized flowers. But in good seed years, beeches are very prolific.

Beech nuts are an important wildlife food for both mammals and birds. In addition to gamebirds and woodpeckers, blue jays and nuthatches peck open the shells with their strong beaks to dig out the tasty kernels inside.

In autumn, beech nuts build up layers of fat in all four eastern species of squirrels, as well as raccoons and porcupines. Before set -

Beech nuts are rich in protein and calcium.

tling in for their winter snooze, black bears rely on calcium- and protein-rich beech nuts as part of their well-balanced fall diet of fruits and nuts. To squirrels, a good crop may mean the difference between a full or bare pantry for the winter, or possibly one stocked with acorns and hazelnuts instead. Fortunately, in nature, all nut-producing trees and shrubs do not normally have crop failures in the same year.

It might come as a surprise to some folks that at least five species of ducks nest in cavities in old trees. Equally surprising is the fact that some are vegetarian. The strikingly handsome wood duck fits both bills. Beech nuts are one of their favorite foods in preparation for their migration south.

putting the mice to work

First Nations people ate beech nuts fresh, dried and stored them for winter, roasted and pounded them into flour, or added them whole to soups. The Potawatomi in Michigan apparently found an easy way to stock their larders. An eighteenth-century adventurer reported that they raided the winter stashes of deer mice, in hollow logs and trees, scooping up beech nuts by the quartful, which the mice had meticulously — and graciously — shelled in advance.

Rappahannocks steeped beech inner bark in salt water, and applied the tea to relieve poison ivy. Iroquois brewed a decoction of beech and basswood leaves for application to burns, scalds, and frostbite.

White Ash
(*Fraxinus americana*)

American ash
Canadian white ash

frêne blanc
franc frêne
frêne d'Amérique

Meskwaki (Fox): *wi'sūkak*

Leaf
- compound, opposite; composed of 5–9 oval stalked leaflets, tapering at each end;
- leaflets in opposite pairs, 6–14 cm (2–5") long; basal leaflets shortest; on hairless central stalk;
- edges smooth, or with a few wavy teeth above the middle; tips often curved;
- upper side dark green; underside silvery green, with raised midrib and downy veins;
- one of the latest deciduous trees to leaf out in spring;
- turn yellow or deep burgundy in autumn; leaflets fall one at a time, then main stalk.

Flower
- male purple, before leaves emerge;
- female yellowish green, on hairless stalk, as leaves unfold;
- male and female on separate trees (dioecious); both fairly inconspicuous.

Fruit
- winged samara, paddle-shaped, 3–5 cm (1–2") long; in large hanging clusters;
- green in summer, turn brown at maturity; wind-dispersed;
- begin bearing seed at age 20; good crop every 3–5 years.

Twig
- stout, purplish, glossy or with gray film; smooth, with lenticels; not completely round, but somewhat flattened in cross-section;
- uppermost pair of lateral buds almost touching terminal bud;
- terminal bud rusty brown, pyramidal, 5–14 mm (¼–½") long; blunt;
- leaf scars U-shaped, with lateral buds in the notch.

Bark
- on younger trees, light gray, smooth;
- on older trees, furrowed into thin ridges forming diamond pattern.

Wood
- heavy, hard, strong, stiff, straight-grained; impact resistant; odorless;
- heartwood light or grayish brown; thick sapwood creamy white;
- annual growth rings distinct.

Height
18–25 m (60–80')

Diameter
60–90 cm (24–36")

Longevity
150–200 years

In autumn, leaves turn yellow or deep burgundy.

ash confusion

The dozen or more species of ash native to North America are members of the olive family, and are distantly related to the lilac, introduced here from Europe centuries ago. The three common ashes native to eastern and central Canada are white, black, and red. A fourth, blue ash, is limited to a few isolated locales in the Carolinian zone north of Lake Erie, and has been listed as "threatened" by the Committee on the Status of Endangered Wildlife in Canada (COSEWIC). Blue ash is more common south of the border.

The physical similarities among the three ashes outweigh their differences — even foresters are occasionally stumped to tell the difference. All three have compound leaves in opposite formation on thick twigs, and are composed of 5 to 11 leaflets. From

there, the differences among the three are at best subtle. So how does the non-botanist differentiate among them?

Let's begin with black ash, the easiest to distinguish from the other two. Its bark is soft and corky, and can be rubbed off by hand. Its 7 to 11 leaflets have fine sharp teeth and no stalks. On the winter twig there is a space between the black cone-shaped terminal bud and the nearest pair of lateral buds.

Black ash usually grows on the edges of swamps, and along the banks of streams and rivers. So one can recognize black ash by its corky bark, un-stalked toothed leaflets in summer, black buds in winter, and its wet habitat.

White ash's 5 to 9 leaflets have smooth or slightly wavy edges. There are no teeth and no hair, except for a little along the veins underneath, and the leaflets are clearly stalked. The rusty brown terminal bud is

The compound leaves contain from five to nine stalked leaflets.

closely flanked by the lateral buds, and the twig is hairless and glossy or filmy. White ash grows on moist well-drained upland sites, along with sugar maple, red oak, beech, ironwood, and other tolerant hardwoods. To summarize: toothless leaflets with definite stalks; three buds at the end of the twig almost touching one another; and growing in a typical sugar maple-beech environment.

Red ash, on the other hand, has dense hairs on the underside of its 5 to 9 leaflets, with noticeable rounded teeth above the middle. The twigs are fuzzy, and the bark of young trees is pink gray. It is typically found alongside streams, rivers, and lakes, along with silver maple, elm, and Manitoba maple.

To confound things a wee bit more, botanists consider red ash as one species with two varieties: one with hairless leaflets and leaf stalks grows in Manitoba, Saskatchewan, and the Plains states, and is commonly called green ash; the other, with toothed leaflets, is common in eastern Canada, and is officially named northern red ash.

In Newfoundland, where life is generally less complicated, the identification problem disappears — only black ash grows on the island. On the prairies, only the green ash variety grows. From Ontario to Nova Scotia, where all three species grow, positive identification can be problematic. In the south, white and red ash grow down to northern Florida and Texas; the range of black ash ends around Delaware.

from seed to shade tree

If space allows, white ash should be considered in any long-range landscaping plans. Over time it blossoms into a tall, straight, handsome, broad-crowned shade tree. Fall colors range from honey yellow to deep burgundy.

The decision to plant a male or female is an individual one. Males, of course, produce no seeds, so there is no litter to clean up in the spring. Females, after about age 20, bear hanging clusters of winged seeds (samaras) from early summer to well past leaf fall in autumn, attracting songbirds such as pine grosbeaks and purple finches. Red-eyed vireos, home from wintering in the Amazon, often nest in the sturdy branch forks among thickets of ash saplings.

To plant from seed, gather clusters of samaras in late autumn, separate, and sow in the garden bed. Cover with 6–8 mm (¼") soil, and mulch with straw. In spring remove the mulch, and provide partial shade. Leave in the bed for two seasons, fertilizing with nitrogen in the spring of year two. While still dormant the following spring, transplant the biggest and best-shaped to the permanent site, in full or partial sunlight.

Young white ash grow straight and quickly, with a prominent central leader and even branch distribution. On moist well-drained soils rich in nitrogen and calcium, they reach 8–12 meters (25–40') in 20 years. Since white ash is susceptible to a number of insects and diseases, close observation and occasional maintenance may be required. Any pruning should be done in the fall.

the wood of Ruth, Ashe, and the Rocket

Nothing in sports can be more exasperating than a defenceman lining up at the blue line for a slap shot, only to have his stick break and the puck dribble toward the net. Likewise a batter who swings at a fastball, only to see the end of his bat soar over third base, while the ball bounces harmlessly to the pitcher. It would happen more often, were it not for white ash.

White ash wood is heavy, hard, and straight-grained, and absorbs shock extremely well without breaking. Since the dawn of baseball, it has been the wood of choice for the Louisville Slugger. The same properties have made it ideal for the best hockey sticks.

White ash also has tremendous steam-bending ability, and has been used to produce quality tennis and badminton rackets. The best snowshoes are still made from white ash.

Ash is second only to hickory for tool handles — shovels, axes, hammers, and farm tools. When stained, it greatly resembles the more expensive red oak, and is used in fine furniture, kitchen cabinets, interior finish, and bentwood chairs. Veneer sliced from both the sapwood and the heartwood is used in furniture and paneling. In the lumber yard, no distinction is made between white and red ash wood, although the latter is not as heavy·or strong.

serpents, superstitions, and sweat baths

European folklore dating back to Pliny the Elder (23 BC – AD 74) attributed to ash the power to ward off serpents. It was said that snakes would prefer to slither into a fire rather than cross a circle of ash leaves surrounding it. Whether European immigrants carried the superstition with them to North America, or whether it arose simultaneously among Native people, the ash-snake relationship surfaced in many Native cultures.

Hunters of some tribes carried ash leaves to avoid crossing paths with snakes. In the Appalachians and elsewhere, ash bark tea and poultices were used to remedy snake bites. The Omaha considered red ash wood sacred, and chose it to construct their religious poles. Plains tribes crafted the long stems of their ceremonial smoking pipes from young white ash, ornately decorated with porcupine quills.

The strength and flexibility of ash wood made it ideal for bows, arrow shafts, snow

Paddle-shaped ash seeds hang in clusters.

shoes, sleds, canoe ribs, and paddles. Some Ojibway covered their dwellings with black ash bark, while eastern Natives chose black ash for baskets, fans, and hats. The Penobscot and Ojibway derived a yellow dye from ash bark.

Ash leaves, inner bark, and roots found their way into all Native people's pharmacopoeias. The Mi'kmaq and Penobscot prescribed a strong bitter tea of white ash leaves to cleanse new mothers after childbirth. Leaf teas were used to combat rheumatism, arthritis, and gout.

Native people's use of ash trees was a combination of practical, superstitious, religious, and medicinal. From 1916 to 1926, the *U.S. National Formulary* of drugs listed ash as a tonic and astringent, and the *Canadian Pharmaceutical Journal* included both black and white ash as medicinal plants. With the advent of synthetic drugs early in the twentieth century, many natural and traditional remedies were de-listed, despite their proven power to cure, or at least relieve symptoms. Progress.

sap-sucking scales

White ash entertains a host of midges, mites, leaf miners, loopers, sawflies, and scales. Among the most common are oystershell scales, which at first glance appear to be tiny silver-gray growths on the twigs and branchlets. Closer examination reveals that the insects' mouth parts are securely ensconced in the bark, as they suck out the sap which nourishes them. Despite numerous predators and parasites, scale infestations can be severe enough to literally sap the strength out of a tree, and cause its death.

Ash sawflies and fall webworms are leaf feeders, the latter building a rather ugly nest in late summer. Boring insects such as carpenterworms and ash borers pierce through the bark to the living tissue inside, opening the door to fungus infections.

Black Ash
(*Fraxinus nigra*)

swamp ash
brown ash
basket ash
hoop ash
water ash

frêne noir
frêne gras
frêne à feuilles de sureau
frêne de grève

Mohawk: *ehsa*

Leaf
- compound, opposite; composed of 7–11 leaflets in opposite pairs; each 8–13 cm (3–5") long;
- leaflets oval, tapered to long slender tip; stalkless; finely and sharply toothed from base to tip;
- upper and lower surfaces hairless; tufts of hair at junction of leaflet and central stalk;
- upper surface dark green; underside paler;
- turn rusty brown in autumn; whole leaves fall intact.

Flower
- male and female in same flower, or on separate trees; at tips of twigs; inconspicuous.

Fruit
- broad, sometimes twisted wing, 3–4 cm (1–1½") long, fully enclosing seed; seed not obvious within; blunt or rounded at the tip;
- somewhat spicy odor; in hanging clusters; shed late fall, early winter;
- good seed crops irregular, from 4 to 7 years.

Twig
- thick, round, hairless; bright green and purple when young; becoming dull ash gray;
- uppermost pair of lateral buds well below black, conical terminal bud.

Bark
- on younger trees, light grayish brown, with corky texture; easily indented with fingernail or rubbed off;
- on older trees, scaly.

Wood
- moderately heavy, hard, strong, stiff; straight-grained; high impact resistance;
- heartwood dull brown; narrow sapwood almost white;
- annual growth rings distinct.

Height	**Diameter**	**Longevity**
12–20 m (40–65')	30–50 cm (12–20")	75–125 years

wet feet? not a problem

Black ash does not range as far south as its cousins, the white and red ashes. Delaware is its furthest penetration south. However, it grows further north than the other two, and, like white cedar, occurs in isolated pockets deep in the boreal forests of northern Quebec and Ontario. In the west, it reaches into eastern Manitoba and North Dakota.

Large stands of black ash are rare; small groups congregate around wetlands or line the shores of waterways. Black ash doesn't mind "getting its feet wet," it withstands spring flooding, and grows best where nearby water is flowing. Not a component of the deep forest, its need for full sunlight relegates it to the fringe.

Black ash fills two important ecological roles. Its shallow and thirsty roots help control soil erosion on wet sites, where many other trees cannot grow. And its leaves, rich in nitrogen, calcium, and magnesium, help build up these important elements in the soil. Black ash thrives under a very wide range of soil pH conditions, from very acidic to quite alkaline. Typical associated trees and shrubs, also adapted to poorly drained land, are alder, white cedar, elm, red maple, and red osier dogwood.

black ash baskets

For millenia, First Nations people have woven decorative and practical baskets from black ash. The process is simple, but it requires skill, experience, and a considerable amount of work. With the bark peeled off, black ash logs are immersed in water until saturated. Then they are pounded with a mallet until the wood separates into splints along the annual growth rings. Since black ash grows slowly, the splints between its rings are thin and pliable, but strong, ideal for weaving.

In some jurisdictions, Native people still have the right to harvest black ash on government land, to ensure that this important part of their culture, as well as a source of their income, is not lost. But agriculture, urban development, overcutting, and possibly pollution have made quality black ash, never a common forest tree, increasingly scarce.

In recent years, the Mohawk at Akwesasne, on the St. Lawrence River straddling the Canada–United States border, Mi'kmaq at Millbrook, near Truro, Nova Scotia, and the Maine Abanaki Confederacy have all initiated black ash planting programs, to ensure that future generations will have access to the raw materials to continue this traditional art and craft. A coalition of eastern Native peoples, the Maine Basket Makers Alliance, is devoted to preserving the tradition through training, education, and marketing.

a tree worth preserving

Black ash is not normally recommended as a shade tree around the home. It grows slowly, will not tolerate dryness, and has minimal ornamental value in any season. Wet areas, however, may benefit from its shallow roots. As an ornamental, it might be considered a novelty tree.

If one owns a woodlot with black ash present, it is well worth preserving or propagating, if for no other reasons than its scarcity, its contribution to biodiversity, and its ability to bind soils. When harvested, it sprouts from the stump. Clumps of sprouts may be thinned to concentrate growth on fewer stems, and may require protection from bark-eating mice and voles. Deer and hares are prone to browse the nutrient-rich leaves.

Black ash can be grown from seed gathered and sown in October, and covered with mulch for the winter. Germination may take two years.

sawflies and loopers, webworms and mites

Most of the insects and diseases that afflict the other ashes do not spare black ash. Three leaf-

Leaflets are toothed and stalkless — the key to identifying black ash in summer.

eating insects that prefer black ash are the spiny ash sawfly, the variable redmarked looper, and the fall webworm. Colonies of webworms are easily spotted in August, when the long-haired caterpillars, after skeletonizing the leaves near the branch tips, spin a large, rather ugly tent. Within its shelter they finish their feeding frenzy undisturbed. Infested branches should be pruned off just above the nearest pair of leaves below the tent, and the nests, along with their contents, burned.

The tiny ash flower gall mite attacks male flowers in spring, turning them black. Aborted flowers are visible on the twig tips throughout summer and into winter, long after the leaves have fallen. Aside from preventing pollination of female flowers, this pest is not considered a serious threat.

seeds and sprouts

None of the three common ashes are considered important wildlife trees. However their seeds, which are usually abundant, are one of the preferred foods of evening grosbeaks and purple finches, and are also eaten by wood ducks, cardinals, pine grosbeaks, and red-winged blackbirds.

In some areas, stump sprouts of white and black ash are important winter food for white-tailed deer. Since the sprouts are usually very vigorous, they may be able to withstand browsing and continue growing. Where deer populations exceed the carrying capacity, they can be a serious threat to young black ash, as well as other vegetation. Beavers capitalize on the proximity of black ash to streams, rivers, and wetlands, especially where aspen is unavailable.

cabinets yes, fuelwood no

The brown heartwood of black ash is more attractive than that of white ash, but it lacks its luster and size. Its straight grain and good color transform into handsome cabinetry and interior finish.

When properly seasoned, black ash yields firewood about on a par with white birch. It splits easily, and produces a glowing bed of coals. Rightfully, however, healthy and well-formed black ash should never be used as fuelwood. It is just too scarce. If cut, it can be put to much better use.

leaf and bark remedies

First Nations people drank black ash leaf teas to induce sweating, promote urine flow, and rid the intestines of worms. In addition to serving as an astringent tonic and stimulant, black ash bark decoctions were taken to relieve constipation, stomach cramps, and fevers. Black ash was one of the seven healthful barks that the Mi'kmaq steamed in their sweat lodges. The Ojibway soaked the inner bark in warm water and applied the liquid to relieve sore eyes.

Red Ash
(*Fraxinus pennsylvanica*)

green ash
river ash
water ash

frêne rouge
frêne vert
frêne de Pennsylvanie
frêne de rivage
frêne de savane

Lakota: *cansuska*

Leaf
- compound, opposite; 5–9 leaflets (usually 7) on hairy central stalk; 15–20 cm (6-8") long;
- leaflets oval, pointed at tip; toothed above the middle; on downy stalks 5 mm (¼") long;
- upper side bright yellowish green; underside slightly paler, with dense blondish hairs;
- leaflets turn yellowish brown in autumn, shed one at a time.

Flower
- male and female on separate trees; when leaves unfolding; inconspicuous;
- begin flowering at age 10–15; flower almost every year.

Fruit
- samaras, winged seeds 3–6 cm (1–1½") long; wing often notched at tip;
- seeds start to fall as soon as ripe, and continue all winter.

Twig
- thick, grayish brown, densely hairy, with lenticels;
- terminal bud reddish brown, hairy;
- uppermost pair of lateral buds close to terminal bud.

Bark
- on younger trees, pinkish gray;
- on older trees, slightly raised ridges, forming irregular diamond pattern.

Wood
- heavy, hard, moderately strong, brittle, stiff, coarse-grained;
- heartwood light brown; thick sapwood lighter, streaked with yellow;
- annual growth rings distinct.

Height	Diameter	Longevity
12–18 m (40–60')	30–50 cm (12–20")	80–100 years

Note Many taxonomists consider red ash as a single species, with two distinct varieties: northern red ash in the east, and green ash in the west.

Newly unfolded leaves in a typical riverside environment.

the range of red ash

Red ash, combined with its two varieties, northern red ash and green ash, ranges from Nova Scotia, west through southern Quebec and Ontario, then up through the middle of Manitoba and Saskatchewan, and south as far as the Florida panhandle and eastern Texas. It is absent in some parts of New England, New York, and Pennsylvania, but otherwise blankets the eastern two-thirds of the United States. On the prairies, green ash is a smaller, slower-growing tree. In the south, it may grow .5 meters (20") a year for the first 50 years, and reach heights of 40 meters (130'). An isolated patch of red ash surrounds Lac St. Jean in northern Quebec.

from rural riverside to city sidewalk

Red ash is not a tree of the deep forest. Its natural habitat is confined to bottomlands and alluvial soils along streams, rivers and lakes. It withstands spring flooding, while its roots stabilize the soil and prevent erosion. However, when planted in an urban environment, red (green) ash shows tremendous adaptability to a wide variety of soils, climates, and stresses. It tolerates poor soils, excessive heat and drought, as well as road de-icing salt.

Native red ash and its dozens of cultivated varieties, or cultivars (usually seedless males), have been planted extensively — some say too extensively — in planting pits on city sidewalks, along boulevards, in parks and cemeteries, and around industrial parks and golf courses. It transplants readily and grows fast, especially on good sites. It has even been planted to reforest coal strip mine spoils in the central states, with high survival and fair growth rates.

Leaflets, usually seven in a leaf, are toothed above the middle.

green ash on the prairies

When an easterner thinks of the prairies, what might come to mind, aside from friendly people, are flat endless seas of wheat and other grains. But meandering through the square patchwork sections of farmland is a network of rivers and streams, oases for a handful of trees and shrubs. The most prominent among these are Manitoba maple and green ash.

It was logical that one of the first species planted in prairie field shelterbelts would be green ash. There the hardy native provides respite from the harsh winter winds, protects the soil, encourages wildlife, and creates a more pastoral setting.

From its humble beginnings in 1901, the tree nursery at Indian Head, Saskatchewan, now called the Shelterbelt Centre, has distributed over 600 million trees and shrubs to prairie farmers. It cultivates 26 species and varieties of trees and shrubs, for field, roadside, and farmstead shelterbelts, distributing seven million seedlings a year. Green ash is still the most popular shelterbelt hardwood produced and planted. Aside from its fast growth and winter hardiness, farmers favor it because it does not occupy too much of their valuable cropland. Its upright, compact crown and deep tap root do not compete with, but rather protect, the crops beside it.

Green ash is the state tree of North Dakota.

red ash antagonists

Red ash, like the other ashes, is subject to a number of insects that attack the twigs, devour the leaves, and bore into the trunk. Tiny scale insects suck the sap from twigs and branches; if the infestation is severe, they can cause mortality. Wood borers, like the rather lengthy carpenterworm, tunnel into the wood, weakening trees and exposing them to decay. Sawfly larvae feed on the leaves of all three species of ash.

Ashes are also host to various leaf spots, rusts, and anthracnose fungi, which discolor and disfigure the leaves; in extreme cases, defoliation can lead to death. The proximity of red and black ash to streams and tributaries attracts beavers, who fell the trees to build their dams. The flooding that results can suffocate small stands.

Butternut
(*Juglans cinerea*)

white walnut
oilnut

Menominee: *pûka'nawe*

noyer cendré
arbre à noix longues

Leaf
- compound, alternate; fragrant; somewhat sticky; 30–60 cm (12–24") long;
- composed of 5–8 pairs of stemless, finely toothed, pointed leaflets on a stout oval stalk;
- lowest 2–3 pairs smaller than the rest; single leaflet at the tip;
- underside of leaflets densely hairy;
- one of latest hardwoods to leaf out in spring;
- leaflets turn brown and shed early in autumn, often leaving only end leaflet attached to stalk.

Flower
- males and females on same tree; when leaves are emerging;
- males in bright green drooping catkins 6–14 cm (2–5") long;
- green females, topped by red stigmas, in erect clusters of 3–5, at end of new shoots.

Fruit
- lime-shaped husks 5–7 cm (2–3") long, sticky, fuzzy, green; single or in clusters of 3–5; on long stems;
- nutshell very hard, dark brown/black, with irregular jagged ridges, 3–4 cm (1½–2") long;
- nut sweet, oily, edible; husk dark greenish brown when ripe in autumn;
- begin bearing nuts at age 20; good crop every 2–3 years.

Twig
- stout, downy, buff-colored; pith chambered, chocolate brown;
- pale yellow terminal bud fuzzy and elongated; lateral buds smaller, round;
- large leaf scars fur-topped.

Bark
- on younger trees, ash gray and smooth; later separating into narrow dark shallow crevices;
- on older trees, with irregular flat-topped intersecting ridges;
- inner bark yellow, bitter.

Wood
- light, soft, weak, straight-grained;
- heartwood chestnut brown, wide; sapwood white, narrow;
- annual growth rings distinct.

Height	**Diameter**	**Longevity**
15–25 m (50–80')	30–60 cm (12–24")	70–80 years

102

Hanging male flower catkins appear while leaves are unfurling.

white walnut

Butternut is smaller and shorter-lived than black walnut, the only other species of *Juglans* in North America. It bears a close resemblance — long compound leaves, fuzzy roundish husks, and stout winter twigs. But both the bark and wood are considerably lighter in color — hence one of its common names, white walnut.

A little hardier than its cousin, butternut grows farther north and east, at higher elevations, and on moister sites. Fertile loamy soils and streamsides foster the most robust trees, but butternut is quite at home on dry rocky sites rich in limestone. Like ironwood, it is a loner, and is rarely found in pure stands or groves. Isolated trees or small groupings are typically scattered within stands of maple, beech, black cherry, and oak. Its range stretches from Arkansas, northeast to a few river valleys in New Brunswick, and west through the Great Lakes–St. Lawrence forest in southern Quebec, Ontario and the Lakes states.

Butternut is intolerant of shade. Nuts buried by squirrels germinate and grow only where sunlight reaches the forest floor. The shade cast by its own leaves renders interior branches almost bare, giving the crown a light airy appearance.

Like walnut, butternut roots exude the chemical juglone, which can kill other plants and seedlings whose roots come into contact with them. This may be a self-defense mechanism to ensure its own need for sunlight.

the beauty of butternut

Butternut has been one of the favorite native hardwoods of furniture and cabinet makers, cottage craftsmen, and artists for centuries. Since its outer circle of pale sapwood is narrow, most of the wood is attractive chestnut-colored heartwood. Straight-grained and satiny, the heartwood transforms into beautiful interior trim and molding, doors and windows, handrails, mantel pieces, and picture frames. Its soft texture lends itself well to sculpting and carving.

Butternut finishes nicely, and can be stained to closely resemble the more expensive walnut. It works easily with wood tools, and its lack of taste or odor is perfect for kitchen woodenware. A number of small mills throughout the east peel a beautiful veneer from high quality butternut logs.

Butternut is not ranked high on the list of firewoods; its low calorific value of 17 million BTUs per cord is about equal to that of white pine and trembling aspen. Regardless, it would be somewhat of a sin to burn clear pieces of butternut in the family fireplace or furnace.

fresh, roasted, or pickled

Sweet oily butternuts have long been a staple in the diet of Native Americans. Archeological digs in New Brunswick have unearthed charred butternut shells in prehistoric hearths. Smaller but tastier than walnuts, butternut meats are rich in calories, fat, riboflavin, and protein, and, like walnuts, contain twice as much iron per gram as raisins. Picking butternuts poses two minor problems: when they are ripe, simply touching the sticky husks stains one's hands brown; gloves are recommended. And they are, literally, one hard nut to crack. Soaking overnight in water softens the bony shells. Resist the temptation to pop them in the microwave — they will explode with a bang.

A common colonial custom was to gather immature nuts — husks, shells, and all — and pickle them in vinegar. The butternut pickle recipe is best described by Julia Rogers in her book, *Trees Worth Knowing* (1924):

> *The green nuts are tested with a knitting needle. If it goes through them with no difficulty, and yet the nuts are of good size, they are ready. Vigorous rubbing removes the fuzz after the nuts are scalded. Then they are pickled whole, in spiced vinegar, and are a rare, delectable relish with meats for the winter table.*

Fully ripe and fresh, roasted and salted, or green and pickled, butternuts are a delicious and nutritious bounty from nature.

as a medicinal

Throughout its range, Aboriginal tribes, from the Maliseet in New Brunswick to the Ojibway in Ontario and Minnesota, prescribed the yellowish brown inner bark of butternut as a cathartic and purgative. Nineteenth-century doctors confirmed its medicinal value as a bowel cleanser, and an extract of the inner root bark was officially listed in the *U.S. Pharmacopoeia* from 1820 until 1905. When medical rations were in short supply during the Revolutionary War, surgeons turned to butternut as one of their sources of medicine.

butternut brown

The Ojibway boiled the leaves, bark, and roots of butternut and hazelnut together to create a natural black dye, or used butternut alone for a brown dye. Native people introduced the practice of dying with butternut husks to white settlers. During the Civil War, Confederate soldiers wore homespun woolen garments dyed butternut brown.

Compound leaves are composed of 11 to 17 leaflets.

butternut blues

Nut weevils, lacebugs, sawflies, caterpillars, and loopers prey upon butternut leaves and nuts, but none of the insects pose as serious a threat as butternut canker. A fungus disease suspected of arriving from Europe, the canker was first detected in 1967 in Wisconsin. It has spread rapidly and has nearly eradicated the species in North Carolina and Virginia. The disease has already infested 70 to 90 percent of the butternuts in Minnesota, Wisconsin, and eastern Ontario, has surfaced in nurseries and plantations in Quebec, and has recently crept into the Maritimes. In Michigan, the number of living butternuts, healthy or diseased, has declined by over 80 percent in just 15 years. The U.S. Department of Agriculture has tentatively listed butternut as an endangered species, pending further study.

Rainsplash, and possibly beetles, spread the deadly spores, which infect leaf scars, lenticels, buds, and exposed wounds. There is even evidence that the nuts themselves carry the disease.

Dying branch tips or dead tops are the first symptoms of the problem. In spring, an inky liquid seeps from the cankers; by summer they are covered with sooty patches, usually with a whitish edge. Trunk bark often shreds on older cankers. By then it is too late. When they meet, cankers girdle the tree, choke off its life supply, and ultimately cause death.

To save the species from extinction, nuts and cuttings from canker-free trees, which may be genetically resistant strains, are being preserved or propagated. Meanwhile, the biodiversity of hardwood ecosystems with a butternut component is in serious jeopardy.

wait and see

Aesthetically, butternut is not a superb ornamental or shade tree. Branches are bare of leaves until very late spring, flowers are small and inconspicuous, and fall foliage is a dud. It grows fast, and its long compound leaves cast a nice light shade in summer, but the branches are brittle and susceptible to storm damage.

There are few trees that do not have some redeeming quality as an ornamental. Unfortunately, butternut is often considered one of them. Until the widespread problem with butternut canker is (hopefully) resolved, it is inadvisable to plant, unless there is absolute certainty that the seed came from parents with inherent disease resistance. One should certainly not gather nuts where the canker is rampant, to plant in an area that is still disease-free. The fungus is spreading fast enough on its own; it doesn't need any assistance from people.

"Wait and see" is the best advice for the prospective butternut planter.

déjà vu

There is one glaring omission within these pages: American chestnut (*Castanea dentate*). It is not an oversight; had this book been written a century ago, chestnut would have been a tree of prominence. A magnificent ornamental, pillar of the deciduous forest, provider of sweet edible nuts for people and wildlife alike, its thick bark was a major source of tannin for the leather industry, its decay-resistant wood superb for fences and railway ties, and its leaves and bark a Native cure for colds, rheumatism and heart disorders.

Thick fuzzy winter twigs, with unusually shaped buds, are characteristic of butternut.

All that changed in 1904, when a deadly fungus arrived with a shipment of Asian chestnut ornamentals in New York City. From the Bronx Zoo the chestnut blight spread rapidly, leapfrogging ahead of efforts to isolate it, its tiny spores borne on the feet and feathers of countless birds. In 40 years it had mowed down every chestnut in its path, from southern Maine to Georgia to southern Ontario. Today all that linger are sprouts from old stumps and a scattering of seedlings, hangers-on destined to die from the blight within a few years.

We have to hope the butternut will not go the way of the chestnut. Touch wood.

Black Walnut

(*Juglans nigra*)

American walnut

noyer noir
noyer noir d'Amérique

Teton Dakota: *cha-sapa*

Leaf
- compound, alternate; 30–60 cm (12–24") long; composed of 15–23 leaflets in pairs, 5–12 cm (2–5") long;
- leaflets pointed, finely toothed, almost stemless; aromatic;
- upper side yellowish green; underside paler, slightly fuzzy;
- middle leaflets largest; end leaflet small or absent; main stem downy;
- turn yellow in autumn; one of earliest hardwoods to shed leaves.

Flower
- males in hanging green catkins 6–12 cm (2½–5") long;
- females green and reddish, less conspicuous, erect; solitary or in small clusters;
- both sexes on same tree, often on same twig; wind pollinated.

Fruit
- nut kernel sweet, edible, slightly oily; encased in round, bony, ridged shell;
- husk round, yellowish green, spongy, slightly downy, aromatic; diameter 5–8 cm (2–3");
- single or in bunches of 2–4; ripen in 1 season; fall to ground at maturity in October;
- begin bearing nuts at age 12–15; good crop every 2–3 years.

Twig
- thick, slightly fuzzy; pale to orange brown; dotted with lenticels;
- pith alternately hollow and partitioned; orangey buff color;
- terminal bud gray, downy, 7–9 mm (¼–⅓") long; lateral buds smaller, roundish;
- conspicuous leaf scars heart-shaped.

Bark
- on young trees, pale brown, becoming scaly;
- on older trees, thick, blackish brown; deeply fissured; intersecting ridges round-topped.

Wood
- heavy, hard, strong, stiff, close-grained;
- heartwood chocolate brown, decay-resistant; thin sapwood almost white;
- annual growth rings indistinct.

Height
20–30 m (65–100')

Diameter
60–120 cm (24–48")

Longevity
150–250 years

Long compound leaves may have up to 23 leaflets. Often the end leaflet is absent.

the matriarch

Black walnut is the matriarch of the North American *Juglandiceae* family. Relatives include butternut and the various hickories, including pecan. It is closely related to the Persian or English walnut (*Juglans regia*), the source of walnuts found packaged and in bulk in our stores — a blander, less wild, but meatier and more easily shelled variety.

Black walnut is distributed throughout the eastern and central states, with a little spillover into Canada north of Lakes Ontario and Erie. Like many other hardwoods of the deciduous forest region, it grows best on moist, rich, well-drained bottomlands, floodplains, and fertile hillsides. While it ranges from western Massachusetts to Minnesota and Nebraska, and south to Texas and the Florida panhandle, the best specimens grow in Indiana and the surrounding states. Rarely found in small pure stands, it is most commonly associated with black cherry, white ash, basswood, oaks, and hickories. Iowa has designated black walnut its state tree.

as an ornamental

Black walnut has been widely planted, both within and beyond its natural range, as a nut tree, a timber tree, and an ornamental. In the forest, it grows straight, tall, virtually untapered, and free of branches for two-thirds of its height. In the open, the trunk usually forks a few meters (5–10') from the ground into massive branches spreading high and wide, creating a round, but open, crown. The fern-like foliage is light and airy, allowing partial sunlight to filter to the ground below. Lower limb tips hang within reach, where the nuts can be picked by hand.

The tallest black walnut on record in Canada, in the Halton region of southern Ontario, is a rather impressive 30 meters (100'), considering it is at the northern limit of its range. The champion walnut in the United States is 40 meters (130'). It grows, of all places, in Oregon, planted thousands of kilometers from the heart of its natural range.

Below the surface, walnut tap roots penetrate quickly and deeply to absorb a steady source of water, and the lateral roots may extend 15 meters (50') from the trunk. Walnuts are well-anchored — an asset for the stability of the tree, but a liability if trying to transplant.

Seeds sown in a nursery bed should be outplanted the spring following the first growing season, before the roots become too unwieldy. Alternatively, nuts can be planted directly into their permanent site, in a sunny location. In either case, roto-tilling the sod and soil as deeply and widely as possible, as well as adding bone meal to the soil, is recommended. If the soil is acidic, incorporating lime helps seedlings acclimatize. Walnuts prefer a neutral (pH 7) or slightly alkaline soil. Cover the unhulled nuts with 5 centimeters (2") of soil, and encircle them with a temporary screen partially buried to keep out burrowing rodents. Mulch with sawdust, but not walnut sawdust. Remove the screen after germination.

Black walnut can be grown beyond its natural range if it has the deep, fertile, well-drained soil it needs, and is sheltered from damaging winter winds. It is well worth trying. An option is the Carpathian walnut, a cultivar of *Juglans regia*, native to the mountains of southern Poland. It is hardy in northern climates, and available from most nurseries.

an organic herbicide

. . . the shadow of walnut trees is poison to all plants within its compass . . .
Pliny the Elder, AD 77
Historia Naturalis

Walnut trees act as a natural herbicide through a process called allelopathy. Juglone, a chemical in its leaves, husks, and roots, stunts or kills other plants growing nearby. Tomatoes, apple and pear trees, red and white pines, blueberries, blackberries, and even young walnuts are susceptible. It was once thought that the roots exuded the chemical, but today scientists believe the roots must contact one another for damage to occur. The problem is compounded on wet, poorly aerated soils.

Nitrogen-fixing plants such as speckled alder fertilize walnuts if they are planted nearby, and the walnut provides shelter while they are young. Alders eventually die off from lack of sunshine or allelopathy, their purpose having been served.

from fence post to pillar of the church

We must confess that there are vast Forests to be rid up, which reach from Canada to the Country of Louisiana, all along the River of Meschasipi; so that it would require a great deal of time to clear the Ground. But this is incident to all new Establishments.
Father Louis Hennepin, 1698,
A New Discovery

Settlers in North America were confronted with an array of unfamiliar flora — species of plants unknown in the "old country." They learned, through trial and error, word of mouth, and with the help of Native people, how to adapt to these new ecosystems. There was no manual to guide them.

They found that walnut heartwood, like

*Walnut and butternut twigs are similar —
the terminal bud of the former is gray, the
latter yellow.*

that of cedar and chestnut, did not rot when exposed to the soil or the elements. So they cut it for fence posts and shingles. They were practical people. A roof over their heads and fencing for their livestock were priorities. There was little time for visions of elegant walnut furniture or cabinetry. They had no idea how relatively little walnut there was, how valuable it would become, or that it would one day be hailed as "the queen of North American cabinet woods."

Such was the genesis of black walnut's use. In time it was used for water wheels for grist and saw mills, charcoal for gunpowder, and railway ties to support transportation of people and products. Only later were the glories of walnut recognized, as it found its way into the altars, pillars, and paneling of nineteenth-century churches and cathedrals.

Few considered the limits to the resource until World War I erupted. Suddenly loggers had to venture deeper into the forest to find the walnut needed for rifle stocks and aircraft propellers.

No one visualized that, less than a century later, walnut furniture, cabinetry, and veneer would be in such demand that auctions would be held for standing trees, that wood brokers would flock to bid for the right to harvest them, and that a single tree might generate $3,000. The value of black walnut spawned a new breed of criminal, the tree rustler, who with sophisticated techniques — even helicopters — swooped in at night to poach prime trees from private woodlots.

Competition for prime walnut between domestic and foreign mills eventually became so intense that the price skyrocketed, making it uncompetitive with other hardwoods. Domestic mills turned to more affordable species. Walnut peaked around 1970, and has never regained its status. It takes a back seat to black cherry, oak, pecan, and even sugar maple as the wood prized by furniture manufacturers. Today it captures less than 2 percent of the hardwood market.

Walnut's heartwood is a deep chocolate brown, often with purplish streaks. The sapwood, almost white, can be darkened to the tone of the heartwood by steaming. Walnut works well with hand and power tools, glues adequately, holds screws securely, turns well on a lathe, and has only a moderate blunting effect on tools. The handsome grain finishes and polishes to a beautiful luster and is highly resistant to impact.

Walnut has been transformed into every expensive piece of furniture imaginable — bedroom sets, coffee tables, office desks, dining room sets, bookcases, mantel pieces, and entertainment consoles. Its elegance and resistance to decay has found it a niche in yacht building. Fifty percent of walnut harvested is sliced into veneer, on average about .6 mm thick. Some Japanese mills now produce American walnut veneer a mere .25 mm thick. At that thickness, one would not dare sand it.

A perfect veneer tree is 100 years old, has a 50-centimeter (20") diameter at the top, little or no taper, is perfectly straight, and has no defects. Veneer manufacturers shy away from backyard walnuts. At $50,000 to replace a blade, they cannot afford to slice up a tree that might contain nails, bullets, or even horseshoes.

The trend today in North America is to the lighter woods, but these trends have proven cyclical in the past.

caterpillars and cuckoos

Black walnuts are relatively free of life-threatening insects and diseases. The walnut caterpillar is their principal pest. Be on the lookout for clusters of white eggs on the underside of leaflets in June or early July; then colonies of brick-red larvae skeletonizing the leaflets; in late summer, larger (2 cm [1"]) black caterpillars with long white hair devouring all the leaves on one branch and marching on to the next; and finally, large groups molting on the trunk or large branches, leaving behind their castoff skins.

Several consecutive years of walnut caterpillar attacks can kill branches and occasionally trees. Black-billed and yellow-billed cuckoos are their natural predators. Wild grape vines are the favorite nesting habitat of the latter. If present, keep them; if not, consider planting them.

On the disease front, walnut anthracnose creates large dead blotches on the leaflets. Particularly virulent in wet weather, the fungus weakens trees and shrivels the nuts. To prevent re-occurrence, remove fallen leaves in autumn and incinerate them.

walnut soup and sandblasting

Walnuts were a staple in the diet of Native people who dwelt within its natural range. They are rich in protein, fat, phosphorus, iron, and vitamin E. They were eaten fresh and ripe from the tree, plain or with honey, boiled, baked, made into soups, or dried and ground into flour. Settlers pickled soft unripe nuts for a winter relish.

Winnebago, Cayuga, Ojibway, and many other tribes produced dark brown dyes from the husks or shoots, and black dyes from the roots.

In recent years, walnut shells have proven to be as valuable as the nuts. Ground up, they are used as abrasives to sandblast metal in the automobile and aircraft industries, drilling fluid additives in the oil industry, cleaners for jet engines, and fillers for textured paint.

nuts to the animals

Despite their thick hard shells, black walnuts are a preferred food for nearly 20 species of birds, from red-bellied woodpeckers to gray catbirds. Most, however, rely on the squirrel population to do the hard work — cracking open the shells — before they peck out the tasty morsels inside.

Three species of squirrels — red, gray (including the black version common in Toronto and elsewhere), and their larger cousins, the fox squirrels, farther south — harvest walnuts as soon as they ripen, eat as many as they can, and cache away the rest for a snowy day. By burying the nuts, squirrels are responsible for most of the natural reforestation of black walnut.

Eastern Redcedar
(*Juniperus virginiana*)

red juniper
eastern juniper
red cedar

genévrier rouge
genévrier de Virginie
cèdre rouge

Comanche: *ekawai:pu*

Leaf
- 2 forms: scales and needles; both dark bluish green in summer;
- overlapping scales cling to twigs on 4 sides, forming a square;
- needles sharp-pointed, 12–16 mm (¼–⅓") long; in whorls of 2 or 3; on young trees and vigorous older trees;
- turn bronze, coppery, or slightly purplish in late autumn and winter;
- persist on tree for 5–6 years.

Flower
- minute inconspicuous catkins in spring; male yellow, female violet;
- males and females usually on separate trees.

Fruit
- berries round, blue at maturity, with dusty white bloom; 6–8 mm (½–⅔") diameter;
- fleshy, with firm skin; sweet, resinous taste; contain 1–2 brown oval seeds;
- mature in 1 growing season; remain on tree all winter;
- begin fruiting at age 10–15; heavy fruit crops irregular.

Twig
- slender, brownish red, covered with green leaf scales; appearing square in cross-section;
- buds minute, inconspicuous.

Bark
- on younger trees, thin, dark reddish brown, peeling;
- on older trees, reddish brown to gray; in long, narrow, fibrous, shreddy strips.

Wood
- moderately hard and heavy; close-grained; aromatic; impact resistant;
- heartwood dull or deep red, decay resistant; narrow sapwood almost white;
- annual growth rings distinct.

Height	Diameter	Longevity
8–15 m (25–50')	20–40 cm (8–16")	200–300 years

Blue berries are characteristic of junipers — officially, they are "berry-like cones."

conifer without cones

Eastern redcedar has a few idiosyncrasies. First, it is not a true cedar; it is actually a juniper. Its closest relative, common or ground juniper, is a straggly shrub less than a meter (3–4') in height. Its leaves have two completely different forms: most are scales, some are needles. Its trunk is rarely round — it is often almost heart-shaped.

History tells us that redcedar was once much more common than it is today and that it reached much larger sizes. Yet today we find it growing in poor soils on exhausted old pastures. In its western range, it is creeping onto rangeland, where trees did not exist in the past.

Although botanists classify its fruit as a "berry-like cone," it looks like a berry, tastes somewhat like a berry, and has skin and flesh and seeds like a berry. For all intents and purposes, it is a berry. It bears no resemblance whatsoever to a pine, spruce, or hemlock cone. . . or any other cone for that matter. Which raises the quasi-rhetorical question: if redcedar does not bear cones, is it indeed a conifer?

Redcedar is most at home in the south central states, where it achieves its best growth. It is the most widely distributed softwood tree in the eastern U.S. forest, ranging from the bottom of North Dakota down to eastern Texas, and northeast through Georgia, the Carolinas, as far as southern Maine. In Canada, it is limited to the Thousand Islands area, the top of Lake Champlain, the Carolinian zone north of Lake Erie, the shores of Georgian Bay, with a few isolated patches near Ottawa-Hull.

Early *Canadiens* called the tree *bâton rouge*, or red stick. When they rediscovered it in Louisiana, the name stuck, and today the state capital bears the name. Redcedar is the state tree of Tennessee.

redcedar the pioneer. . .

Like gray birch, pin cherry, and alders, redcedar is a pioneer, an early succession species on former farmlands. Its seeds are sown by resident and migrating birds, who pluck the fruit from trees in nearby fencerows. Pioneers rehabilitate old fields, preparing them for the forest of the future. During their brief occupation of the site, their leaves add organic matter to the soil, and their shade reduces competition from grasses and weeds, allowing more tolerant trees to establish themselves beneath them.

Speckled alder, an old field pioneer that invades poorly drained sites, is a natural soil fertilizer. Nodules on its roots release nitrogen into the soil, replenishing it after years of cultivation. Redcedar performs a similar function in succession. Its calcium-rich leaf litter raises the pH level near the soil surface. The litter encourages earthworm activity, and worms break up the organic material and mix it with mineral soil, creating a porous textured soil ideal for the establishment of other trees.

On very poor sites, redcedar may continue to grow to its age potential — 200 to 300 years. On better sites, it is eventually replaced by more tolerant trees, especially hardwoods, which shade out the redcedars until they die a natural death. Their ecological role as soil enhancers is complete, as nature reclaims the farmland back to the forest it once was.

a natural ornamental

Redcedar is a natural-born ornamental. Without cultivation, it grows slowly into a compact well-shaped columnar or conical tree. It can stand alone, add visual and structural diversity mixed and mingled with other trees and shrubs, or provide a dark green backdrop to more showy plants. Along with its dozens of cultivated varieties (cultivars), it is one of the most popular landscape evergreens in North America. Its horticulturally altered allies are available from nurseries in any size or shape imaginable — globular, pyramidal, spreading, columnar, or dwarf — as well as in a range of foliage colors from deep green, to blue, to silver.

Redcedar can be pruned and sheared into any shape, from a bowling ball to a candlestick to a building block, or it can be left au naturel. At close spacing, it produces an excellent thick hedge and natural screen.

Redcedars thrive on infertile soils, where most other trees wouldn't stand a chance. They are at home on deep, dry, sandy and gravelly sites, with a pH range from slightly acid to slightly alkaline. Redcedars are extremely drought-resistant. All they require is full sunlight and good air circulation. They are immune to both salt and air pollution.

the resilient forest

Trees may visually dominate a forest, but forests are much more than a collection of trees, just as cities are more than a conglomeration of buildings. Forests are communities of animate and inanimate objects that constantly interact with one another. Forests are dynamic, always changing, always evolving.

Contrary to popular opinion, forests are not in a delicate balanced state that must never be disturbed. Disturbances, caused by both nature and humans, occur all the time. Forest fires, windstorms, ice storms, hurricanes, tornadoes, floods, drought, and insect and disease epidemics change the nature of forests dramatically, sometimes for centuries. Similarly, logging, highway and railroad construction, energy exploration and development, mining, farming, and urbanization have long-term impacts. Hydroelectric dams and pollution spills may have effects that will last for millennia.

But the forest is, if nothing else, resilient. One cannot help but be amazed to stumble upon a long-abandoned asphalt road — a road initially built by cutting the forest, then bulldozing, grading, gravelling, and paving — to find wildflowers, shrubs, and even trees growing in the cracks and potholes. At some time in the future, there will be little evidence the pavement ever existed.

Redcedar, as an early succession species, is one of the first steps in this natural restoration process.

the redcedar-apple connection

A new forest is even more dynamic. It evolves from early to late succession species, and in the absence of a disturbance, may reach what is commonly called a climax state. At all stages of its evolution, the thousands of plants and animals — from oaks to orchids, earthworms to microscopic soil bacteria — interact with one another to form a community we call a forest ecosystem.

Some of these relationships are fascinating. One such interaction is the curious relationship between two totally unrelated plants that share a common disease. The fungus, a rust, requires two host species to survive and proliferate. White pine blister rust, for example, depends on the presence of both white pine and currants or gooseberries. Sweet fern blister rust needs jack pine and sweet fern as its alternate hosts.

Another is cedar apple rust, whose alternate hosts are eastern redcedar and apple trees. Spores from 5-centimeter (2") galls on redcedar, initiated by spring rains, are borne by wind and insects to nearby apple trees. There they attack the leaves and fruit, causing early leaf fall and undersized, deformed apples. In late summer, spores return to the redcedars, where they spend the winter. The next year they produce more galls, and the following spring they re-infect the apple trees. Damage to redcedar leaves is mostly cosmetic, but damage to an apple crop can be disastrous.

There are four options for control. Ensure that no redcedar grows within a kilometer or more (up to a mile) of apple trees; manually pick galls from redcedars, and destroy them; plant only rust-resistant redcedar or apple cultivars; or spray fungicides on both hosts.

The most serious threat to redcedar is fire. Its thin fibrous bark and compact crown of volatile foliage make it very susceptible even to grass fires.

redcedar medicine

Indigenous people in North America relied on redcedar to treat respiratory ailments. The aromatic heartwood was one of seven herbal ingredients that the Meskwaki steamed and inhaled for bronchitis. In the sweat lodge, the Omaha laid the leaves on hot stones and inhaled the vapors for head colds. Other Plains nations boiled the berries and leaves together into a cough syrup. Rappahannucks drank an infusion of the berries and wild ginger for asthma. The Mohawk boiled a blend of redcedar leaves and those of five other conifers, and drank the compound for both coughs and colds. All conifer needles are rich in vitamin C.

Choctaw women in Louisiana drank a redcedar tea to regulate menstrual flow. The Seneca of upstate New York drank the liquid from boiled leaves as a spring diuretic to cleanse the kidneys. The Ojibway boiled redcedar and yew (ground hemlock) twigs together, and drank the decoction for rheumatism. Pawnees breathed in the leaf smoke for nervousness and nightmares, Creeks for neck cramps, and Natchez for shoulder and back pain.

First Nations people in Quebec and the Maritimes, who lived beyond the natural range of redcedar, substituted common or ground juniper, its diminutive cousin, for relief from many of the same ailments.

It is reported that Oglalas, during an epidemic of Asiatic cholera in 1849–50, successfully fought the disease by drinking a redcedar leaf decoction. The Mohawk used redcedar, which they considered high in insulin, for diabetes.

Ontario Ojibway boiled the inner bark into a mahogany dye, with which they colored the bark strips in their woven mats. Several tribes carved their dugout canoes from redcedar — they were light, waterproof, and durable. Merchant vessels that sailed the waters of Lake Ontario were built of redcedar near Kingston, the northern limit of the species.

Cedrol, an oil distilled from the leaves, twigs, and heartwood, was employed as a medicine to promote healing of wounds, and was used as a perfume and polish.

a wildlife retreat

For some 50 to 70 songbirds, redcedar just about does it all. Whether in a fencerow, windbreak, on old fields, or planted around the home, its dense foliage, which often extends to the ground, offers cover and nesting habitat to cedar waxwings, robins, and mockingbirds, all creatures of open spaces. Along with bluebirds, they rate the berries number one on their food preference list. Juncos, myrtle warblers, chipping sparrows, and song sparrows roost amid the thick foliage.

In exchange for free food, birds obligingly disperse the seeds far and wide. Waxwings, robins and bluebirds perched on fences digest the fruit and deposit the seeds, making redcedar a typical fence-row tree. Straight rows of tall redcedars can be found today where the fences below have long since disappeared.

Grouse, quail, pheasants, and turkeys gobble the berries, and seek cover under the sheltering branches. Four-legged fans of the fruit range from the tiny meadow mouse to the black bear. Other berry buffs are rabbits, foxes, raccoons, skunks, opossums, and coyotes. White-tailed and mule deer browse the calcium- and iron-rich foliage, in some regions an important winter food.

the price of literacy

Most of us learned in elementary school that there is no lead in a lead pencil. But no one really gave any thought to the wood — except those involved in what was a huge industry in the southern states. At the turn of the twentieth century, pencil mills were manufacturing 315 million pencils a year, consuming over 100,000 tons of wood annually. The wood was redcedar.

> How long the supply will last is hard to say, but it is certain that some of the mills now in operation must shut down inside of a dozen years, and this regardless of any measures which may be taken in the meantime to protect the young growth. . . . Though the supply of cedar suitable for pencils has been greatly depleted, and though it is certain that before long it will be practically exhausted, no steps have been taken to provide for a future supply.
>
> USDA Forest Service,
> *Circular 102, 1907*

This is just another example of the short-sightedness and excesses of the past when it came to our forests. Only the best quality logs were highgraded from mixedwood forests. And only clear knot-free heartwood was used. It was common practice to leave the logs in the mill yard for several years, until the thin sapwood rotted away. The quality specs for pencil wood were very high — as a result, 90 percent of the wood, by weight, was wasted. As predicted, the supply ran out. By 1940, only 10 percent of pencils were made of redcedar; today other species and wood composites have all but replaced it.

cedar chests and cigar boxes

Redcedar's soft aromatic heartwood lent itself to two specialty products — cedar chests and cigar boxes. Presumably because of its aroma, wool blankets and clothing stored in chests, wardrobes, and closets lined with unfinished redcedar are safe from moths. It was selected for cigar boxes for its softness, light weight, low shrinkage, ease of working, color, and aroma. Cigars remained fresher longer when packed in redcedar.

Redcedar heartwood is highly rot resistant and splits easily. Ergo that staple of the countryside, the traditional split rail fence, with posts and rails of cedar. Other rural uses included house and barn sills, milking pails, and wash tubs.

In some areas, redcedar's full compact foliage and conical shape have made it a very popular Christmas tree.

In making gin, grain is distilled over juniper berries; in fact the word "gin" is derived from the French *genévrier*, for juniper, as is the name Geneva gin.

Redcedar wood has a fine, uniform and straight grain, except around the plentiful knots. It saws and glues exceptionally well, and has good nail-holding capability. Its rich color takes a high polish. Like black cherry, its heartwood, if left unfinished, will darken with exposure to sunlight. It is one of the softwoods preferred by carvers and whittlers.

Tamarack
(*Larix laricina*)

eastern larch
hackmatack
American larch
juniper

mélèze
mélèze laricin
épinette rouge
tamarac
violon

Abenaki: *akemantak*

Leaf
- needles soft, flexible, light green; triangular in cross section; 2–5 cm (1–2") long;
- in two different configurations;
- on older twigs, in clusters of 15–30 radiating from stubby spur shoots;
- on new twigs, single and arranged spirally around twig;
- turn golden yellow in late autumn, then shed.

Flower
- males small, oval, yellow, and slightly drooping; females bright red;
- both male and female on same tree, in late spring.

Fruit
- cones small, stalked, erect; light brown at maturity; 1–2 cm (⅓–½") long;
- open late summer to release winged seeds, dispersed by wind;
- empty cones, resembling tiny wooden roses, may remain on tree for several years;
- begin bearing cones at age 12–15; good seed crop every 3–6 years.

Twig
- orange brown, slender, and flexible; spur shoots give twigs knobby appearance;
- terminal buds reddish brown, shiny.

Bark
- on younger trees, thin, smooth, and bluish gray;
- on older trees, reddish brown and scaly.

Wood
- moderately heavy, hard, strong; odorless; often with spiral grain; impact-resistant;
- heartwood yellowish brown, oily, decay-resistant; thin sapwood whitish;
- annual growth rings very distinct.

Height
16–20 m (50–65')

Diameter
30–40 cm (12–16")

Longevity
60–80 years

The annual growth rings are very distinct; the wide spacing between them indicates rapid growth.

breaking all the rules

Ten species of larch exist around the world, all in the northern hemisphere. Of these, three are native to North America. Tamarack — often referred to as eastern larch — has the greatest range. It grows from Maryland north to the taiga, the transition zone between the boreal forest and the treeless Arctic tundra. Next to white and black spruce, tamarack is the widest-ranging conifer on the continent, stretching from Newfoundland and Labrador to the Alaska interior.

Despite its broad distribution, tamarack comprises only one percent of the softwood volume of Canada, and even less in the United States. It rarely forms pure stands of any size, tending instead to occupy sites where no other tree will grow.

Tamarack is an anomaly in the otherwise orderly world of trees. It is a softwood, but its wood is hard and heavy. It is a conifer, but not an evergreen. Like southern bald cypress, it sheds its leaves each fall. Other conifers shed their needles after two to ten years, thereby remaining "evergreen." Tamarack has not only one needle configuration, but two distinct patterns on the same branch. Unlike other softwoods, it yields firewood equal or superior in heat value to many of the hardwoods. It grows best on moist well-drained upland soils, but in the wild is usually found growing in wet conditions at the edges of bogs and other wetlands. Its root system is shallow, yet it remains windfirm.

The species is locally called, in English and in French, by at least ten different names, including "juniper" and "violon" in the Maritimes, and "épinette rouge" in parts of Quebec and New Brunswick. All three are misnomers.

landscaping with larch

Landscaping with larch makes good sense. Its soft apple-green foliage and small rosy flowers in early spring, airy and delicate crown throughout summer, and brilliant golden color in late autumn, when other deciduous trees stand naked, make tamarack a three-season delight. In the early days of November, its leafless but living skeleton signals the onset of winter.

Tamaracks tolerate a broad range of temperatures, precipitation, and daylight length. They survive virtually any conditions, except shade and flooding. Soil depth is not a consideration; their wide-spreading roots rarely penetrate more than a meter (3') below ground. They are very fast growing, frost hardy, require little maintenance, and under ideal conditions can reach a height of 12 meters (40') in 20 years. They can be planted from seed, from cuttings from terminal shoots, or easily transplanted from the wild.

ship's knees and trunnels

The use of tamarack's strong and decay-resistant wood is woven into the colonization and development history of North America. In the era of sailing ships, the naturally L-shaped stumps and upper roots became the "knees" of ships, the large brackets which fixed the deck timbers to the hull.

The knees of the original *Bluenose*, the schooner depicted on Canada's dime, were created from Nova Scotia tamarack stumps. When the *Bluenose* finally hit a reef and sank in 1946, the trunnels — tree nails — foot-long spikes of tamarack that held the key joints of the ship together, were still sound and solidly entrenched, after 25 years of ocean sailing. Today on the east coast, boat builders still steam and bend tamarack for the ribs of Northumberland wooden fishing boats.

Tamarack's decay resistance, coupled with its strength, made it the ideal wood for railway ties, and laid the groundwork for the nineteenth-century western expansion of both Canada and the United States. The last spike was likely driven into a tamarack tie.

These same qualities led farmers to use tamarack for fence posts and barn sills, miners for pit props, builders and engineers for durable piles and piers, and woodlot owners for culverts and bridges to access their forests. Tamarack also stood for thousands of kilometers of telephone and utility poles, providing vital communications links and sources of energy to homes and factories across the continent.

tamarack threats

At the turn of the twentieth century, vast areas of eastern North America almost lost a component of their forest ecosystems. The cause was a larch sawfly epidemic. It eventually subsided, at least temporarily, but not before tamarack had become locally endangered and had to be literally "born again." Today, the regions affected are devoid of mature tamaracks.

Unquestionably the most destructive of the more than 40 insects that attack larch, colonies of sawfly larvae eat themselves out of house and home on one branch, then migrate en masse to other limbs, until whole trees are defoliated. They reproduce abundantly; female sawflies, 98 percent of the population, do not require mating to lay fertile eggs. Manitoba had initial success combating sawflies by importing and releasing parasites from Europe, but unfortunately the parasites were found to have their own parasites.

Another threat is the larch casebearer, introduced into North America in Massachusetts in the 1880s. The larvae of this curious moth eat the center out of a needle, then chew off both ends to form a portable home, which they carry on their backs while searching for other needles to eat.

The tiny eastern larch beetle preys upon weakened trees. It bores tunnels in the wood, girdling the tree, and causing needles to turn prematurely yellow and the bark to peel, often resulting in death of the tree.

Last on this short list of tamarack threats is the larch cone maggot, the larva of a fly resembling a small housefly. At pollination time maggots hatch within young cones and bore through them, destroying seeds as they go.

fauna loves flora

In many regions, porcupines, tree climbers extraordinaire, are the most prickly threat to tamarack. They love the inner bark, and devour large patches, leaving bare wood exposed, permanently scarring and sometimes killing the tree. The ponderous, heavily armoured rodent is almost invincible. Few forest creatures are willing to risk the pain of its quills to feast on its tender meat. Fishers, as well as red foxes, bobcats, and owls, have learned the secret — roll it over to expose its unarmed belly. Other carnivores and domestic dogs (the prudent ones, at least) have learned by experience not to mess with porky.

Tamarack bogs provide habitat for snowshoe hares, which in turn are preyed upon by lynx, fox, fishers, martens and great grey owls. Bears, mink, bobcats, and otters are also at home in tamarack habitat. Tamarack bogs in Ohio were one of the last roosting areas of passenger pigeons before their senseless extinction early in the twentieth century.

In the fall, spruce grouse gorge themselves on both the needles and the buds. Crossbills, purple finches, and kinglets feed on tamarack seeds as soon as the cones mature. Connecticut warblers and yellow-bellied flycatchers are two of the songbirds who nest on the ground among bog tamaracks.

a cure for all manner of ills

A man who lives and dies in the woods knows the secret life of trees.

Chief Dan George,
My Heart Soars, 1989

The inner bark of tamarack was universally considered "good medicine" by Aboriginal people, but each tribe prescribed a different use for it. The Menominee peeled and applied it fresh as a poultice on wounds and inflammations. The Potawatomi made a bark extract to treat bronchitis and chronic inflammation of the urinary tract. The Ojibway considered it a laxative, tonic, headache remedy, and diuretic, and also applied it on burns. The Mi'kmaq and Maliseet steeped it as a tea for colds, consumption, or general debility.

Decoctions of the needles were said to cure piles, haemoptsis (spitting of blood), menorrhagia (abnormal menstrual flow), diarrhea, and dysentery. Flambeau Ojibway steamed the needles over hot rocks and inhaled the fumes for congestion.

Doctors and pharmacists were not oblivious to the medicinal benefits of tamarack. It was included in the *Materia Medica* in the 1820s, the *Canadian Pharmaceutical Journal* in 1868, the *U.S. Pharmacopoeia* in 1905, and the *U.S. Dispensatory* in 1916.

Tamarack had other applications for Native people. Northern Saulteaux of Ontario decorated their clothing and pouches with porcupine quills dyed red with tamarack bark. The Mohawk on the St. Lawrence crafted snowshoes from the flexible and durable wood.

tamarack and wetlands

The clearest way into the Universe is through a forest wilderness.

John Muir,
1838–1914

Immature cones are purple, and erect on the twig.

The shallow, wide-spreading roots of tamarack protect the edges of wetlands, binding fragile soils, preventing erosion and stabilizing water levels. Wetlands are one of our most precious natural habitats, whose value has been little understood until recently. North American experts list five classes: fens, marshes, swamps, peat bogs, and shallow open water; but many wetlands have characteristics of several types. Tamarack is commonly found growing in fens, a less advanced and less acidic form of bog.

Wetlands have traditionally had a bad rap: useless for farming, impossible to build upon, a poor place to try to grow trees, and home to a million mosquitoes. But wetlands play a pivotal role in our ecosystem. They act as giant sponges, absorbing snow and rain, filtering it, and slowly releasing it in drier times.

Wetlands are home to hundreds of our less familiar and less cuddly critters such as salamanders, water bugs, frogs, toads, and shrews. They in turn are prey for species further up the food chain, such as otters, cranes, and ducks. Marsh wrens and swamp sparrows build their nests of grasses and sedges that are found only in wetlands. Wetlands host unique flora as well, species adapted to the harsh conditions which cannot survive anywhere else.

Since the settlement of North America by our European ancestors, millions of hectares of wetlands have been filled in, drained, or otherwise swallowed up by progress. Preservation of those remaining is essential. One quarter of the carbon sink (storage) provided by the Earth's wetlands lies in the bogs and fens of Canada, where carbon dioxide is absorbed from the atmosphere and stored or sequestered in sphagnum peat moss. Conservation of wetlands may have significant implications in buffering possible global climate change.

The Carolinian Forest

Tree species that in Canada grow naturally only in the Carolinian forest zone are:

black-gum	*Nyssa sylvatica*	nyssa sylvestre
blue ash	*Fraxinus quadrangulata*	frêne anguleux
cherry birch	*Betula lenta*	bouleau flexible
cucumber-tree (magnolia)	*Magnolia acuminata*	magnolia acuminé
dwarf hackberry	*Celtis tenuifolia*	micocoulier rabougri
flowering dogwood	*Cornus florida*	cornouillier fleuri
honey-locust	*Gleditsia triacanthos*	févier épineux
hoptree	*Ptelea trifoliata*	ptéléa trifolié
Kentucky coffeetree	*Gymnocladus dioicus*	chicot févier
pawpaw	*Asimina triloba*	asiminier trilobé
Ohio buckeye	*Aesculus glabra*	marronier
pignut (red) hickory	*Carya glabra*	caryer glabre
pin oak	*Quercus palustris*	chêne des marais
pumpkin ash	*Fraxinus profunda*	frêne pubescent
redbud	*Cercis canadensis*	gainier rouge
red mulberry	*Morus rubra*	mûrier rouge
sassafras	*Sassafras albidum*	sassafras official
shellbark hickory	*Carya laciniosa*	caryer lacinié
Shumard oak	*Quercus shumardii*	chêne de Shumard
tulip-tree (yellow-poplar)	*Liriodendron tulipfera*	tulipier de Virginie
wild crab apple	*Malus coronaria*	pommier odorant

Tree species that grow predominantly in the Carolinian forest zone, but occur naturally in other isolated locations in southern Quebec, Ontario, or Manitoba are:

American (wild) plum	*Prunus americana*	prunier d'Amérique
American (sweet) chestnut	*Castanea dentata*	châtaignier d'Amérique
black maple	*Acer nigrum*	érable noir
black oak	*Quercus velutina*	chêne noir
black walnut	*Juglans nigra*	noyer noir
blue-beech (hornbeam)	*Carpinus caroliniana*	charme de Caroline
Chinquapin oak	*Quercus muehlenbergii*	chêne jaune
northern pin (Hills) oak	*Quercus ellipsoidalis*	chêne ellipsoïdal
swamp white oak	*Quercus bicolor*	chêne bicolore
sycamore	*Platanus occidentalis*	platane occidental

Carolinian Canada

*Woe unto them that join house to house
   and field to field
Till there be no place in the midst of the
   earth.*

Isaiah 5:8

The Carolinian forest zone earns its name from being the northernmost outpost of the American deciduous forest, whose roots lie in North and South Carolina. It stretches across the top of Lake Erie, from Windsor in the west, to Grand Bend near the foot of Lake Huron in the north, and east to the shores of Lake Ontario. Within the zone lie the cities of Toronto, Hamilton, Niagara Falls, London, Sarnia, and Windsor. One quarter of Canada's population lives within the Carolinian zone, an area only twice the size of Cape Breton Island.

The Carolinian zone, or Carolinian Canada, is no longer the almost continuous forest it once was. Three-quarters of this region is prime agricultural land, producing soybeans, market and canning vegetables, fruit, ginseng, and tobacco, and it is served by numerous nurseries growing trees, shrubs, and flowers. Most of the remainder is urban or industrial. Only 11 percent is still forested — isolated islands of tree-cover scattered amid a sea of farmland and development. The forest is fragmented, to say the least. One of the largest blocks of forest in the region, Backus Woods, covers only 260 hectares, or 500 acres, the equivalent of a standard farm section on the prairies. The largest woodlot in Essex County, near Windsor, is 133 hectares (330 acres).

Its southern latitude, which includes the most southerly points in Canada, and the moderating effect of Lake Erie, the warmest of the Great Lakes, combine to give the region the highest year-round temperatures, the longest growing season, and the most frost-free days in Ontario. Little wonder it is popularly referred to as the Banana Belt.

As a result of its climate, the Carolinian zone is home to many plants and animals that cannot survive elsewhere in Canada. There are, for example, double the number of tree species in Carolinian Canada (which represents less than 1 percent of Canada's land base) than in all the Atlantic provinces combined. The region is also home to numerous shrubs, grasses, ferns, wildflowers, birds, mammals, reptiles, amphibians, and insects — even cactus — that exist nowhere else in the country. Carolinian Canada is the habitat of 40 percent of Canada's rare, threatened, and endangered species.

why all the fuss?

Restoring and preserving the Carolinian forest is not just a matter of protecting species. With some very notable exceptions, most of the flora and fauna are in danger, not of extinction, but rather of local extirpation. If we can for a moment overlook the international boundary that separates the United States from Canada, we can see that these species, albeit rare in Canada, are commonplace further south in the heart of the deciduous forest. So why all the fuss?

The Carolinian region is part of our natural, and our national heritage. The plants and animals here are as much a fabric of what constitutes Canada as the pine martens, tuckamores, and puffin colonies of Newfoundland and Labrador; the red spruces, lobsters, and Atlantic salmon of the Maritimes; the whales and dolphins of the Bay of Fundy; the woodland caribou of *la Gaspésie*, the beluga whales of the St. Lawrence; the maple sugar bushes of *la Beauce*; the old-growth white pines of Temagami; the millennium-old stunted cedars on the Niagara Escarpment; the black spruce bogs of the boreal forest; the sloughs, shelterbelts and aspen parklands of the prairies; the bison and whooping cranes of Wood Buffalo National Park; the lodgepole pines and grizzlies of the Rockies; the fruit orchards of the Okanagan Valley; the majestic sitka spruces of the Carmanah Valley; the hardy jack pines of the Territories; the polar bears of the Arctic Circle; the peregrine falcons who now nest on our downtown skyscrapers; and the caribou herds migrating across the barren tundra that blankets the north of our country. These living treasures, like those of the Carolinian forest, are part of what makes Canada Canada.

Although the Carolinian zone contains countless species of plants and animals that are unique to the area, the whole must be viewed as a functioning ecosystem in which each species interacts with the others. The ultimate goal of conservation is not to save a fern, a snake, or a tree, but to restore or preserve a natural community that was intact little more than a century ago, one which will once again furnish habitat for the fern, or snake, or tree.

Carolinian Canada is a stunning example of biological diversity, where north meets south. Where black gums, tulip-trees, and flowering dogwoods grow amid red maples, basswoods, and yellow birches. Where the ranges of the Louisiana and the northern waterthrushes converge. Where opossums and mink co-habit the same forest. Where western tall grass prairie and southern oak Savannahs share the same peninsula as northern white pines. Over 500 species of plants flourish in the Carolinian zone; one-fifth of them occur nowhere else in Canada. This is biodiversity at its best.

much more to learn

It is not within the scope of this book to describe in detail each of the tree species indigenous to the Carolinian forest zone. That task has been admirably accomplished by Gerry Waldron, in his book entitled *The Tree Book — Tree Species and Restoration Guide for the Windsor-Essex Region.*

For those who want to know more about the species of plants, birds, mammals, amphibians, reptiles, and insects listed under the five categories of wildlife at risk by the Committee on the Status of Endangered Wildlife in Canada (COSEWIC), Environment Canada has such a publication in its excellent Hinterland Who's Who series. The most current listing includes the cucumber magnolia and red mulberry as endangered; the chestnut and Kentucky coffeetree as threatened; and the hoptree, dwarf hackberry, blue ash and Shumard oak as of special concern. A future list might well include butternut, rapidly falling victim to a fatal imported canker disease.

To learn more about the area, its natural history, its current status, the myriad local conservation measures currently underway, and the dozens of government and non-government organizations, large and small, that are working together to address the situation, contact the Carolinian Canada Coalition in London, Ontario.

Ironwood
(*Ostrya virginiana*)

hop hornbeam
leverwood
deerwood

ostryer de Virginie
bois dûr
bois à levier
bois de fer

Cayuga: *teo:ji'*

Leaf
- simple, alternate; oval with pointed toothed tip and heart-shaped base; 6–12 cm (2½–5") long;
- thin, with silky texture; edges saw-toothed, veins leading to larger teeth; on short pale green stalks;
- upper side dull dark green; underside paler; with raised midrib fuzzy at vein junctions;
- opaque yellow, then brown, in autumn.

Flower
- male catkins reddish brown, 2–3 cm (1") long;
- in groups of 2–3 at end of twigs all winter;
- double their length in spring and hang downwards, dispersing yellow pollen;
- tiny green females in clusters at end of new shoots;
- both sexes on same tree; pollinate when leaves unfolding.

Fruit
- seeds tiny, flattened, teardrop shaped; encased singly in pillowy sacs; pale yellow in summer, brown at maturity in autumn;
- sacs hanging in compact bunches of 10–20, on short stems, at end of new shoots;
- remain on twigs after leaf fall; fall singly or in bunches over winter;
- begin bearing fruit at age 20–25; good seed crop most years; occasional bumper crops.

Twig
- slender, wiry, mahogany color, shiny, with tiny lenticels; often coated with gray film;
- buds greenish brown, pointed, slightly fuzzy at the tip; angling away from twig at 30°.

Bark
- on younger trees, dull brown with lenticels;
- on older trees, grayish brown, with long narrow vertical plates; easily rubbed off;
- on very mature trees, curling out at ends, giving shreddy appearance;
- sometimes spiraling around tree.

Wood
- very heavy, hard; tough, durable; close grained; impact-resistant; odorless;
- heartwood light brown with reddish tinge; thick sapwood nearly white;
- annual growth rings indistinct.

Height
8–12 m (25–40')

Diameter
20–40 cm (8–16")

Longevity
75–100 years

a tree of the understory

Ironwood is a tree of the forest understory. It can live its entire life in the shade of taller hardwoods such as maple, oak, and ash. Like its overshadowing partners, it requires moist, fertile, well-drained soil. A bit of a loner, ironwood is usually scattered here and there, rarely, if ever, in pure stands.

Very young ironwoods may be difficult to identify. The leaves are very similar to those of yellow birch. Sapling bark resembles the rest of the birch family — smooth and brown, with lenticels. Soon the birches develop their characteristic papery texture, while ironwood becomes rough and scaly.

Ironwood fruit is unique. While the birches produce cone-like structures that bear their seeds, ironwood develops clusters of pale yellow sacs — with the texture of flower petals — much like those of the unrelated hop vine. Thus its other common name — hop hornbeam.

The range of ironwood is extensive. From its northern limits in Atlantic Canada, across southern Quebec and Ontario, to the southeast corner of Manitoba, it stretches through most of the eastern states to Arkansas, Texas, and down into central America, showing remarkable adaptability to a wide range of climates.

wood-be medicine

Native people produced a cornucopia of medicines from our native trees and shrubs, mostly from the inner bark, but often from the twigs, roots, and leaves. With ironwood, they used the wood itself. They sliced the reddish heartwood into chips, sometimes pounded it into a crude powder, and boiled it into a healthful tonic and treatment for fevers, scaly skin, and indigestion.

The Ojibway drank a heartwood tonic for kidney ailments. Both they and the Onondaga Iroquois included ironwood in their cough syrup. In the mid-1800s, iron-wood was recognized in the *U.S. Pharmacopoeia* and in Canada's official list of medicinal plants.

tiny but tough

Anyone who has tried to split ironwood understands where it gets its name. Without adequate power and the right technique, the ax bounces off with a twang, as if it had hit a steel beam. Mercifully, ironwoods are small and don't require much splitting. Forget the ax — use a wood splitter.

Ironwood is not considered a commercial species, but in the past it was used locally to make wagon wheel hubs, mill cogs, sleigh runners, mallets, pestles, tool handles, ladder rungs, and a host of farm and home implements. Its strength as a lever, one of the most basic and useful of tools, was the source of its less common name, leverwood.

Ironwood is not recommended for the average home handyman. It doesn't take nails or screws easily, and blunts tools quickly, but it takes on a nice finish if one can get the project to that stage.

from mergansers to mockingbirds

Ironwood's sheltered niche beneath the forest canopy is ideal nesting habitat for songbirds to protect their eggs and offspring from predators. Its horizontal branches provide a platform on which vireos, tanagers, and warblers construct their nests.

Where ironwood grows within the range of the ruffed grouse, its nutritious buds and male catkins help the big birds survive the rigors of winter. In autumn, grouse supplement their diet with ironwood nutlets, and return the favor by dispersing the seeds far and wide, ensuring future generations of ironwood in the hardwood ecosystems they call home.

Ironwood seeds are tiny but tasty morsels for a diverse group of feathered feeders —

Narrow vertical strips of bark, often loose at the ends, flake off when rubbed.

mergansers, turkeys, grosbeaks, woodpeckers, finches, pheasants, and mockingbirds.

an anchor in the landscape

If you are seeking a fairly small and hardy tree to fill a shaded spot, ironwood is worth considering. Completely at home in the shade, it will thrive in full sunlight as well. In the open, the breadth of its spreading crown often exceeds its height. The U.S. record holder, in Grand Traverse County, Michigan is 23 meters (74') tall, and its crown spans 34 meters (111').

The long horizontal branches dip slightly at the tips, where the male catkins preparing to pollinate in early spring, cast a faint yellowish glow. Throughout summer, the branch tips are bedecked with bunches of pale yellow fruit tucked neatly amid the dark green foliage.

Even on ideal soils, ironwood is slow to grow. But patience is rewarded with a pleasant little tree to anchor other more flamboyant ornamentals and add diversity to the home landscape.

Planting from seed is straightforward — collect the seed sacs when brown in the fall, dry, and remove the nutlets. Wear gloves — the sacs bear minute hairs that irritate the skin. Sow the seeds about a centimeter (½") deep in the soil, and mulch for the winter. Next spring, remove the mulch when the nutlets germinate, and water if there is a prolonged period without rain.

Young trees are generally slow to acclimatize to their new home; transplanting very early in spring helps the root system adjust.

Ironwood is tough and highly resistant to damage by wind, snow, or ice. However, it will not tolerate flooding or salt damage. It has no insect or disease enemies of consequence, except the introduced gypsy moth when local populations hit epidemic levels. Tiny but tough, ironwood is a solid, if unspectacular, choice for an ornamental.

the other ironwood

Alongside streams in the forest understory grows another, even smaller, member of the birch family, blue beech (*Carpinus caroliniana*), which also goes by the names of hornbeam and ironwood. Its leaves might be confused with those of ironwood, but they are firmer and bluer. The bark, however, is very different. Even on old trees, it is thin and smooth like beech, only bluer, and has long vertical rounded ridges like rippling muscles — earning it yet another name: musclewood.

Blue beech's range is slightly more limited than that of ironwood. It grows from southern Maine to Minnesota, down to eastern Texas and northern Florida. In Canada, it is restricted to the St. Lawrence and Ottawa River valleys, north of Lake Ontario, the Carolinian forest, and Manitoulin Island in Lake Huron.

Blue beech's short narrow trunk limits its commercial use, but its hard heavy wood is excellent for tool handles.

White Spruce
(*Picea glauca*)

Canada spruce
cat spruce
field spruce
pasture spruce
skunk spruce

épinette blanche
prusse blanche
épinette grise
épicéa blanche
épicéa glauque

Ojibway: *zesegaandag*

Leaf
- needles bluish green, covered with whitish film; 1.5–2 cm (⅔–¾") long;
- square in cross section; tips pointed; stiff; straight or curved;
- pungent odor when crushed;
- persist on tree 7–10 years.

Flower
- males rosy red, 1.5–2 cm (⅔–¾") long; near end of twig; shed yellow pollen at maturity;
- females red or yellowish green; erect; oval;
- males and females on same tree, on previous year's twigs.

Fruit
- cones slender, cylindrical, hanging; beige brown at maturity; soft to the touch;
- ripen in 1 season; disperse seeds within weeks of opening, then fall;
- seeds thin-winged; about 140 per cone;
- in bumper year, 8,000 to 10,000 cones on large trees;
- begin bearing cones at age 20–30; good seed crop every 2–6 years.

Twig
- slender; beige; hairless;
- rough where short stubs remain after old needles shed;
- in spring, expanding buds covered with thin brown onion skin.

Bark
- on younger trees, thin, somewhat smooth; light gray;
- on older trees, ash gray; scaly;
- exposed bark silvery.

Wood
- light, soft, straight-grained; odorless; fine-textured;
- pale yellowish white; no contrast between heartwood and sapwood;
- annual growth rings distinct.

Height	Diameter	Longevity
20–25 m (65–80')	40–80 cm (16–32")	100–200 years

Fertilizer will accentuate the lush bluish green foliage in open-grown white spruces.

a tree of the northern boreal

The distribution of white spruce is transcontinental. Its evergreen spires bedeck the forest landscape from Newfoundland and Labrador west, hugging the northern tree limit, to the interior of Alaska, including much of non-coastal British Columbia. It is predominantly a Canadian tree, with spillover into the upper regions of the Lakes states, New York, and New England.

With such a broad span, with extremes of soils, climate, and a host of other factors, including genetics, it is natural that white spruce is variable in size and form. The largest specimens grow in Wood Buffalo National Park, where giants 50 meters (165') tall line the fertile floodplains of the Peace River. Prairie spruces, historically the region's chief source of softwood lumber, are commonly found in mixed-wood stands, suppressed under the canopy of trembling aspen. With time, the spruces push through the short-lived aspen and dominate the site. Further south in farming country, where winters are long and winds severe, white spruce is planted as a hardy ornamental, and in windbreaks and shelterbelts. It is the provincial tree of Manitoba and the state tree of South Dakota.

Along the shores of the east coast, scattered specimens are found clinging to clifftops, battered by bitter salt-laden winds from the North Atlantic. Their exposed sides may be brown and bare of needles, but the leeward side remains green, under some of the harshest winter weather imaginable.

sprucing up your property

Where space allows, white spruce should be considered essential in any residential landscape plans. When grown in the open, its dense boughs of blue-green foliage reach to the ground, creating a stately tree with a full pyramidal crown. In the city it will help reduce noise and sight pollution, afford privacy, and encourage wildlife.

At maturity in early fall, white spruce cones open and release their seeds to the wind. To plant a spruce, collect seed from cones as soon as they become soft to the touch, before they open and are consumed by birds and squirrels. Sow in a prepared bed — a small corner of the garden will do — cover with a thin layer of topsoil, and mulch for the winter. As with all trees planted from seed, sow more than required, allowing for infertile seeds and raiding by rodents.

Alternatively, if you wish to get a head start, (with permission from the owner) dig up a young white spruce from a field, forest edge, or roadside, keeping all the roots intact, and transplant to your home site. Plant slightly deeper than its original depth. A third option is to purchase a native white spruce, potted or bound in a root ball, at a local nursery or garden center.

Once established, a fertilizer rich in nitrogen will accelerate the growth rate and enhance the blue color of the foliage. White spruce, closely spaced and well maintained, can also produce a thick handsome hedge.

curing the Cartier crew

In 1535, on Jacques Cartier's second expedition to Canada, his three ships became locked in the ice at the Iroquois village of Stadacona, at what is today Quebec City. His crew, at sea for months, was suffering from scurvy — 25 had already died.

Cartier inquired of a local Indian chief what could be done, and the Indian brought boughs of an evergreen tree he called "annedda." The branches were boiled, and Cartier's men drank the juice every second day. By the sixth day they were cured. Native people may not have heard of vitamin C, but they knew from experience that whatever

spruce and other evergreens contained was good medicine for the ills of scurvy.

For centuries both historians and botanists have debated the nature of the Cartier cure, with no conclusive agreement. It is safe to say that *annedda* was either spruce, cedar, hemlock, or pine — all evergreens whose needles are rich in vitamin C.

a farmstead abandoned

Since the end of the nineteenth century, a socioeconomic phenomenon has pervaded many areas of eastern North America. The financial and physical hardships of farming, and the lure of the city have taken their toll — in Nova Scotia alone over 400,000 hectares (1 million acres) of farmland have been abandoned in the last century.

Nature wastes little time reclaiming fields as forests. It is called forest succession. The tree and shrub species that invade idle land vary from region to region. In the Maritimes and New England, seeds from white spruces in fencerows and adjacent forests are blown onto the site, where they quickly germinate. Within a decade or two, the grasses disappear, and young thickets of even-aged white spruce abound. As time goes on and the trees grow taller, the ground below becomes carpeted with thick mosses, with a scattering of tiny wildflowers. In dense old stands, were it not for white spruce's habit of retaining its lower dead branches, the setting would be park-like.

At about 50 years of age, long before their normal life expectancy, many pasture spruces begin to decay at the stump and roots. They must be cut down if the owner is to salvage any economic benefit, or they will be lost. After the harvest, the fields are not re-colonized by white spruce or any other pioneer tree, but revert to grasses, herbs, and shrubs, and remain that way for years. Although theories abound, no one quite knows why.

The beige-brown cones are soft to the touch when mature.

waste not

When Native people cut down a white spruce, no part of the tree went to waste. They used the needles, twigs, limbs, pitch, outer bark, inner bark, wood, gum, and roots. From these they derived food, drink, shelter, and medicine, as well as materials for sewing, building, cleaning, cooking, and heating.

In spring and summer, some tribes dried and ground the inner bark, which they stored as an emergency flour. Teas steeped from the young needles and twigs, sometimes sweetened with maple syrup or flavored with dried berries, yielded not only a refreshing drink, but a healthful and antiscorbutic tonic.

Inner bark decoctions were drunk for general stomach disorders, and twig decoctions, sometimes mixed with mosses and ironwood chips, were steamed to relieve rheumatic pains. A salve derived from the inner bark was applied to cuts, sores, and wounds.

The outer bark was used for roofing and for fire tinder, the branches as brooms, and the branch tips mixed with balsam fir for bedding. Spruce boughs were placed under wigwams as "good medicine" for the inhabitants of the dwelling.

White spruce roots were soaked, split, and chewed to form the thread that bound the birchbark canoes, baskets, and snowshoes. The light but strong wood formed part of the inner structure of the canoes; boiled or chewed spruce gum was used to caulk the seams. The gum was also chewed as a digestive, or purely for pleasure, especially by women and children. This prompted seventeenth-century explorer Nicolas Denys to comment, "In consequence they never had a toothache and their teeth were well kept and white as snow." Spruce was also one of the medicinal herbs used in sweat baths.

Indians passed on the tradition of brewing spruce beer to the settlers, and it became a staple beverage in their diet. The wealthier of the colonists mixed brandy and maple syrup with spruce beer; those less fortunate drank it straight. Spruce beer is definitely an acquired taste.

Stradivarius, but not the Spruce Goose

The highly resonant wood of white and red spruce is prized for its quality of transmitting vibrations, and is the eastern wood of choice for crafting musical instrument components. Carefully selected for uniformity of structure, and seasoned under exacting conditions, spruce wood is used for organ pipes, and the sounding boards of pianos, violins, guitars, and other stringed instruments. The improvement in the quality of violins is attributable to long usage, not age, as the years of playing enable the wood to vibrate more readily.

Contrary to popular belief, the infamous and immense *Spruce Goose* aircraft designed by Howard Hughes, now preserved in California, was constructed not of spruce, but of laminated white birch.

Throughout its range, white spruce is one of the most common sources of softwood lumber; its lightness and strength, as well as its ease to work with, make it a favorite among carpenters. But it does tend to be knot-ridden. Its long fibers and low resin content make it ideal for pulp and paper; it has been one of the prime pulpwood species since the first pulp mills were built in the mid-1800s.

a place to call home

Mature white spruce is a critical habitat for the spruce grouse, whose diet consists mainly of spruce needles. Commonly called the "fool hen," this rather goofy grouse has not yet grasped the concept that a person wearing an orange vest and toting a rifle is likely a hunter. Unlike that of the ruffed grouse, the breast meat of the spruce grouse is dark and tastes — understandably — rather sprucey.

White spruce's dense foliage is the prime nesting habitat for robins, mourning doves, chipping sparrows, and mockingbirds, along with some 20 other species of songbirds. In the fall, the seed eaters — white-winged crossbills, evening grosbeaks, red-breasted nuthatches, and goldfinches — congregate to await the cone-ripening season.

Red squirrels are always on the spot whenever any forest nut or seed ripens. When their numbers are high and the cone crop is low, they snip off the cone-bearing branch tips, to ensure that they alone consume its contents.

New England porcupines have a thing for white spruce and sugar maple bark, and in Alaska black bears strip off the bark to munch on the sweet sapwood. Snowshoe hares, when their cyclical populations peak, cause significant damage to young trees by nibbling off the shoot tips. Of course, Canada lynx live for the years the hare population soars.

wormy buds and rotten roots

The needles and buds of white spruce and balsam fir share the dubious distinction of being the favored food fare of the eastern spruce budworm, arguably the most destructive tree insect in North America. Budworm populations rise and fall in irregular cycles. At their peaks, even their predators and parasites cannot control their devastation. At epidemic levels, budworm larvae, rather attractive caterpillars in their own right, can devour every young needle and bud in weeks.

Fortunately white spruce, unlike fir, can survive attacks for three or four years without high mortality. By then the budworm population has usually collapsed from starvation or disease, with help from its natural predators and parasites. Or it has moved on to greener pastures — clouds of migrating moths are sometimes so thick, they are picked up on radar screens.

Other troublesome insects are the spruce budmoth, a particular problem in Quebec and New Brunswick plantations, the yellowheaded spruce sawfly, and at times the white pine weevil. All three prefer open grown, roadside, or plantation trees in full sunlight.

There are a dozen or so diseases that afflict white spruce, most of which are not considered threatening. Three that can cause serious injury or death are the velvet top fungus, tomentosus root rot, and armillaria root rot. All three can be detected by their mushrooms at the base of the tree. By then it is too late.

Black Spruce
(*Picea mariana*)

swamp spruce
bog spruce

épinette noir
épicéa marial
prusse noire

Beothuk: *traw-na-soo*

Leaf
- needles dull bluish green; stiff; tips blunt; 1–1.5 cm (⅜–⅔") long;
- square in cross-section; roll between the fingers like a wooden match;
- spirally mounted on tiny pegs which remain after needles shed;
- persist on tree 7–10 years.

Flower
- males oval, tiny, bright red;
- females purple; on previous year's twigs; in upper branches;
- males and females on same tree.

Fruit
- cones stubby, oval, 2–3 cm (about 1") long; ripen in one season; purple; brown at maturity;
- single or in pairs, near top of crown; some turn gray, remain unopened on tree 5–10 years;
- relatively resistant to fire when closed;
- seeds small, winged, dark brown; released gradually over several years;
- begin bearing cones at age 10; good seed crop every 2–6 years.

Twig
- slender, hairy, various shades of brown; rough where short stubs remain after older needles shed; buds small, sharp-pointed;
- branches short, slender, horizontal; sometimes drooping with upturned tips.

Bark
- on younger trees, thin, gray or reddish brown; scaly;
- on older trees, darker gray, with large thin scales;
- inner bark olive green.

Wood
- moderately light in weight, soft, relatively strong, resilient, straight-grained;
- nearly white to pale yellowish brown; little contrast between heartwood and narrow sapwood;
- heaviest of the three eastern spruces;
- annual growth rings distinct.

Height
10–20 m (30–60')

Diameter
15–25 cm (6–10")

Longevity
200 years

The stubby, oval cones, usually close to the main stem, mature in one growing season.

symbol of the north

All day the sun has shone on the surface of
some savage swamp,
where the single spruce stands . . .
Henry David Thoreau (1817–1862)

Black spruce is truly a tree of the north country. From Newfoundland's Bonavista Bay to the Bering Strait of Alaska, it has adapted to the gamut of growing conditions. It is equally at home on the edges of muskegs, on rocky hillsides, on sandy loams, on bare mineral soil, or in the middle of peat bogs. It frequently grows where no other tree will survive. Its versatility results in a variety of shapes and sizes, from stunted shrub on the tundra to towering spire on a fertile slope half a continent south.

The classic black spruce is found in and around bogs in the boreal "spruce-moose" forest, where its short, slender trunk, and stubby, leafless limbs are capped by a dense dark green crown resembling a Scots Guard bearskin busby, or, as some suggest, the Pope's hat. Beneath the spruces, sphagnum mosses and lichens are usually prevalent.

The solemn image of moonlight over a black spruce wetland somehow seems to personify Canada's northern wilderness, and has been captured by countless poets, photographers, and artists.

a survivor

Black spruce is one of the hardiest trees in North America. Wind and wildfire are its principal threats. Its shallow roots render it susceptible to blowdown, especially when neighboring trees are removed and their mutual support system breaks down. Beaver or human dams that cause flooding will kill black spruce.

Its thin, scaly, resinous bark, tiers of dead dry branches, and compact crown of needles rich in volatile oils make black spruce a prime candidate for forest fires. But the species adapts well. Scorched by fire, its cones open and release viable seeds, the lightest of all the native conifers, which are borne afar by the wind to establish a new forest. In pure stands or as solitary sentinels at the edge of a bog, black spruce ensures its perpetuation.

Black spruce has few serious insect or disease enemies. Since it flushes late in the spring, it avoids frost damage and most of the feeding frenzy of the spruce budworm, whose timing is more attuned to balsam fir and white spruce. Dwarf mistletoe can be a problem to individual trees, resulting in curious conglomerations of woody branches called "witch's brooms."

tuckamore

In addition to reproducing from seeds, black spruce has the ability to propagate by layering. When dormant buds on bottom branches contact soil or mosses, they establish roots of their own and develop into new trees. Layering taken to its extreme occurs in alpine areas and on the barren but spectacular coast of Newfoundland, where literally kilometers of stunted and windswept black spruce proliferate, interconnected by their roots, in what Newfoundlanders call "tuckamore."

Black spruce is the arboreal emblem of Newfoundland and Labrador.

snow blindness and spruce beer

With the prevalence of black spruce in the north, it was inevitable that Native people would discover a multitude of medicinal and other uses for its various parts. The Dene people applied twig resin with a feather to cure snow blindness and other eye damage. The Chipewyan and Cree boiled young cones and gargled the liquid for oral maladies ranging from bad breath to toothache to sore throat. Further east, Montagnais, Mi'kmaq, and Maliseet boiled the twigs for a cough and cold remedy. The Potawatomi applied poultices of the inner bark on infections. The Ojibway brewed the needles and crushed bark into a decoction for headaches. The Northern Saulteaux sucked the cones like candy as a treatment for diphtheria, and drank the liquid from boiled cones to combat dry scaly skin.

Birch bark canoes were sewn together with strong and pliable spruce roots, and then caulked with spruce resin boiled with tallow. Young spruce was shaped into spear handles and other hunting and fishing implements. New shoots were brewed into spruce beer, rich in vitamin C, sometimes flavored with maple syrup, a practice still carried on in parts of Quebec.

spruce, paper, and people

. . . the object of intelligent forestry is not simply to preserve the forest, but to utilize it so as to produce the greatest benefits to the public.

Elihu Stewart, 1901
First Secretary,
Canadian Forestry Association

Black spruce is one of the most important Canadian trees in the manufacture of pulp and paper. Its long and strong fibers give strength to newsprint, tissues, and paper towels. Its high cellulose content, density,

low resin level, and near-white color (which necessitates less bleaching) are ideal for paper production. Canadian newsprint has long been recognized worldwide for its quality, primarily due to its spruce content. Canada supplies 30 percent of the world's newsprint.

Forestry provides jobs for almost 900,000 Canadians. Over 250 Canadian communities, large and small, rely on spruce, pine, and aspen forests for the raw materials to supply local mills and provide employment. Many might become ghost towns if the spruce forests were not sustainably managed. Another thousand communities are partially dependent on the forest industry for their survival. In the boreal forests of Ontario, Quebec, and Newfoundland, black spruce is the backbone of the forest industry.

other uses of spruce

Rarely a large tree, black spruce converts nicely into 2x4 studs and smaller-dimension lumber. It is perfect for laths used in snow fences, as stickers to dry lumber, and, in older homes, as the foundation behind plaster walls. It was once extensively used in the box and container industry, and because of its lack of odor or taste, was ideal for food containers.

For home projects from bookshelves to decks to doghouses, black spruce wood is light, soft, resilient, and straight-grained. It does not split when nailed, and takes paint and varnish well. In Canada it is marketed in a lumber category called SPF, which includes all the spruces and balsam fir.

The needles contain one of the richest sources of bornyl acetate, a basic ingredient in most "pine-scented" perfumes and cleaners.

critters of the bog

Boreal black spruce bogs and their surroundings are the summer home and breeding grounds for many migratory songbirds. In spring, the tiny ruby-crowned kinglet attaches her nest to hanging twigs in the thick foliage at the ends of spruce branches. The female blackpoll warbler single-handedly builds her nest snuggled close to the trunk, where the obliging male feeds her while she incubates her eggs (perhaps out of guilt for not helping build the nest). Yellow-bellied flycatchers and Tennessee warblers nest in the sphagnum moss at the foot of black spruce, or among the roots of blown-over trees. Further north, near the timberline, the gray-cheeked thrush flies all the way from the West Indies and South America to nest amid the branches of stunted black spruce.

Wetlands are home to one out of three species at risk in Canada. Black spruce bogs provide habitat for countless other wild creatures whose survival depends on their existence, and who in turn contribute to the functioning of the wetland ecosystem. They may not be pretty or furry or cuddly, but frogs, toads, turtles, salamanders, newts, and thousands of species of insects and plants interact with one another to ensure the continued vitality of their wet world. In turn, bogs act as a giant sponge, capturing and filtering the water that feeds our rivers and streams. Canada is home to 24 percent of the world's bogs, swamps, and marshes.

Facing page: The needles, like those of all spruces, appear round, but are actually square in cross section. The oval cones, the smallest of the native spruces, mature in one season, but may remain on the tree for years.

Red Spruce
(*Picea rubens*)

yellow spruce
maritime spruce
eastern spruce
he-balsam

épinette rouge
épinette à bière
prusse rouge

Mi'kmaq: *kawak*

Leaf
- needles bright yellowish green; shiny; curved; stiff; tips pointed; square in cross section; 1–2 cm (⅜–¾") long; underside with prominent midrib;
- attached singly to twig on short pegs; encircling twig; angling toward end of twig;
- persist on tree 5–7 years.

Flower
- males bright red, oval, pendent; near end of last year's growth;
- females purplish green, small, erect; at tips of twigs; in upper half of crown;
- males and females on different branches of same tree.

Fruit
- cones oval, cylindrical; green to purplish green; shiny reddish brown at maturity;
- 3–5 cm (1¼–2") long; hanging on short stalk; with thin smooth rounded scales;
- mature in 1 growing season; open when ripe in autumn;
- release dark brown winged seeds from fall to early summer; seeds wind-disseminated, mostly in the fall;
- begin bearing cones at age 20–30; good seed crop every 3–8 years.

Twig
- yellow or orange brown; slightly hairy; rough where short stubs remain after older needles shed;
- buds cone-shaped.

Bark
- on younger trees, thin, reddish brown, finely scaly;
- on older trees, dark brown and furrowed;
- inner bark yellowish or reddish brown.

Wood
- soft, strong, light; stiff; resilient; straight-grained; odorless; not decay-resistant;
- nearly white to pale yellowish brown; little contrast between heartwood and sapwood;
- annual growth rings distinct.

Height
20–25 m (65–80')

Diameter
30–60 cm (12–24")

Longevity
250–400 years

The cones, which take one season to mature, are reddish brown in autumn.

spruce of the east

Of the three spruces native to eastern North America, red spruce has the most limited distribution. It thrives in the cool moist climate of Nova Scotia, where it is honored as the provincial arboreal emblem. From there it extends through Prince Edward Island and New Brunswick, southern Quebec, New England and New York. From Pennsylvania on, it occurs only in isolated pockets at higher elevations in the Appalachians, as far south as Tennessee. Its best growth is in the Great Smoky Mountains of North Carolina. There the American Forests' national record holder is an imposing 45 meters (146') tall. To the north, outlying stands of red spruce grow in Algonquin Park and the Haliburton area of eastern Ontario.

Red spruce occurs both in pure stands and mixed with other softwoods and hardwoods, including white pine, sugar maple, beech, hemlock, and yellow birch. It is commonly, but not always, found on moist upland sites. The presence of bunchberries and wood-sorrels on the forest floor usually indicates a good site for red spruce. Pure old-growth stands often originate from spruce mixed with balsam fir or white birch regeneration, where the firs and birches have long since died out, leaving only the much longer-lived spruces.

kissin' cousins

Where the ranges of red and black spruce overlap, they interbreed, producing natural hybrids that have characteristics of both parents. Identifying them can be tricky. Forestry academics have developed elaborate mathematical formulae, but the simplest, if not the most scientific or infallible, rule of thumb is this: if a spruce is in or around a bog, it is black; if it is on an upland site, it is red; if it is in between, it could be either, or more likely a hybrid. Hybrids have characteristics (twigs, needles, cones, and so on) of one or the other species to varying degrees.

Two processes of succession commonly occur in our eastern spruce-fir forests. One is a gradual evolution resulting from older trees dying, creating an opening, and being replaced by new seedlings or already-existing younger or shade-tolerant trees below. These are uneven-age stands, in which individual trees took root periodically over a long span of years. They are best managed by periodic selection cuts, in which trees approaching maturity (sometimes, but not necessarily, the largest trees) are harvested, leaving the younger (but not necessarily the smallest) trees room to grow.

Far more common in northern forests is the even-age stand, the result of a major disturbance such as a spruce budworm infestation, clearcut, forest fire, or windstorm that killed or removed all the standing trees, so that the forest was literally reborn. These forests often regenerate with balsam fir and red spruce, along with pioneer hardwoods such as white birch, gray birch, pin cherry, or aspen. All the trees, regardless of size, are roughly the same age.

Prior to the disturbance, balsam fir and red spruce may have already been sitting in the understory as seedlings; or they may germinate after the disturbance. Young fir rapidly outgrow red spruce and soon dominate the stand. Spruce, very tolerant of shade, are content to sit patiently in the shadow of the fir, healthy, but growing very slowly, like theater understudies waiting for lead actors to die off, so they can seize the opportunity. When the shorter-lived fir eventually succumb to old age or another insect infestation, the spruce are released. They respond to the sudden availability of sunlight, and grow rapidly. Red spruce are very patient — they can wait over 100 years for release.

Forest managers accelerate the succession process by spacing or "cleaning" young spruce-fir thickets when the trees are 4–5 meters (15') or smaller. The operation removes most of the fir and other softwoods, spaces out the thriftiest spruce so each has room to grow to its potential, and leaves scattered hardwoods and other conifers for biodiversity and wildlife.

Another option is to wait until the firs reach commercial size, and harvest them for lumber or pulpwood, and leave standing the spruces, in what is called a release cut. Either way, red spruces get a boost earlier than they would if nature were allowed to take its course.

around the home

In regions with cool climates and moist, well-drained, slightly acidic soils, red spruce makes a splendid ornamental. Without competition from neighboring trees, its full pyramidal crown extends almost to the ground. The shiny yellow green foliage is attractive on its own, in contrast with the blue green of white spruce, or with autumn hardwood hues. Planting red spruce has its wildlife rewards: colorful crossbills like to nest and raise their families in the shelter of its foliage.

Where permitted, digging up a few small roadside wildlings to transplant at home is one option for planting. It is not difficult — red spruce roots are shallow. Or they can be planted just as easily from seed. Gather seeds when the cones mature in autumn, and sow immediately in a partially shaded garden bed. Cover lightly with less than 1 cm (½") of soil, the shallower the better, and mulch for the winter. When the seeds germinate in spring, remove the mulch. The next fall, re-mulch

Needles are typically yellowish green, stiff, and curved, and encircle the twigs. At first glance they appear round, but closer examination reveals they are actually square in cross section. They remain on the tree for five to seven years, then shed; the first to fall are those closest to the main stem.

up to the height of the seedlings. Leave in the bed for two growing seasons, and transplant to a sunny site the following spring.

a carpenter's delight

Red spruce lumber is one of the most valuable of our eastern softwoods. Light but strong, it is used from top to bottom in house construction — from rafters, to studs, to floor joists. It is easy on carpenter's tools, holds nails and glues well, and doesn't split or warp.

It has much higher value in the crafting of sound boards of stringed musical instruments. Its high resonance provides excellent acoustics for guitars, mandolins, violin bellies, pianos, and organ pipes.

In the era of wooden ships, straight and tall red spruces were used for masts and spars. Nova Scotia red spruce formed the ribs, ceiling, and deck beams of the original *Bluenose* schooner.

Red spruce was once a favored wood for food containers — such as butter boxes — because it imparts no foreign odor or taste to its contents. Its light weight and strength makes it ideal for ladder rungs, oars, and canoe paddles.

Red spruce also transforms into world-class newsprint, facial tissues, toilet paper, and a host of other paper products. Its long, straight fibers provide strength, and, with its light color, it requires less bleaching than many other woods.

use of spruce — wise and otherwise

Red spruce needles and twigs, like most evergreens, are a good source of vitamin C. In winter, when fresh fruit was non-existent, scurvy posed a constant threat to native people. Spruce needle teas were a preventative medicine staple in their diet. European settlers took it one step further. They added molasses, honey, or maple syrup, fermented it, and created North America's first alcoholic beverage — spruce beer. Still medicinal, but now with a kick.

The Montagnais of Quebec boiled red spruce inner bark with roots of sourgrass, and drank the liquid for throat and lung disorders. In the southern Appalachians, red spruce pitch was rubbed into rheumatic joints to ease the pain.

Spruce gum, exuded from broken tree limbs or wounds in the bark, was long a favorite with kids and lumberjacks. At one time, it was produced commercially in Maine, and marketed as "State of Maine Pure Spruce Gum." The advent of chicle-based gums (as in Chiclets) from the Central American sapodilla tree rang the death knell for the small labor-intensive industry. By the mid-twentieth century, chicle itself was replaced with synthetics.

bugs, blowdown, fire, and acid fog

Fortunately, red spruce buds flush rather late in spring, and miss the majority of the feeding onslaught of spruce budworm caterpillars, whose development is more closely attuned to white spruce and balsam fir. Where balsam fir is mixed with red spruce, however, the fir attracts the budworm and renders the spruce more susceptible to the voracious budworms.

The shallow root systems of red spruce make them prone to blowdown in heavy winds. Their thin bark, high resin content, and volatile needles also make them vulnerable to forest fires.

The most serious threat to red spruce is a widespread dieback phenomenon, most predominant in mountainous regions throughout the east. Extensive studies indicate that acid fog and air pollution from heavy metals such as aluminum are the culprits, perhaps in association with other environmental factors and the age of the spruces.

Jack Pine
(*Pinus banksiana*)

Banksian pine
princess pine
princy pine
scrub pine
gray pine

pin gris
cyprès
pin divariqué
pin des rochers
pin de Banks

Woods Cree: *oskahtak*

Leaf
- needles in pairs, spreading from a papery sheath; straight or slightly twisted;
- stiff and pointed; yellowish green; 2–5 cm (1–2") long;
- persist on tree 2–3 years.

Flower
- male flowers beige; in vertical clusters at ends of young branches; females purple;
- males and females on same tree (monoecious); wind-pollinated.

Fruit
- cones stemless; straight or curved; in clusters of 2 or 3; 4–7 cm (2–3") long;
- yellowish brown when mature at end of second growing season; hard and serotinous (sealed with resin);
- older cones gray; may remain unopened on tree up to 20 years;
- seeds dark brown; 3 mm (⅛") long;
- begin bearing cones as early as age 3–10; good seed crop every 3–4 years.

Twig
- slender; ridged and grooved;
- yellowish green to purplish brown, becoming dark grayish brown with age;
- buds brown, resinous;
- on branches in annual whorls around stem; often with shorter "false whorls" in between.

Bark
- on younger trees, thin, reddish or grayish brown; becoming flaky;
- on older trees, dark grayish brown; furrowed, with plates or scales.

Wood
- moderately hard and heavy; weak; knotty; resinous odor;
- heartwood light yellowish brown; thick sapwood almost white;
- annual growth rings distinct.

Height
18–25 m (60–80')

Diameter
30–40 cm (12–16")

Longevity
100–150 years

In spring, the male flowers stand erect on the twigs before releasing their pollen.

the history and range of jack pine

Pines and pines and the shadow of pines as
far as the eye can see;
A steadfast legion of stalwart knights in
dominant empery . . .

Robert Service, 1874–1958
The Pines

In the late 1760s, British naturalist Sir Joseph Banks, a member of Captain Cook's expedition charting the east coast of Canada, encountered a conifer unknown in Europe. Upon his return to England, he reported his discovery, and the name *Pinus banksiana* was bestowed on the tree in his honor. Little did he or anyone know that his discovery would turn out to be the most widely distributed pine species in North America. Jack pine grows from northern New England westward to the Lakes states, and from central Newfoundland to the Yukon; it is also one of the widest-ranging trees on the planet.

Throughout its range, it shows tremendous variability in size and form, and adaptability to a multitude of sites. On the northern taiga, the transition zone between the boreal forest and the treeless tundra, it struggles as a stunted tree on acidic soils. It achieves its best growth on fertile sandy sites in the northern prairie provinces, often reaching heights of 25 meters (80'). It grows in mixed stands, along with aspen, white birch, and spruce, and very commonly in pure monocultural even-aged stands resulting from forest fires. In western Alberta it is replaced by, and often interbreeds with, lodgepole pine, the provincial tree of Alberta; at its southern limit Virginia pine takes over. Both species are close relatives.

The serotinous cones of jack pine are sealed tight with resin, which melts only when temperatures exceed 50° C (120° F), releasing the seeds locked within. Unopened cones may persist on a tree for 20 years, still containing viable seeds. The oldest jack pine on record is a 230-year-old specimen near Lake Nipigon in northwestern Ontario. Since the retreat of the glaciers some 10,000 years ago, jack pine stands have undergone repeated cycles of birth from seed, growth, destruction by forest fire, and re-establishment from seeds freed by the fires.

Jack pine is short-lived, by tree standards, but in the boreal forest it seldom reaches maturity. On average, stands of jack pine burn every 40 to 80 years. The cause is usually lightning. Foresters today believe that the practice of harvesting by clearcutting, followed by seedbed preparation to expose mineral soil, and planting or seeding jack pine most closely replicates the natural history, evolution, and succession of jack pine stands. Jack pine is a very important reforestation species on the drier sites of the boreal.

Since it is very intolerant of shade, and quickly regenerates burnt sites, jack pine is considered a pioneer, an early succession species. In the north, its removal by fire merely repeats the cycle; in more southerly regions it is sometimes replaced by red or white pine, or hardwoods. Because of its broad geographic range, its genetic diversity within that range, and its temperature, daylight, precipitation and soil requirements, it is virtually impossible to generalize about jack pine — its growth habits, form, size . . . or its future.

The Northwest Territories share onetime northern resident Robert Service's reverence for jack pine and have declared it their official arboreal emblem.

a wild and woolly touch

In wildness is the preservation of the world.
Henry David Thoreau (1817–1862)

Those who wish to instill a wild and woolly touch to their landscape might consider planting jack pine. Otherwise it is not recommended as an ornamental. As an open-grown tree it is short, irregular, and scraggly. Lower limbs remain on the tree and spread wildly. A jack pine on an open site in Minnesota measured a mere 18 meters (60') tall, with a crown 38 meters (125') wide. They appear unkempt, and the yellowish needles seem unhealthy, except perhaps as a contrast to darker green conifers. One author perhaps best described the jack pine as "homely."

In its defense, jack pine is a hardy and rugged tree, is easily planted, grows rapidly for the first 20 years, requires little maintenance, and is adaptable to almost any site that is dry or sandy.

the endangered and the dangerous

On Michigan's lower peninsula, young jack pine stands are one of the last remaining nesting habitats for the globally endangered Kirtland's warbler. This little gray-backed and yellow-breasted songbird builds her nest on or in the ground, under the cover of the lower branches of jack pine, among ground shrubs such as blueberry, bearberry, and sweet fern.

Jack pine seeds are eaten by bronzed grackles, chipping sparrows, goldfinches, and juncos. Red squirrels, chipmunks, white footed mice, and red-backed voles are among the rodents who dine on the seeds as well. Snowshoe hares eat the young bark, porcupines eat the older bark, and deer and moose browse the needles and twigs. Throughout winter, jack pine needles are a favorite food of spruce grouse.

from tree to wood to paper

At one time considered a weed by the forest industry, jack pine has grown into a staple in the manufacturing of kraft pulp and paper. Harvested trees, often combined with recycled paper and wood chips from sawmills, provide mills throughout its range with their requirements for raw materials or "furnish."

Canada is the world's largest producer of newsprint, and the United States its largest consumer. The demand for newspapers, magazines, and advertising material in the United States is insatiable, and the fast-growing jack pine helps meet the need.

Sawn into lumber, jack pine is used in construction framing, sheathing, interior woodwork, boxes, and crates. It was used extensively in the construction of those totems of the prairies, the grain elevators. Not naturally resistant to rot, jack pine converts into poles, posts, and railway ties only when treated with preservatives. In the workshop, jack pine glues readily, holds nails well, and accepts paint and varnish adequately.

clearcutting

Clearcutting is without doubt the most controversial forestry issue today. Impassioned debate erupts whenever the topic arises. Almost everyone has a strong opinion.

Most of us look at recent clearcuts and see nothing but ugliness. Where once stood a proud forest, we think, now lies an unsightly pile of organic rubble, not unlike the aftermath of a tornado. The professional forest manager, who, through training and experience, thinks long term, perceives a clearcut as a forest of the future. The average person, however, feels only a sense of loss of something beautiful that was there in the past, anger at the apparent destruction of our forests, and perhaps resentment that some multinational is wreaking havoc on our environment. These sentiments are not only understandable, but commendable.

Clearcuts are ugly, at least until the next generation of young trees — natural or planted — re-greens the site. They are an affront to anyone's aesthetic sensibilities. But are they a legitimate, environmentally sound forest harvesting practice?

A simple, hypothetical, but typically realistic example might shed some light on the question.

A pure jack pine stand on a gently rolling sandy site in the boreal forest is 80 years old, having originated from a forest wildfire that destroyed the previous pine forest, opened the sealed cones, and re-seeded the new forest. Our forest, like almost all pure jack pine stands, is even-aged. All the trees, regardless of size, are the same age, their seeds having germinated the same summer as the fire. On this site all trees are showing signs of deterioration from old age. Each year, the loss of trees from natural mortality exceeds the new growth. Our stand is going downhill.

There are three options available to the forest manager: leave the forest untouched, harvest all the trees, or undertake some form of selective cut whereby some trees are harvested and others are left standing. Let's examine the options.

If left undisturbed, the trees will continue to age and deteriorate, unfortunately much like the health prospects of 84-year-old Aunt Bertha. They are mature, perhaps overmature. It is a fact of life — unfortunately, trees do not live forever. More trees will die each year, and those that survive will continue to lose vigor until they too inevitably succumb. An attack by jack pine budworm, a common insect in the boreal forest, like pneumonia to people Aunt Bertha's age, would speed up the process. Dead trees are a very dry fuel waiting for the next lightning bolt to ignite, and our forest will inevitably be lost to fire — much as it was 80 years ago. This is the pattern that has been repeated in jack pine forests for the past 7,000 to 8,000 years. It is perfectly natural.

Enter people, the other element in the environment/economy relationship. The historic Brundtland Commission gave us the yardstick by which we measure sustainable development — maintaining the delicate balance of the environment and the economy, that is, people coexisting with nature so that future generations may have the same opportunity.

Individuals, families, and whole communities rely on forest management for their survival. Direct employment in the woods — planting, tending, and harvesting, collectively called "silviculture" — ensures the economic and therefore social stability of 250 communities in Canada alone. Let's assume our forest is located near one of these communities.

At the same time, there is a steadily growing worldwide demand for wood and paper, which must be supplied from somewhere on our planet. It seems preferable to fulfill that demand where forests are truly considered a renewable resource, where it is economically beneficial to our community and to our country, where ever-stricter government guidelines exist, and where the process is managed by professional foresters, technicians, and wildlife managers, rather than slash-and-burn, cut-and-run operations in some other region of the world — perhaps the tropical rainforest.

Some forests like ours should be preserved, under a protected areas strategy, as living museums, study and research areas, and representative examples of the natural jack pine/forest fire successional ecosystem. But certainly not all of them.

From both an environmental and an economic point of view, now is the time to harvest our stand, before it deteriorates further, so the amount of wood recouped is maximized. Or worse, before it goes up in flames, endangering surrounding forests, wildlife, people, property, or possibly whole communities.

This leaves our other two options: clearcutting, or some form of selective cutting. Let's look at the latter first.

Since all the trees, both large and small, are the same age, cutting only the large trees would certainly be profitable to all involved, but it would leave standing the genetically inferior trees to serve as parents to the next generation. To paraphrase the Bible, the weak would inherit the earth. This is referred to as highgrading — taking the best and leaving the rest — arguably the worst forestry practice imaginable, and the cause of most of the forest degradation in eastern North America.

The reverse — harvesting only the smaller trees — would not only be uneconomical, but would have no beneficial effect on the remaining large trees, for they are too old to respond to the increased space, nutrients, and sunlight. It would be akin to thinning the garden carrots in late September when it's simply too late. The remaining trees will continue to deteriorate, and worse, with the stand having been thinned, their mutual support system would be removed, rendering them more susceptible to blowdown by the wind. After the next major storm, it would be essentially a clearcut. Selection cutting is clearly not appropriate in our jack pine stand.

Clearcutting, removal of all the trees, large and small, leaving standing dead trees or snags for wildlife, is the only acceptable option in this case, and many others like it. It must be thoroughly planned, with strict adherence to government guidelines, and carefully executed to minimize negative environmental impacts. An after-harvest prescription must be put in place and implemented to ensure the healthy regeneration of the next forest. No doubt it will be ugly for several years — until the logging residue, or "slash," breaks down and decomposes into the forest soil, and the young trees grow into a healthier, better-managed forest than the one harvested.

This is by no means a blanket prescription for clearcutting. In numerous other forest situations, for example, on steep slopes, along waterways, and in wetland areas — clearcutting is absolutely inappropriate. Uneven-aged stands should be harvested under the selection cut system, harvesting the old trees and allowing the young trees to take advantage of the increased sunlight, reduced competition, and available soil nutrients.

There is no doubt that in the past clearcutting has often been misapplied. We have all seen examples of this. But its misuse has decreased dramatically in the last decade, and hopefully will continue to do so, as forest managers employ all of the forest management tools in their silvicultural toolbox — shelterwoods, seed tree cuts, group tree selection, crop tree selection, commercial thinning, release cuts, strip cuts, patch cuts, and all the permutations and combinations of these that are appropriate for a specific forest stand. Clearcutting is one of these tools.

poultices and baby powder

First Nations people derived medicines from the needles, roots, bark, resin and cones of jack pine. Sealed cones were boiled by Michigan's Potawatomi, and the liquid resin was used as an ointment. The Cree melted the pitch to fumigate dwellings of the sick. The Ojibway dried and pounded the needles into a powder for dusting on sores, burns, cuts, and frostbite. The Woods Cree applied inner bark poultices on deep cuts, and brewed a bark tea for coughs, colds and the flu. Ojibway women sprinkled powder made from rotten pine wood to relieve baby diaper rash. Pine oil and pine tar were considered disinfectants, antiseptics, insecticides, and deodorants. Today they are still ingredients in some commercial cleaning and personal hygiene products.

sweet fern and sawflies

The delicate and fragrant sweet fern — not a true fern, but very similar in appearance — is one of the most pleasant little plants in our northern forests. It has served as a natural remedy for the irritation of poison ivy for centuries.

Unfortunately, it is also the alternate host of sweet fern blister rust, whose other host is young jack pine. The two species often share the same dry sandy sites. Rust-infected sweet ferns release powdery orange spores in early summer; by fall, the first signs of the disease appear on nearby jack pine. Vertical orange cankers appear on the lower trunk, and cankers on the branches form galls of swollen bark. As older trees are rarely affected, the remedy is to eliminate sweet fern from the vicinity until the jack pines are 2–3 meters (6–10') tall.

Another serious threat to young jack pine is scleroderris canker. Yellowing at the base of the needles is the first sign of the disease; prolonged exposure can lead to a tree's death.

Among the injurious insects are the white pine weevil, jack pine sawfly, and jack pine budworm, close cousin of the notorious spruce budworm. The budworm, occasionally reaching epidemic levels, devours needles, buds, and male flowers, robbing the tree of its photosynthetic capability. Jack pine sawfly larvae tunnel into the wood and girdle the tree, cutting off the flow of nutrients and starving it. The weevil, whose larvae kill the previous year's leader — the top vertical shoot — of young trees, causes a crooked or forked tree, but rarely kills a tree.

Facing page: Jack pine bark is gray, thin, and scaly. It is very susceptible to fire, but nature has prepared it well. The cones are sealed with resin, which will only open under the heat of a forest fire. The seeds are then released, germinate, and a new jack pine stand begins. This has historically been the nature of the boreal forest for over 7,000 years, where forest fires at average intervals of 40 to 80 years remove the old stand, and a new generation begins.

Red Pine
(*Pinus resinosa*)

Norway pine

pin rouge
pin de Norvège
pin résineux

Maliseet: *pa'-si-akw*

Leaf
- needles slender, straight, shiny, dark green, 10–16 cm (4–6") long; in bundles of 2;
- flat on one side, rounded on the other: semi-circular in cross section;
- joined at base in papery sheath; in tufts near ends of branches;
- somewhat flexible, but will snap when bent;
- remain on tree for 4–5 years.

Flower
- in May-June; both sexes on same tree; females in upper branches, males lower;
- males purple, in groups around base of new shoot; pollination by wind;
- females red, at tips of new shoots; takes 2 seasons to ripen into mature cones.

Fruit
- cones oval, 4–6 cm (1½–2½") long; often in pairs; cone scales not prickly;
- turn from green to purple to brown at maturity;
- open and release winged seeds in early fall; remain open on tree until spring;
- begin bearing cones at age 15–25; good seed crop every 3–7 years; bumper crop every 10–12 years.

Twig
- thick, rough, orange to reddish brown;
- on branches in distinct annual whorls around trunk;
- buds resinous, chestnut brown, pointed.

Bark
- on younger trees, pink and gray, scaly;
- on older trees, pink and grayish brown; thick; with broad, flat ridges and flaky scales.

Wood
- light, moderately hard, fairly strong, straight-grained; resinous;
- heartwood pale brown with pink tinge; sapwood wide, yellowish white;
- annual growth rings distinct.

Height
20–30 m (65–100')

Diameter
50–80 cm (20–30")

Longevity
200–300 years

Cones take two growing seasons to evolve from fertilized flowers to maturity.

beauty 10; biodiversity 2

Nothing is quite so inspiring as a stroll through a pure stand of tall red pines. Gray and coral columns — straight, clear, virtually taperless — unfold into a canopy of lush dark greenery. Over the lifetime of a red pine stand, literally tons of litter, primarily needles, create a plush carpet on the forest floor. With little or no undergrowth, it presents a natural park setting. Biodiversity it may not be, but beauty it is.

As the stand approaches maturity, depending on the site and soil, plant and animal diversity gradually increases. Gaps in the canopy create opportunities below for wildflowers, shrubs and tree seedlings, as well as a more hospitable habitat for wildlife.

Pure and mixed stands of red pine span a fairly narrow band across the east side of the continent, on both sides of the border. Southeast Manitoba and northern Minnesota — where it is the state tree — are its western limit. It follows a path east through southern Ontario, Quebec, and the border states to Nova Scotia. A few isolated pockets pop up on insular Newfoundland, north of Lake Superior, and in the mountains of West Virginia. Wherever it grows, red pine displays little variation in appearance.

altering an ecosystem

Because of its beauty, ease of planting, adaptability to a variety of soils, and its value for wood products, millions of red pines were planted on abandoned farm fields over the last century, many to prevent erosion on sandy soils. Pine plantations are one of the most simple but dramatic examples of how humans can change a local ecosystem. Within a decade or two, gone are the grasses and wildflowers, replaced by a bed of fallen needles. Not only do the flora change, but the small mammals, insects, earthworms, and other field fauna disappear. Take a few steps outside of the plantation, and the grassland ecosystem abruptly re-appears, much as it was before the planting.

to plant a pine

To plant a pine . . . one need be neither god nor poet; one need only own a shovel.
Aldo Leopold, 1949
A Sand County Almanac

Open-grown red pine is equally delightful. Shorter in stature than its forest kin, it sports a dome-shaped crown of dark green foliage that contrasts with the colorful bark. Pine transplants easily, thrives in full sunlight, and is not overly choosy about its growing medium. It is most at home on well-drained and aerated, sandy, acidic soils, where its roots dig in deeply to firmly anchor the tree. Red pine is not affected by either weevil or blister rust, the nemeses of its cousin the white pine.

Rows of red pines create a handsome and practical screen or windbreak. However the species is susceptible to sea and road salt, as well as city pollutants.

Most nursery outlets carry balled and burlapped pines, and younger bare root stock is available for reforestation purposes from some provincial, state and forest industry sources, usually requiring a minimum order.

If it is called 3-0 stock, that means seedlings have spent three growing seasons in a seedbed; 2-2 stock is four years old — two years in a seedbed, and two years in a transplant bed. Thrifty 3-0 red pine is usually able to survive competition from grasses and hay on old fields.

Planting from seed is simple and straightforward, but cones may be difficult to locate and gather. Fall sowing of seeds 1 centimeter (½") deep in a prepared well-drained sandy loam, with mulching over the winter, will produce tiny but healthy seedlings the following summer. They should be held over at least one more growing season before outplanting. Beware of rabbits and mice.

the perfect telephone pole

Arguably the most valuable end product of red pine is poles. Its height, straightness, lack of taper, and self-pruning limbs are unmatched within its range. Pressure treating with preservatives gives poles the decay resistance the species lacks in nature. The same qualities make red pine ideal for piling, posts, railway ties, and log homes. Like white pine, it was once highly valued for masts, spars, and decks of wooden sailing ships. In the early 1800s, British importers preferred red pine lumber over white pine, and were willing to pay twice the price.

Red pine is moderately light, strong, is worked easily with hand and power carpentry tools, and takes glue and holds nails well. As the species name *resinosa* implies, its resin is sometimes an impediment to painting and varnishing. Doors, sashes, and interior and exterior trim are commonly made from red pine.

red pine poultices and puppets

For medicinal purposes, Native people made little distinction between red and white pine. The Ojibway in the Great Lakes area applied crushed or boiled needles, or inhaled their steaming vapors, to relieve headaches. The Menominee steeped a tea of the inner bark of young trees, and drank it for chest pains. They also applied bark poultices to sores and wounds. Red pine resin was boiled with tallow to produce a waterproof pitch for caulking birch bark canoes. Ojibway children created dancing puppets from the needles.

scleroderris, sirococcus, shoot moths, and snow

At one time red pine was considered relatively insect- and disease-free. Hundreds of millions of trees were planted in eastern North America, on cutovers, forest fire sites, and on abandoned farmland. But red pine has proven to have its share of enemies — diseases, insects, and weather.

Scleroderris canker, a fungus with an affinity for red pine, has two strains. The North American race attacks saplings less than two meters (6–7') tall; the more virulent European variety infects trees of all sizes and ages. Browning at the base of the needles in late spring is the first telltale symptom. By August, needles are completely brown, and the fungus has begun to slowly work its way toward the main stem, where it inflicts its worst damage. Tiny canker cups on the trunk open when wet to release spores that spread the disease, and then close in dry weather. Mortality sets in above the canker. The only method of control, other than fungicides, is to prune and destroy the lower limbs under heavy attack.

Sirococcus shoot blight, another unwelcome import from abroad, infests new shoots of red pine, spruce, and tamarack. Within weeks the needles wilt, collapse at the base, and droop. Young red pines near older trees are most susceptible. Repeated attacks over a few years can be fatal.

The European pine shoot moth arrived on this continent early in the twentieth century. Larvae of the rust-colored moth mine

Attractive pink and gray bark tones set red pine apart from the rest of the pine family.

needles near their base, then shift to devouring the buds. Severe infestations create crooked or multi-topped little trees, permanently deforming them and destroying their value as potential poles.

Weather too can be damaging to red pine. Heavy wet snows or ice can overload limbs, tearing them out of their sockets, leaving gaping holes in the trunk that open the door to infection. Late spring frost damage to buds and tender shoots is common in low-lying areas and frost pockets.

In a pure stand of red pine, the forest floor is blanketed with fallen needles, and little else grows.

the seed-eating set

Pine seeds may represent over half the diet of some songbirds. Pine siskins and crossbills, for example, are strict vegetarians — no bugs, worms, or caterpillars for them. In good seed years, they flourish; in off years, life gets tougher. Red breasted nuthatches and chipping sparrows are also pine seed consumers. Red pine, especially in plantations, serves double duty for the sparrows, as both a food source and nesting habitat. Whatever seeds birds don't clean up, chip-munks and voles eagerly await on the ground.

Red pine may not be as important a wildlife tree as white pine — there are fewer of them, they bear fewer cones, and once dead, they decompose quickly, rarely remaining standing as a wildlife snag. A southeast Ontario study determined that pure 30-to-40-year-old red pine plantations supported only one quarter of the songbird diversity of nearby mixed and hardwood stands. But they are still a good food source for the seed-eating set.

Pitch Pine
(*Pinus rigida*)

hard pine

pin dur
pin à feuilles rigides
pin rigide
pin des corbeaux

Leaf
- needles yellowish green; stiff, twisted, blunt-tipped, 7–12 cm (3–5") long; in bundles of 3;
- often in tufts on short twigs along trunk; persist for 2 years, then shed.

Flower
- males yellow, at base of long new shoots;
- females pale green with rosy tint, single or in clusters;
- both sexes on same tree, wind-pollinated.

Fruit
- cones oval, pointed, with prickly scales, 4–8 cm (1½–3") long, on short stems; often in clusters of 2–3;
- take 2 years to ripen; may open at maturity in autumn, remain closed until fire, or open irregularly;
- open, gray, weathered cones may persist for many years;
- some cones attached directly to trunk by short twigs;
- seeds 4–5 mm (⅙–⅕") long; long-winged;
- begin bearing cones as early as age 3–5, especially on stump sprouts; good seed crop every 4–9 years.

Twig
- thick, hairless; from green to orange to dark brown; ridged and grooved;
- buds sharp-pointed, resinous, brown.

Bark
- on younger trees, reddish brown, smooth, becoming scaly;
- on older trees, furrowed into thick irregular flat dark plates with reddish tinge.

Wood
- moderately heavy, hard, strong, resinous; brittle, fairly decay resistant;
- heartwood reddish brown; sapwood pale yellow;
- annual growth rings distinct; may produce more than 1 growth ring per year.

Height	Diameter	Longevity
10–20 m (30–60')	30–45 cm (12–18")	150–200 years

Tufts of needles, and even cones, can grow directly on the trunk.

a Canadian rarity . . . and an oddity

Pitch pine, the only three-needled pine in eastern North America, is indeed rare in Canada. Like the Carolinian hardwoods bordering Lake Erie, it is at the absolute northern limit of its range, which extends from southern Maine to just past South Carolina. It grows naturally in Ontario on about 150 isolated spots on the northeast shore of Lake Ontario, around Charleston Lake, and along the St. Lawrence River. In Quebec, two small populations grow south of Montreal. There is some concern that these outlying populations may be genetically deteriorating due to inbreeding.

Finding a specimen has been made easy by Parks Canada, who have erected a large wooden sign denoting its presence alongside the Thousand Islands Parkway, and Quebec has established a pitch pine ecological reserve near Chateauguay.

Stragglers this far north are not the epitome of forest beauty. Misshapen and gnarled, they bear a profusion of cones on dead and dying branches scattered throughout the sparse crown. They would look more at home in a desert setting. Further south in the Carolinas, pitch pine has a healthier, straighter form, and grows to a height of 25 meters (80').

Pitch pine thrives on poor soils — shallow, sandy, and acidic — but often grows in cedar peat bogs or in hardwood stands. It is an ideal tree to plant on shifting sands, where it stabilizes the soil. A little precocious, it begins to produce viable cones as early as three years of age. Some cones open at maturity, some remain closed for a few years, and others, like those of its cousin the jack pine, open only with the heat of a forest fire. Its thick bark, a rougher version of red pine, protects the trunk from fire. Even when all the crown foliage is burned, pitch pine can reproduce from dormant buds on the trunk.

These develop into new branches, and the tree resumes growth. It is also the only conifer in the east that regenerates from stump sprouts, a trait usually restricted to broadleaf trees.

a conversation piece

If one lives near the tree's northern limit, planting pitch pine is worth the experiment. But don't expect a beautiful tree. Consider it more a living conversation piece than a lovely ornamental.

Gather seed when the cones turn from green to brown in the fall. If the scales are sealed tight by resin, try dipping in boiling water for a minute, or heating in the oven at 50° C (120° F) until the resin melts. Plant in the fall by pressing seeds firmly into the soil, and cover with 1 or 2 centimeters (¾") of sand, soil, or mulch. If rodents don't discover and devour them, viable seeds should germinate in the spring.

Pitch pine is well-adapted to cold, but is susceptible to winter damage. Insects such as the pitch pine looper and the European pine shoot moth are also potential enemies. Like jack pine, young pitch pine is vulnerable to sweet fern blister rust.

Deer browsing, nibbling of seedlings by mice and hares, and gnawing of the bark by porcupines are all threats to the southern Canada and northern New York populations, already stressed by their position at the most northerly limit.

railroad ties and locomotive fuel

Much like other southern pines, pitch pine wood is heavy, hard, stiff, and strong — qualities that make it ideal for structural timbers, mine supports, piles, and railway ties. Its resin emits a distinctive odor. It does not take and hold paint and varnish well, but it seasons easily, glues well, and holds nails and screws securely. Where it grows in abundance, it is pulped by the sulfate process to produce kraft paper, by-products of which are turpentine and rosin.

Pitch pine was at one time considered a choice wood for grist-mill water wheels, fuel for steam locomotives, and charcoal for blacksmiths.

naval stores

At one time, turpentine and rosin were important products derived from standing trees, branches, and stumps of pitch pine. They were termed "naval stores" because the pitch, cooked into a thick tar, was used to preserve ropes and caulk the seams of wooden ships. Production of naval stores was a booming business in New England until the late seventeenth century, when the longleaf pines of North Carolina were discovered to yield more pitch, and the whole industry shifted south.

Off the Barbary Coast, captains of cargo vessels bought off pirates with naval stores, in exchange for safe passage. In the early 1900s, production in the southern United States peaked at 750,000 barrels of turpentine, and nearly 2 million drums of rosin.

Turpentine has varied medicinal properties and has been used as an astringent, diuretic, stimulant, antispasmodic, and vermifuge. Rosin is an ingredient of paints and varnishes, soaps, and solder flux, and it is used to treat violin bows and ballet slippers. Rosin bags give baseball pitchers a better grip on the ball.

for boils, burns, and bowel movements

The Seneca and Cayuga in upper New York collected the pitch by boring a hole in the bark, and applied it as a salve for boils and burns. It was also used to draw out thorns and slivers. A teaspoonful of the pitch with a sweetener added, taken twice a week, reportedly had a mild laxative effect.

Eastern White Pine
(*Pinus strobus*)

white pine
Weymouth pine
northern white pine

pin blanc
pin de Weymouth
pin jaune
pin du lord

Ojibway: *zhingwaak*

Leaf
- bluish green needles in bunches of 5; 5–15 cm (2–6") long;
- straight, flexible, soft to the touch; minute teeth; pointed at tip;
- triangular in cross-section; remain on tree 2–4 years.

Flower
- male flowers at base of new shoots; release yellow pollen;
- females pink or purplish, at end of shoots;
- males and females on same tree, females usually nearer the top.

Fruit
- immature cones 10–18 cm (4–7") long; green, cigar-shaped, sticky, straight or curved, aromatic: often oozing white resin;
- take 2 years to mature; at maturity light brown, hanging from thick round brown stem;
- discharge winged seeds in early autumn, then shed;
- begin bearing cones at age 5–10; good seed crop every 3–5 years.

Twig
- green, fuzzy in first year;
- buds reddish brown, pointed, 15 mm ($\frac{2}{3}$") long;
- flexible branches in distinct annual whorls, usually 5.

Bark
- on younger trees, gray green and smooth;
- on older trees, dark gray brown, furrowed, 2–5 cm (1–2") thick.

Wood
- soft, light, somewhat strong, straight-grained, even-textured;
- heartwood light brown; sapwood almost white;
- annual growth rings distinct.

Height
30–50 m (100–160')

Diameter
60–150 cm (24–60")

Longevity
200–400 years

A common sight on the forest floor of a northern mixed wood forest.

the best of pines, the worst of times

The New World's history has been largely the story of man's struggle with nature. It is the war with the wilderness which has constituted its epic . . . shaping the mentality and the conduct of every inhabitant.

A. R. M. Lower, 1938

The history of eastern North America, from the colonization by the first Europeans until the end of the nineteenth century, was inextricably interwoven with the monarch of the forest — the white pine. A paragon of grace and beauty, its sheer stature dominated the landscape. And the liquidation of its biggest and best affected our economic, social, political, and ecological development.

To the settlers the pines, indeed all trees, represented a mixed blessing. They were the major obstacle to successful farming — and therefore to survival. At the same time they furnished families with houses, barns, churches, furniture, tools, and the firewood needed to survive winter. Yet there was simply too much of it — in clearing the land for the farm homestead, what they couldn't use they simply burned. Thus began the onslaught.

To the British, as with the French before them, the magnificent pines of the colonies were prized for shipbuilding. Even before Napoleon had blocked England's access to the timbers of the Baltic, the motherland had turned to the forests of her colonies for the pines she desperately needed for the masts and spars of her ships. To rule the waves, Britannia needed masts for the sails of her brigantines.

Government surveyors combed the countryside, branding the King's Broad Arrow on all white pines of mast quality — the tallest and the straightest — for the exclusive use of the Royal Navy. Severe penalties were inflicted on any settler who dared to cut one down for his own use. The Broad Arrow was a thorny issue with New England colonists, and added fuel to the tinderbox of rebellion.

The scale of activity was enormous. In 1811 alone, 23,000 masts were loaded onto schooners bound for England from Quebec, then the largest timber port in the world. Many were 120 feet long and 4 feet in diameter, the biggest and the best the forest had to offer. In foresters' parlance, the forests were being systematically "highgraded." First the masts, then the huge and extremely wasteful hand-hewn "squared timbers," then "deals" (slabs of pine at least 3" thick), and ultimately sawn lumber for the North American market.

In 1850, J. S. Springer of Maine prophesied: *Thirty years ago it was unnecessary to search for a locality for a lumber camp on the Penobscot, for a man could step from his house to his day's work, the pine, that forest king, abounding on every side. Fifty years hence the vast pine forests through which the Penobscot flows will be on the eve of destruction.* His prediction proved to be conservative. Within 100 years, from the Maritimes to Minnesota, white pine of commercial value was all but obliterated from the landscape.

In 1871, Prime Minister Sir John A. Macdonald wrote to the premier of Ontario: *The sight of the immense masses of timber passing my windows every morning constantly brings to mind the absolute necessity there is for looking at the future of this great trade. We are recklessly destroying the timber of Canada and there is scarcely the possibility of replacing it.* It was 40 years later that the last white pine left Ottawa, all the best gone from an area spanning some 400 miles on either side of the Ottawa River and its tributaries. Bernard Fernow, the first Chief of the U.S. Forest Service, estimated that by the turn of the century, only 15 percent of the original virgin pine forest on the continent remained.

To some it was a wonderful chapter of exciting romantic adventure — remote lumber camps in winter, cooks serving up a steady diet of salt pork and beans and hot tea, lumberjacks felling gigantic trees with only ax and crosscut saw, teams of massive horses and oxen hauling huge loads of logs over treacherous roads of ice, spring river log drives that imperilled the lives of hundreds of *draveurs*, rafts of timber the size of football fields floating down rivers, and tall ships setting sail for the motherland laden with timbers.

It had all the exuberance and frenzy of the Yukon Gold Rush. After all, it was frontier time. There would always be more white pine over the next hill. By today's standards, however, it evokes the same sense of regret as the wanton eradication of the prairie buffalo, or the senseless slaughter that sent millions of passenger pigeons into extinction. But it is very easy to judge the actions of the past by today's values.

White pine spawned the forest industry in North America. Through trade of masts and spars, squared timbers and deals, and finally sawn lumber, the economy boomed and government coffers swelled, communities and towns sprang up, roads and schools and hospitals were built.

To move the wood, transportation networks exploded, providing new modes of travel for both passengers and cargoes. Canals such as the Hudson, the Champlain, the Erie, the Welland, the Oswego, and the

Female flowers, usually at the top of the tree, take two growing seasons to mature into woody cones.

Chambly were built at great expense to barge pine from the forest to the urban consumer. Railroads were constructed to ship lumber — the New York Central, the Bytown and Prescott, the Boston and Albany. Each new railroad sprouted a string of sawmills along its route, and villages grew up around the mills, at least until the supply of white pine was exhausted. Some remained, adapted, and grew; others became ghost towns. It was the opening of eastern North America, and white pine was the stimulus.

But the pine necessarily took its toll in the process. By 1860 the best was gone from New Brunswick; by the end of the century, almost all old-growth pine stands had been liquidated everywhere white pine grew, from Nova Scotia to western Ontario and Minnesota. Thousands of people were employed, timber barons grew wealthy, governments generated substantial revenues, and countless spin-off industries were born, but all at the expense of the pine.

The final word goes to Sir Henri Joly de Lotbinière, later to become the first president of the Canadian Forestry Association, who wrote in 1875:

In a very short time since the beginning of this century we have overrun our forests, picking out the finest pine, and we have impoverished them to a serious extent, and, what makes it worse, impoverished the country too.

the original cough drop

It is not surprising that today's commercial cough syrups contain active ingredients derived from white pine. For centuries and throughout pine's range, Native medicine people had been prescribing the inner bark, needles, or gum as an expectorant for coughs, colds, sore throats, and related lung problems.

The Mohegan, Menominee, Shinnecook and Mi'kmaq steeped a medicinal tea of the inner bark; the Montagnais used the gum and the Tadousac, the needles. The Mohawk mixed pine needles with those of spruce, tamarack, fir, hemlock, cedar and yew — all conifers rich in vitamin C. The Onondaga boiled the bark and inhaled the vapors; the Seneca mixed pine needles with black cherry bark and maple sugar to make their cough syrup. North America's first cough drop was likely produced by Long Island's Shinnecook, who sucked on dried pine pitch for relief.

Other uses of white pine were a baby powder from pulverized rotten wood, a vapor inhalant for headaches and backaches, poultices of the pounded inner bark applied to wounds and sores, a bark beverage for kidney and bladder ailments, and the addition of the male flowers to meat stews. Aging baby boomers should note that in 1672 John Josselyn reported from New England: *The distilled water of the green cones taketh away wrinkles in the face, being laid on with cloths.*

white pine bed-and-breakfast

Among the many songbirds who eat white pine seeds, the most dependent is the red crossbill, whose eastern range conveniently corresponds to that of the pine. Two-thirds of the crossbill's diet consists of nutritious pine seeds. Crossbills dangle from branches, noisily cracking open the hanging cones with their unique beaks. Since they dine in the pine, they often board there as well. The olive green female, whose plumage blends with the pine foliage, often builds her nest well out on the long branches of pine, sometimes concealing it in a cluster of needles. She rarely leaves the nest during the two weeks she incubates her four eggs, so the male obligingly serves her breakfast in bed.

In addition to crossbills, another 20 or so songbirds prefer the somewhat oily seeds of white pine, including nuthatches, pine siskins, chickadees, cardinals, and grosbeaks. Spruce grouse and wild turkeys eat both the seeds and the needles.

White pine not only provides food for wildlife, but it offers a place to call home for birds and mammals alike. It is the most popular nesting site for mourning doves, and a favorite of robins, wood thrushes, and blue jays. Eagles and ospreys often construct their huge nests at the top of large white pines overlooking the water, the source of their diet of fish. Tops of large white pine are a favorite spot for gray squirrels to build their nests of leaves. Large old hollow pines are ideal cavity den sites for black bears, raccoons, martens, and fishers, as well as a few of the larger birds like the pileated woodpecker and the barred owl.

figureheads and pine boxes

White pine is a wonderful wood to work with. It is slightly fragrant, has a soft uniform texture and a fine grain, and is easy to nail, plane, or even carve. It is lightweight and fairly strong. The wood has a natural smooth satiny finish. For outdoor use it takes preservatives, paints, and stains well. It is the third-most popular-selling wood in North America, behind red oak and black cherry.

Throughout the history of its use in North America, pine has been fashioned into just about anything that can be made of wood. Besides being the resource for items one might expect, such as furniture, trim and molding, window frames and sashes, doors, and siding, it has been used

As white pine matures, the bark may become over 5 centimeters (2") thick.

sumed about a billion board feet of white pine every year. The packing boxes were used to ship all manner of articles, from clothing to machinery, before the era of the corrugated box, metal strapping, pallets, and PVC plastic. At their destination, they were emptied of their contents, broken up, and burned. It is estimated that the original pine forests contained only 750 billion board feet of lumber.

of weevils and rusts

One might assume that, with the near eradication of old white pine in the nineteenth century, a massive reforestation effort would have ensued. But there have been two reasons foresters have been hesitant to plant white pine: one is an insect, the other is a disease.

The white pine weevil, with its long pointed snout, is a rather nasty looking little critter. After a winter of hibernation in the duff beneath a young pine, adult weevils crawl to the top shoot in the spring to feed, meet, and breed. Females lay up to 200 eggs in punctures they make in the leader, the top vertical shoot. Upon hatching, the ravenous larvae systematically form a tight feeding ring inside the bark, tunneling their way down the shoot, killing it as they go. By July, the leader turns brown, keels over and dies, taking on a characteristic shepherd's crook shape.

One or more of the side branches in the top whorl curves skyward to assume the leader role. If only one branch succeeds, it forms a permanent crook in the main stem. If two or more achieve dominance, a forked tree results. Repeated weevil attacks create seriously deformed trees that, though curious to behold, are too misshapen to ever produce lumber. Trees growing in partial shade are less susceptible to the weevil, which needs heat and sunshine to thrive, but they grow more slowly and are more spindly.

Pruning off and burning infested leaders is the most common non-chemical method

to carve ship's figureheads and cigar store Indians, construct coffins (the "pine box" of many westerns), and our now-treasured covered bridges. Pine sawdust mixed with resin has been molded into distributor caps, disc brakes, and toilet seats, and impregnated with asphalt to make roofing paper and shingles. And its long fibers make strong paper.

When white pine was still considered plentiful and inexhaustible, massive amounts were consumed in the disposable box business. In 1905, there were 344 box factories in New England, which collectively conof combating the weevils. Unfortunately the larvae of some wasps and flies inside, who prey upon weevils, are also destroyed in the process. Some feel that a multi-forked tree has more character, so letting the weevils do their thing can provide a creation sculpted by nature.

White pine blister rust is equally insidious. It was introduced to North America in the early 1900s in seedlings imported into New York from Europe, and it spread rapidly. The rust has two hosts; white pine and the *Ribes* family, which includes domestic and wild currants and gooseberries. Wind carries spores of the fungus from one host to the other. They settle on pine needles, and the fungus works its way through the twig, along the branch, to the trunk. There it causes its worst damage by girdling the tree, killing everything above the infection. There is no cure, but eradication of all *Ribes* in the vicinity helps. Removal and burning of infected branches before the rust reaches the trunk can save a tree.

leaving a legacy

It is not exaggerated praise to call a tree
the grandest
And most beautiful of all the productions
of the earth

William Gilpin (1762–1843)

What does one get for the child who has everything? A young living tree, and a little help in planting it, is a gift that will be remembered for generations. Since the life expectancy of white pine is 200 to 400 years, that translates into quite a number of generations.

Most quality garden centers carry native eastern white pine. If not available locally, young pines growing wild in the gravel along roadsides are common throughout its range. White pines under one meter (3–4') transplant readily.

The ideal soil is a good sandy loam, but pine will survive on a variety of sites, as long as it is not too wet or too dry. In choosing the planting spot, look to the future. Ensure that there will be ample space for the long branches to spread. Open grown pines tend to retain their lower branches. The site should have full sunlight or a little shade. A location south of the home or cottage will provide shade in the heat of summer, but will block the warmth of the winter sun. A slightly shady locale will reduce the likelihood of damage by the white pine weevil.

An added incentive to plant white pine, if you are a resident of Ontario, Maine, or Michigan, is that you will be planting your official arboreal emblem.

Balsam Poplar
(*Populus balsamifera*)

Balm of Gilead
black poplar
taca mahac

peuplier baumier
peuplier noir
baumier
liard

Dogrib Dene: *t'ooladzè*

Leaf
- simple, alternate; triangular, with tapered tip and rounded or slightly heart-shaped base;
- thick, fragrant; fine rounded teeth tipped with brown glands; 8–12 cm (3–5") long;
- upper side shiny dark green with brownish tinge; waxy; midrib and veins a little fuzzy;
- underside much paler, silvery green, often with rusty blotches; raised yellow midrib;
- 6–7 veins per side, fork before they reach edge;
- stem round, reddish green, with two brown glands at base of leaf.

Flower
- male catkins elongate to 7–10 cm (3–4") before leaves unfold;
- female catkins green, 6–8 cm (2–3") long; males and females on separate trees.

Fruit
- mature female catkins brown, hanging; 10–13 cm (4–5") long; before leaves fully grown;
- composed of small oval pointed pods that split in two;
- release 2–3 light gray tufted seeds per capsule.

Twig
- slightly thick, somewhat hairy, lightly ridged; red brown when young, then gray;
- slightly angular in cross-section; sparse lengthwise lenticels;
- buds dark reddish brown, gummy, shiny, fragrant;
- lateral buds pressed against twig.

Bark
- on younger trees, grayish green and smooth;
- on older trees, thick, gray, furrowed; with flat scaly ridges.

Wood
- light, soft, weak; not impact- or rot-resistant;
- heartwood grayish brown; sapwood nearly white; transition not clear;
- annual growth rings faint and inconspicuous.

Height
20–25 m (70–80')

Diameter
30–60 cm (12–24")

Longevity
70–100 years

Young balsam poplars have smooth, yellowish or greenish brown bark.

From sea to shining sea

> We have nothing to fear and a great deal to learn from trees, that vigorous and pacific tribe which without stint produces strengthening essences for us. Soothing balms. And in whose gracious company we spend so many cool, silent and intimate hours.
>
> Marcel Proust,
> 1871–1922

Older botany textbooks classified balsam poplar and Balm of Gilead as two distinct species, mostly due to minor differences in the leaves. Today it is routinely, but not universally, accepted that they are indeed one species. For the sake of simplicity, they are treated here as such.

Variations in traits due to genetics or local environment might well be expected in

a tree that grows continent-wide. Balsam poplar ranges from the Newfoundland and Labrador shores of the North Atlantic to the Alaska coast on the Bering Sea. Its southern limits lie in the eastern states bordering Canada, with isolated pockets as far south as Georgia and Mississippi. Unlike most trees, the oldest and the largest specimens are found in the north. In the Mackenzie River valley, trees 30–40 meters (100–130') tall and 175 years old are not rare. Balsam poplar is first and foremost a tree of the vast boreal forest.

Balsam poplar is most at home on rich bottomlands, but it will grow anywhere there is enough, but not too much, moisture. Trees produce a healthy crop of seeds every year; however their viability is very short-lived. If they are not blown onto fresh moist mineral soil, such as shorelines or forest fire sites, they perish within a few days. Root suckering is the primary means of balsam poplar regrowth.

mixed reviews

Balsam poplar receives mixed reviews as an ornamental. On the one hand it is fast-growing, thrives on a variety of soils, survives extreme cold, and its unusual tinted foliage contrasts with that of other broadleaf trees. But its resinous buds may attract wasps, its catkins may be a nuisance to clean up, and its pollen may affect allergies in some people. Because of its wide-spreading roots, it should not be planted near septic systems, wells, or city water and sewage lines.

The sweet scent of balsam on a summer evening may well outweigh these concerns. It can be planted from seed or cuttings, or transplanted from the forest edge.

blight, borers, and miners

No insects or diseases pose a serious threat to the balsam poplar's survival. There are a few, however, that inflict moderate damage in localized areas. Linospora leaf blight and Septoria leaf spot are fungi that produce brown blotches on the leaves, causing them to shed prematurely. If a shade tree is infected, raking and burning the fallen leaves reduces the likelihood of a re-occurrence.

The voracious forest tent caterpillar attacks balsam poplar only after it has defoliated all nearby trembling aspen. Populations of aspen webworm, spiny elm caterpillar, and balsam poplar leaf blotch miner are usually local. Miners inside the leaves can be eliminated only with a systemic insecticide. Webworms can be sprayed with Bt, and colonies of spiny elm caterpillar can be removed by hand. Larvae of the poplar-and-willow borer, a weevil introduced to this continent, tunnel upward from the base of the tree and can seriously weaken it.

Unless an insect is threatening the life of a tree, one should allow its natural predators, parasites, and diseases to control its population.

paper, packing material, and bobbers

Until relatively recently, balsam poplar was not widely used in the forest industry. With its expansion into the furthest reaches of the boreal forest and the development of new pulping technologies, it is now a frequent mix with trembling aspen in paper production. It is chipped to produce particleboard, and its sawn lumber is marketed as northern aspen.

In the past, wood shavings were used for excelsior packing material, its wood for concealed furniture components, and its veneer was used for plywood and fruit baskets. On the prairies, it was commonly used for stable flooring. The wood is light, soft, weak, and not rot-resistant. It will not split when nailed, and was a favorite in the disposable box and crate trade. In the north it is still a common firewood, but its heat value is rather low.

The thick buoyant bark near the base of older trees was once carved into toy boats, fishing bobbers, and floats for fish nets.

the secret is in the bud

Wherewith thei doe cure and make whole many infirmities, which if wee did lack them, thei were incurable, and without any remedie . . . for which cause I did pretend to treate, and to write, of all thynges brying from out Indias, which serveth for the arte and use of Medicine.

Nicholas Monardes,
Physician of Seville,
1493–1598

Throughout the expansive range of balsam poplar, First Nations people made medicine from the resin in its gummy buds. Most tribes whose remedies have been documented prepared the buds in the same way and for similar purposes. The Maliseet in the Maritimes and Ojibway in Ontario boiled them in bear grease or tallow, strained the mixture, and applied the fragrant salve directly, or in poultices, to wounds, sores, boils, eczema, rashes, hemorrhoids, or gout. The ointment was also rubbed onto sore muscles, sprains, and rheumatic joints, as well as on the inside of the nose to clear respiratory passages from the effects of colds and bronchitis.

Native women steeped the roots with those of trembling aspen, and drank the tea to stop excessive flow during pregnancy and to prevent premature births. The Cree used boiled inner bark or fresh leaves to draw out infections and to relieve breathing problems.

The buds are reported to have diuretic, expectorant, and stimulant properties, and contain both salicin (like their distant cousins the willows) and populin, an aromatic glucoside. The leaves and stems contain vitamin C. The buds were officially listed in the *U.S. National Formulary*, the bible of American pharmacists, until 1965.

The Cottonwoods
(*Populus deltoides*)

cotton tree
necklace poplar
eastern cottonwood
eastern poplar
plains cottonwood

peuplier deltoïde
liard
cotonnier
peuplier à feuilles deltoïdes
peuplier monolifière
peuplier du Canada

Omaha-Ponca: *maa zho*

Leaf
- simple, alternate; roughly equilateral triangle-shaped; tip pointed; 5–10 cm (2–4") long and wide;
- thick, with the feel of wax paper; light bright green, slightly paler underneath;
- teeth rounded to naked eye; actually slightly hooked and tipped with tiny brown glands;
- flat stems almost leaf length, yellow with reddish tinge; three or more warty glands at base;
- yellow raised midrib on upper side, flanked by 5–7 veins, usually forked;
- flutter in breeze; turn yellow in autumn; one of the last trees to shed leaves.

Flower
- male catkins densely flowered, 5–7 cm (2–3") long; fall off intact after pollination;
- tiny green and yellow female flowers in hanging catkins;
- males and females on separate trees; before leaves unfold.

Fruit
- like hanging string of beads, 15–25 cm (6–10") long; capsules green, stalked, tapered, pointed;
- brown at maturity, split into 3–4 parts; release tiny brown seeds on tufts of cottony hairs;
- good seed crop most years.

Twig
- thick, yellowish green-brown; smooth, ridged; almost square in cross-section;
- brown sticky buds angled out from twig; fragrant, shiny; terminal bud long, slender;
- on branches rising at 45° angle from trunk, often drooping at tips.

Bark
- on younger trees, thin, smooth, grayish yellow tinged with green;
- on older trees, ash gray, thick, and deeply furrowed, with broad round ridges.

Wood
- light, soft, weak; fine-textured, close-grained, porous;
- heartwood gray-brown; thick sapwood nearly white.

Note The description above applies to eastern cottonwood. Plains cottonwood differs as follows: leaves have only 1–2 basal glands; buds are downy; and twigs are light yellow. Where the two interbreed, trees may have characteristics of each. On the prairies, tree heights will be considerably less than those indicated below.

Height	Diameter	Longevity
25–30 m (80–100')	80–120 cm (30–48")	50–70 years

Thick, smooth, toothed leaves are roughly the shape of an equilateral triangle. Hence the Latin name deltoides.

a cottonwood by any other name

In 1753 the classification of plants into a hierarchy of divisions, classes, orders, families, genera, and species was initiated by Swedish botany professor Carolus Linnaeus (a Latin pseudonym he adopted). He became known as the father of systematic botany. Under his system, tree names are in Latin, a common international standard transcending language differences. They are composed of two words. The first is generic (the genus) and the second is specific (the species) — a descriptor which distinguishes it from other members of the genus.

For example, *Populus* is the poplar genus and *deltoides* means triangular, referring to the shape of the leaf. In textbooks, the Latin name is followed by the abbreviated name or initials of the botanist who named it. *Populus deltoides* becomes *Populus deltoides* Marsh.

But nature being as complex and unpredictable as it is, man's attempts to assign order to it have not been foolproof, and disagreements in the scientific community arise. Species have been renamed and reclassified, subspecies and varieties have been elevated to species level, and species downgraded to subspecies and varieties. Eastern cottonwood is one of these ambiguous cases.

Botanists have been debating cottonwood's place in the order of things botanical for nearly a century. It has been bounced around from species, to subspecies, to variety, and even to natural hybrid of two different subspecies. The only area of agreement is that the tree exists.

The latest Canadian authority, *Trees in Canada* by J. L. Farrar, considers that there are two subspecies of *Populus deltoides*: plains cottonwood, over a broad area in the west, and eastern cottonwood, confined to a few locales in the east, with extensive intergrading of the two in between.

The differences are subtle: leaf characteristics, hairiness of the buds, and color of the twigs. For the purposes of this book (and at the risk of enraging purists), the two subspecies are considered as one, with minor variations in characteristics within its overall range — from southern Quebec and western New England, down to Florida and Texas, and northward through the plains states to southern Alberta.

Plains cottonwood is the state tree of both Nebraska and Kansas.

According to the Manitoba Forestry Association, the largest tree in the province, as of 1987, was a plains cottonwood located in an oxbow of the Assiniboine River near Portage La Prairie. It was 36 meters (115') tall with a diameter of 205 centimeters (almost 7').

instant shade tree

Cottonwood is the fastest growing native tree east of the Rockies. On moist silt or sand loams adjacent to rivers, it has been known to reach 4 meters (13') in its first year. In the Mississippi valley, 35-year-old trees have measured 40 meters (130') tall. Further north, the growth rate is less spectacular, but still impressive. Minnesota cottonwoods commonly grow 30 meters (100') tall in 50 years.

Cottonwoods bear huge seed crops almost every year. An early 1900s scientific journal reported a 13-meter (40') open-grown tree bearing 28 million seeds. Some consider this the major drawback to cottonwood as an ornamental. The silky hairs that carry the seeds litter the landscape, block air conditioners, and cling to window screens, and they may affect allergy sufferers.

Like their distant cousins the willows, cottonwoods can be planted directly from cuttings. Two-to-three-year-old seedlings or young stump sprouts furnish the best cuttings. In early spring, before the buds flush, cut them into 25-centimeter (10") lengths, stick them in moist soil (right side up!) in full sunlight, and watch them grow. Removal of grass competition will give them a boost. To plant from seed, collect only the largest seeds from mature catkins, when the seed capsules begin to open. Sow on bare, moist, partially shaded soil immediately after collection. Do not cover with soil.

absorbent cotton

Most of the native trees supplied medicines of one form or another, both for internal consumption and external application. But how were the topical medicines applied? Enter cottonwood. The Ojibway gathered the fluffy tufts attached to the tiny seeds, soaked them with herbal disinfectants or astringents, and applied them to cuts and open sores — the forerunner of today's absorbent cotton. The Mohawk considered cottonwood inner bark, taken internally, to be a vermifuge; it was boiled and the liquid drunk to rid the body of intestinal worms.

the cottonwood pantry

The resinous buds and caterpillar-like catkins of cottonwood are preferred winter and spring foods of both ruffed and sharp-tailed grouse, and in the summer sharp-tails dine on the protein-rich leaves. Winter resident evening grosbeaks and purple finches derive nourishment and energy from the buds as well. A symmetrical pattern of tiny holes in the bark indicates a yellow-bellied sapsucker has been visiting a cottonwood for sap snacks. Other woodpeckers excavate the soft wood and nest in the cavities they chip out.

The proximity of young cottonwood saplings to rivers and streams makes a handy

source of food and dam-building material for beavers. Seedlings are a tasty morsel to rabbits, and the twigs are a favorite browse for deer.

hybrid poplars

Centuries ago, eastern cottonwoods from North America were introduced into France, where they spontaneously interbred with European black poplar. The offspring of this mixed marriage rapidly outgrew both parents. This was the genesis of what came to be known as Carolina poplar, the most widely planted hybrid tree in the world.

The rapid growth of natural hybrids led to cloning of the best specimens, and in 1912 the first successes were achieved in England. Cuttings were brought to North America as early as 1925, and planted extensively as city shade trees and farm windbreaks.

Today there are over 5,000 genotypes of hybrid poplar; most have no names, only numbers. Tree breeders look for hardiness in a range of climates, good rooting ability, resistance to disease, and of course fast growth. In hybrid poplar plantations, genetically identical monocultures, much like some agricultural strains, are extremely susceptible to disease, so clones are now being bred with resistance to one or more diseases.

In the latter half of the twentieth century, governments, universities, and the forest industry began to experiment with short rotation cropping. The goal was to produce merchantable trees in 8 to 12 years.

In the early 1970s the Domtar paper mill in Cornwall, Ontario, was among the first to pioneer hybrid poplar plantations in Canada. Idle farmland was the target, and intensive management was the technique. The Ontario government developed and supplied the trees, farmers and woodlot owners the land, and Domtar the expertise and labor.

In a blend of agricultural and forestry practices, fields are prepared by brush cutting, plowing, harrowing, and herbiciding. Unrooted cuttings are planted, and followed up with fertilizers, more herbicides, and sometimes pruning and thinning. More environmentally friendly approaches being experimented with elsewhere are planting of cover crops or mulching with polyethylene mats to control competing weeds, and fertilizing with treated municipal sewage.

Products of hybrid poplar plantations include pulp and paper, sawlogs, veneer, waferboard or oriented strand board (OSB), biomass energy, methanol, and even feed for livestock.

Is all the effort and expense worthwhile? Perhaps. To meet the growing world demand for wood and paper, intensive forest management, which includes poplar plantations, is part of the solution. Theoretically, it will help meet short-term demand, and free other forest land for ecological preserves and multiple use management. Only time will tell if this is a wise course to follow, and what the long-term ecological impacts, if any, may be.

Preliminary studies indicate that young hybrid poplar plantations host a greater number and diversity of small mammals and birds than farm fields, but fewer than neighboring natural forests.

The irony is that not so long ago poplars themselves were herbicided as weeds.

Facing page: As cottonwoods rapidly mature, the smooth bark of their youth develops into a thick furrowed bark with broad, rounded ridges. With an average lifespan of only 50 to 70 years, cottonwoods are short-lived by tree standards. In the heart of their range, on the most fertile soils of the Mississipi Valley, they have been known to grow taller than the average bungalow in their first year. Further north and west, their growth is less spectacular. They are the fastest growing native trees east of the Rockies.

Largetooth Aspen
(*Populus grandidentata*)

bigtooth aspen
poplar
popple

peuplier à grandes dents
grand tremble

Onondaga: *nut-ki'e*

Leaf
- simple, alternate; almost round, with pointed tip; 6–10 cm (2–4") long;
- edges undulating with large uneven, slightly hooked teeth;
- upper side dark green with yellow veins; underside pale green, with a touch of fuzz around midrib and veins;
- stalk flat, perpendicular to the leaf; reddish yellow; a little shorter than the leaf;
- silvery green and velvety when unfolding in late spring;
- turn yellow, occasionally reddish yellow, in autumn.

Flower
- male catkin hanging; gray and very fuzzy; before leaves unfold; falls off intact;
- female elongates into hanging smooth green catkin, as leaves emerge;
- males and females on separate trees.

Fruit
- hanging catkin of tiny, cone-shaped, pale green, downy capsules;
- capsules split in 2, 4–6 weeks after flowering; release tiny seeds tufted with white hairs;
- good seed crop every 4–5 years.

Twig
- new twigs reddish or yellowish brown; older twigs grayish green;
- pale lenticels sparse; pith star-shaped;
- buds dark brown, pointed, diverging from the twig; partially downy;
- buds not fragrant or resinous; male flower buds larger than leaf buds.

Bark
- on younger trees, smooth and thin; yellowish brown to greenish gray;
- on older trees, charcoal gray, thick and deeply furrowed.

Wood
- soft, light, weak; straight-grained;
- heartwood light grayish beige; sapwood nearly white;
- annual growth rings inconspicuous.

Height	**Diameter**	**Longevity**
15–20 m (50–70')	30–60 cm (12–24")	80–150 years

an aspen of more moderate climes

Compared to trembling aspen, the range of largetooth aspen is small and limited to more moderate climates — from Cape Breton and Prince Edward Island in the east, to the southeast tip of Manitoba, and as far south as the mountains of Tennessee. It edges into Ontario's boreal forest north to Matheson, in Quebec to Lac Témiscamingue, but is absent in the boreal forest of the prairie provinces.

Largetooth grows best on moist, fertile, well-aerated soils. If a forest fire burns off the top organic layer, exposing mineral soil, largetooth is one of the first pioneer species to seed in. It is highly intolerant and can not reproduce in its own shade. It is commonly found in young tolerant hardwood stands, where it initially outgrows the competition. But its life expectancy is short, and if there is no disturbance, it is eventually replaced by maples, ashes, pines, and other longer-lived trees. Because of its demand for full sunlight, it is commonly found along roadsides and on forest edges.

first the bad news

Most horticulturists do not recommend largetooth aspen as an ornamental around the home. Their reasons are sound. Its shallow wide-spreading roots can play havoc with sewer and water lines. Its propensity to reproduce from root suckers, even at a very young age, means that if you plant one tree, you get a dozen or more, perhaps an unwanted bonus. And largetooth aspen is susceptible to a wide range of insects and fungal diseases, as well as storm damage.

The good news is that if you have the space for the roots to spread and for young clones to create a little aspen grove, largetooth aspen is a rather appealing tree to consider. It is a fast grower. Its smooth grayish green bark is handsome. The leaves quiver and rustle even in the gentlest breezes, and, if it is a male, its dangling flower catkins decorate the tree even before leaves appear in early spring. Its moments of glory come in late spring when the leaves finally unfold into an elegant display of silvery velvet, and in late autumn when they turn bright yellow, often with tinges of red and orange.

Homeowners living near the forest may be rewarded by a winter visit from a ruffed grouse perched in their aspen, munching away at the buds.

poached or scrambled

Largetooth aspen has similar medicinal properties to its close cousin, trembling aspen, and First Nations people employed it for much the same purposes. Algonquins and Iroquois applied poultices of the inner bark or young roots to stop the bleeding of cuts and wounds. The Maliseet drank the steeped inner bark to stimulate the appetite. The Cayuga produced an itch powder from the "dust" collected from the outer bark in early spring. The Ojibway cooked and ate the cambium layer, which is reported to taste like eggs.

of clones and hybrids

Like all members of the poplar family, largetooth aspens are dioecious. There are male trees and female trees. Pollen from male catkins is borne by the wind to fertilize the tiny flowers of females. Within four to six weeks, female flowers mature into hanging catkins of pale green seed capsules. The capsules split in two, and release minute, extremely light seeds attached to tufts of long white cottony hairs. Seeds — up to a million from a single large tree — are dispersed far and wide by the wind, or carried along waterways. In order to germinate, they must land on moist mineral soil. Otherwise they perish within a few days. Most largetooth aspen seeds don't make it. A very small percentage

In late spring, the unfolding leaves are covered with silvery velvet.

germinate, and when they do, even fewer seedlings survive the first year.

Aspen reproduces primarily through root suckering. Dormant buds on the shallow roots, triggered by increased soil temperatures from the removal of shade, surface as new trees — exact replicas, genetically, sexually, and visually, of the parent tree. An aspen clone may be a dozen trees, or it may spread over time to cover a vast area. One clone in Michigan is 8,000 years old, while another in Minnesota covers over 14 hectares (35 acres). Aspen clones are among the oldest and largest living beings on the planet.

Occasionally, pollen from a largetooth aspen may cross the line and develop a meaningful relationship with the flower of a female trembling aspen, or vice versa. The "kissing cousins" spawn a natural hybrid of the two species, with characteristics of each parent.

aspen and the gourmand grouse

Largetooth aspen ranks second, behind trembling aspen, as the preferred winter meal of ruffed grouse. Grouse gorge on the large and nutritious flower buds of male trees at the amazing rate of 30 buds a minute — 350 to 400 buds in a 15-minute evening feeding frenzy. All the while, the large bird is bal-anced precariously on a branch 10–15 meters (30–50') above the ground. Male aspen floral buds are winter's survival package for ruffed grouse, supplemented by the catkins of birch, ironwood, and hazelnut.

Beavers are also highly dependent on aspen. Within its relatively small range, largetooth aspen supplies beavers with the bark and twigs that are staples in their diet. In addition, young largetooth suckers are a browse favorite of white-tailed deer and snowshoe hares, who in turn provide a natural thinning service in thick young stands.

aspen is, well, aspen

Largetooth aspen is 10 percent heavier and denser than trembling aspen; otherwise their wood characteristics are the same. The two species are not differentiated in the marketplace; both are sold simply as "aspen." For the woodworker, largetooth has a fine texture and high luster. It holds nails well, won't readily split, and is easy to glue. It wears extremely well for a light species.

When growing in the forest, aspen is straight, has little taper, and bears few branches. These qualities, coupled with its softness and light weight, make it the choice of many log home builders, when peeled and treated with preservatives.

Trembling Aspen
(*Populus tremuloides*)

quaking aspen
poplar
popple
white poplar

peuplier faux-tremble
tremble
peuplier

Massachusett: *me:twe*

Leaf
- simple, alternate; small, round, with pointed tip; fine toothed; 3–6 cm (1¼–2½");
- upper side deep green; underside duller green;
- on long slender flattened stalk, perpendicular to the leaf;
- turn golden yellow in late autumn.

Flower
- appear before leaves; males and females on separate trees;
- both evolve into hanging catkins; males gray and fuzzy, females green and smooth.

Fruit
- seed pods on central stem of hanging female catkins;
- mature 4–6 weeks after flowering;
- pods split in 2, release tiny light seeds with white tufts of hair;
- good seed crop every 2–3 years.

Twig
- slender, shiny, green or gray/brown, round, with oval lenticels;
- buds dark brown, shiny, pointed, pressed to the twig.

Bark
- on younger trees, grayish green, yellowish green, or chalky white; smooth, with waxy luster;
- on older trees, cracking into dark gray furrows; almost black at base.

Wood
- soft, light, weak; straight-grained;
- heartwood light grayish brown to grayish white; sapwood creamy white;
- transition from sapwood to heartwood not obvious;
- annual growth rings distinct, but not conspicuous.

Height
12–20 m (40–65')

Diameter
30–60 cm (12–24")

Longevity
60–90 years

Trembling aspen's autumn hues of yellow seem to become more intense as one travels west.

poplars in perpetuity

Trembling aspen is more popularly referred to as poplar, popple, or just plain old "aspen."

Its natural range is extraordinary. From Alaska east to Newfoundland and Labrador, and south to the Baja in Mexico, it is the widest-ranging tree species in North America. It grows at elevations from sea level to 10,000 feet in the Rockies, in groves at the edge of the prairies, on mountainsides, on flat lands and in valley bottoms, in pure stands or mixed with dozens of other species, and on sandy or clay or silt soils. Wherever it is not too wet, not too dry, and there is full sunlight, trembling aspen thrives.

Aspen trees are of only one sex, that is, dioecious, the majority males, fewer females, and a tiny percentage hermaphrodites. In peak years a large female aspen may produce a million or more seeds. But most seeds deteriorate in a matter of days, and very few are fortunate enough to find the right conditions of moist mineral soil and sunlight to germinate and grow. Most trembling aspen originate from suckering of the roots of parent trees.

Suckers grow from buds on the long shallow undulating roots, a few centimeters below the surface. Tapping the parent's root system for nutrients, they shoot up rapidly, reaching 2 meters (6') or more in the first year, with leaves several times normal size. Each young tree is genetically identical to the other, and so the entire group of suckers is a natural clone. A clone can be a half dozen trees in the immediate vicinity of the parent, or it can spread to cover hectares. Each sucker in a clone also grows its own roots, but remains connected to the parent's root system, at least for the first 20 to 30 years.

A forest of pure aspen is usually a mosaic of patches of genetically identical clones.

Clones are easily identifiable, when viewed on hillsides or from the air, by their color, gender, size, and other inherited traits such as flowering time, branching habit, and fall foliage color.

aspen in the boreal

In the boreal forest, trees rarely go through a natural succession leading to a climax stage. Forest fires take care of that. Since the retreat of the glaciers some 10,000 years ago, lightning-caused fires have ravaged the forests, on average, every 40 to 80 years. In the boreal, nature unfolds in cycles. Forests grow, are consumed by fire, and are reborn. Trembling aspen plays a pivotal role. In the aftermath of a fire, aspen suckers rise from the ashes like a phoenix. Triggered by increased sunlight and soil temperature, suckers form dense thickets of young trees, as many as 100,000 in a hectare, or 40,000 per acre. Those with some advantage, such as a few weeks' head start, good genes, or a fertile microsite, reach toward the sun and shade out the less fortunate. Eventually aspens thin themselves out naturally.

Further south, in the absence of a forest fire, aspen is often replaced by longer-lived, more tolerant species such as sugar maple. Having rejuvenated the soil and served as a nurse for its successors, the pioneering aspen disappears, its role accomplished.

the weed comes of age

The bitter leaves and bark form a favorite food of the porcupine, who seems to be almost the only friend of the much despised "Popple."

W. H. Muldrew,
Sylvan Ontario, 1905

Until well past the mid-twentieth century, the forest industry considered trembling aspen a weed. It was a species to be eradicated, mechanically or chemically, in order to promote conifer growth. Despite aspen's abundance and broad distribution, its commercial potential was slow to be recognized. Increasing worldwide demand for wood products, coupled with new technology to convert aspen's short fibers into pulp and paper, or to fabricate the many varieties of panel boards, changed all that.

In the 1930s and 1940s aspen was primarily used for excelsior (shavings for packing material), crates and boxes, and a few odds and ends such as chicken coops, bee hives, and washboards. There was a time when half-sawn aspen was used for stable floors, for despite its softness, it wears well.

From 1965 to 1988, the use of aspen increased by 500 percent. Today aspen processing is a multi-billion-dollar business, employing thousands of people and supporting countless communities. Aspen is converted into paper products of all kinds — from tissue to corrugated board to fine printing paper.

At the same time, the panelboard industry has blossomed, developing a broad range of 4x8 products, including aspen plywood, waferboard and oriented strand board (OSB) for construction. The first aspen waferboard, called "Aspenite," was produced in 1962 in Saskatchewan. The prairie provinces, Ontario, Quebec, and the Lakes states are now dotted with state-of-the-art processing plants using aspen from the boreal forest.

Other aspen products are pallets, laths, moldings, Venetian blinds, core stock for doors, hockey stick handles, and kitchen woodenware. Since it cracks or "checks" less than most species, it has become a favorite for stackwall and log homes. Aspen veneer is converted into match sticks and, because the wood is odorless and tasteless, chopsticks, tongue depressors, and ice-cream sticks.

While the life expectancy of trembling aspen may be up to 90 years, trees normally deteriorate long before that. The effects of insects and diseases, and the species' susceptibility to heart rot and stain render the wood of most mature aspens unusable. Healthy young trees, however, produce acceptable framing lumber, if properly seasoned.

The wood is light, soft, straight-grained, finely textured, and easy to work with. It takes nails, glue, paints, and stains well, and does not splinter. It is often a less expensive substitute for basswood for wood carving and sculpting.

If ever there was a tree that could boast of being a "true champion" of multiple use, it is the versatile poplar. In addition to serving a wide variety of man's needs, it provides home and food for wildlife, heals quickly our scarred landscape and provides a bright splash of fall color to dazzle the eye.
Environment Canada Forestry Report, 1974

grouse grub and beaver building material

Many historical events, hitherto explained solely in terms of human enterprise, were actually biotic interactions between people and land.

Aldo Leopold,
A Sand County Almanac

The complex interdependence of the plant and animal community is evident everywhere — lynx and hares, woodcock and worms, budworm and balsam fir, ospreys and fish, dragonflies and mosquitoes, monarch butterflies and milkweed, hummingbirds and wildflower nectar, to name but a few. Two wildlife species, beaver and ruffed grouse, are reliant on trembling aspen.

It is no coincidence that the original range of beaver in North America corresponded exactly with that of trembling aspen. Beaver need aspen. Adults consume 1 to 2 kilograms (2–4 lbs.) of the soft thin bark daily, and they use the branches and smaller trees to construct their lodges and engineer their intricate and virtually indestructible dams. The longest beaver dam on record is 652 meters, or half a mile wide. It takes half a hectare of poplar, over an acre, to support a typical family of five beavers for two years.

Without poplar as the habitat for beaver, the early history of Canada might have been dramatically different. The pursuit of beaver pelts by trappers and traders to furnish the fashionable felt hats of France was the driving force behind the early exploration and development of the country.

The range of ruffed grouse also mirrors that of trembling aspen. Grouse rely on all stages of aspen growth. Under the shelter of thickets of young suckers, the female leads her brood in foraging for protein-rich insects. Grouse breed and nest in mid-size stands. And in winter, adults weighing half a kilogram nimbly maneuver the stiff limbs of older poplars to reach their evening meal of male flower buds. Then a quick dive into their snow burrow to snugly spend the night. Trembling aspen is critical for the winter and spring survival of grouse. The buds are high in fiber, and a good source of calcium and vitamin A.

Other gamebirds, such as bobwhite quail, sharp-tailed grouse, and prairie chickens, rely on aspen as well. In the northern prairie provinces, and elsewhere in the boreal, mature trembling aspen are the exclusive roosting habitat of big brown bats. The bats move in after yellow-bellied sapsuckers have excavated nesting cavities in decaying heartwood.

Snowshoe hares and cottontail rabbits gnaw the bark off young trees, often girdling them in the process. Deer and moose browse the twigs and leaves of young suckers; when their populations are high, overbrowsing can cause young trees to be permanently deformed or die. Elk, or wapiti, supplement their grass diet in autumn with fallen aspen leaves. And porcupines, who show distinct taste preferences in different areas, are aspen bark feeders as well.

Furry male catkins dangle from the leaf tips before the leaves unfurl.

of caterpillars and cankers

There are over 300 insects and 150 diseases that attack trembling aspen; two are particularly noteworthy.

The forest tent caterpillar, a rather handsome little creature, causes widespread devastation when its population soars; outbreaks have covered over 100,000 square kilometers, or 40,000 square miles. Millions of what some people call "army worms" can defoliate a poplar, or a whole stand of poplar, in a matter of days. Standing beneath a canopy of aspen under attack, one can hear what sounds like steady rainfall on the leaf litter — but it isn't rain.

The name tent caterpillar is a misnomer. This critter, unlike its *Malacosoma* cousins, eastern, northern, and prairie tent caterpillars, does not hang around long enough to build a tent.

Having consumed all there is to consume, the army descends the bare trees and marches on, searching for more poplar, but eating anything green in its path — alders, evergreens, even garden plants. Streetwise they are not — their fatality rate in crossing highways and railway tracks is so tremendous that they turn pavement and rails slick and dangerous.

Within weeks the resilient aspens recover. They grow another set of leaves, usually of odd shapes and sizes, and carry out the photosynthesis that keeps them alive. As for the caterpillars, nature takes its course. Within two or three years they die of starvation or attacks by parasites, and virtually disappear.

One such parasite is a flesh-fly, similar in appearance to the housefly, which destroys tent caterpillars by laying its eggs in their cocoons. The maggots, in the millions, then feed on the caterpillars. The fly

Throughout the boreal forest, and as far south as Mexico, autumn aspens lend a touch of splendor to the landscape. Forests of pure aspen are usually a mosaic of genetically identical clones, each with its own subtle shading of yellow.

too can be a nuisance in the woods, for, despite its big red eyes, it doesn't appear to see very well, and buzzes into one's face, eyes, and ears with annoying regularity. Fortunately they last only a few days, before they too are gone, their role in nature's ongoing saga fulfilled.

Hypoxylon canker is the other major threat to trembling aspen. Airborne spores of the fungus enter the tree through wounds such as broken branches. The fungus destroys the inner bark, ultimately girdling and killing the tree. Signs of hypoxylon are orange discoloration of the bark in the first year, blistering and cracking the next year, and finally in the third year hard gray patches that appear within the orange outline of the canker. By this time the damage is done. Trees should be cut down and all wood and branches destroyed or removed.

aspen on the homestead

And softly thro' the altered air
Hurries a timid leaf.
Emily Dickinson (1830–1886)

Some suggest that trembling aspen is not a great choice for an ornamental. But it does have a lot going for it. It's not fussy about the soil it grows in, as long as it's not too wet or not too dry. It is easily planted from root cuttings, grows fast in its early years, and will provide shade long before most other trees will. In early spring male catkins hang like fringe from the boughs; in summer even the slightest breeze will set the leaves fluttering. All year round its yellowish green bark provides a pleasant contrast to the grays and browns of most other species. In autumn, depending on where you live or the genes of the tree you have planted, the foliage will be attractive, ranging from a honey yellow to a pleasant shade of red. Mostly they are golden.

The downside is aspen's susceptibility to a vast array of insects and diseases, its inability to grow in the shade, and the likelihood it will sucker to create a grove of aspen rather than a single tree. The latter may be an asset if one has the space.

In the prairie provinces, aspens and their hybrids have been planted as shade trees around homesteads, and as farm shelterbelts, since the turn of the century. Shelterbelts prevent soil erosion, reduce drifting snows, and provide visual relief to the flatness of the countryside. They also supply critical habitat for a variety of wildlife.

bitter medicine, but it works

Throughout the tremendous range of trembling aspen, Native people discovered the medicinal value of its inner bark. It was removed, scraped, chewed, baked, shredded, dried, or powdered, and then steeped or boiled and drunk for the relief of fevers, earaches, coughs and colds, as a blood-strengthening tonic, and as a vermifuge for children. It made one sweat, it was bitter medicine, but it worked. From the Dene of the north to the Delaware of the south, from the Cree of the prairies to the Penobscot in Maine, Native people knew it worked. Naturally. The active ingredient is salicin, better known to us today as aspirin. Poplars are members of the willow family, the original organic source of ASA.

Astringent salves were also made by mixing bark with animal fat for application in the nostrils for colds, and on cuts and sores for prompt healing. The Tête de Boule boiled the fibrous roots down to a syrup, which they rubbed on painful joints. Saskatchewan's Woods Cree applied fresh crushed leaves to bee stings to soothe the irritation.

The other aspen or poplar species were similarly used by Native people, but each had its own peculiar medicinal niche as well.

The Plums

Canada plum

(*Prunus nigra*)

prunier noir
prunier du Canada
prunier sauvage

American plum
wild plum

(*Prunus americana*)

prunier d'Amérique

Lakota: *kan'tahucan*

Leaf
- simple, alternate; oval, with pointed toothed tip; tapering at base; 6–12 cm (2–5") long;
- teeth sharply pointed (*P. americana*), or rounded with tiny glands at tips (*P. nigra*);
- upper side dark green, smooth; underside paler, with fuzzy midvein;
- leafstalks 8–18 mm (⅓–¾") long, often with 1–3 glands near base of leaf;
- turn orange to purple in autumn.

Flower
- showy, white, 5-petalled, 18–25 mm (¾–1") wide; in loose clusters of 2–4; fragrant;
- before or while leaves unfold; on previous year's twigs;
- *P. nigra* slightly larger, often with pink tinge before fading.

Fruit
- yellow to reddish orange to red; indented on one side; 2–3 cm (approx. 1") in diameter;
- flesh yellow, clings to stone; edible, sour;
- stone oval, flattened, hard, smooth; 14–20 mm (½–¾") long; varying ripening times;
- good crop every 1–2 years.

Twig
- smooth, dark gray or brown; bitter almond taste;
- on branches with thorns or short spur shoots;
- buds grayish brown, small, pointed.

Bark
- on younger trees, thin, smooth, dark grayish brown; with lenticels;
- on older trees, rough, with vertical plate-like scales.

Wood
- heavy, hard, strong, close-grained;
- heartwood reddish brown; thin sapwood paler.

Height
5–9 m (15–30')

Diameter
20–25 cm (8–10")

Longevity
40–60 years

200

Both wild and Canada plums are a treat for wildlife and humans alike.

our native plums

During his 1535 voyage of discovery, Jacques Cartier reported to his king on the indigenous people and flora and fauna he encountered. From Ile d'Orléans, not far from the future site of Quebec City, he wrote: *They also have plums, which they dry as we do for the winter: they call them Honesta.* Four years later, Hernando de Soto recorded in his memoirs, from what is today the state of Georgia: *The plum trees grow in fields without planting or dressing them, and are as big and as rancke as though they grew in gardens digged and watered.*

Cartier had discovered the Canada plum (*Prunus nigra*), and de Soto the wild plum (*P. americana*). Of the ten or so species of plums native to North America, these two are widespread, but scattered, throughout southern Canada and the eastern and southern states. Wild plum is the more southerly of the two. It grows from lower New England to northern Florida and New Mexico, up through the foothills of the Colorado Rockies, the Dakotas to Saskatchewan, and east to the Carolinian forest of southern Ontario.

The hardier Canada plum ranges from southern Manitoba to the provinces and states surrounding the Great Lakes, the St. Lawrence River valley, and parts of New Brunswick and New England. Isolated populations occur beyond the ranges of both species.

For centuries, native plums have captured the interest of amateur and professional horticulturists alike. They have been transplanted both within and outside their natural ranges, crossbred with each other and with European plums, and used as the hardy rootstock for grafting commercial varieties.

Native plum trees are at home along roadsides, on streambanks, in fencerows, in old pastures, and on hilly slopes rich in lime. They are not trees of the forest — they require full sunlight to grow, and their size does not allow them to compete with larger species.

Plums are members of the wide-ranging rose family, and are closely related to cherries, peaches, apricots, and almonds.

beauty and bounty

Both native plum trees merit consideration around the home or cottage, as ornamentals and as fruit trees. The clusters of beautiful white blossoms herald the imminent arrival of summer, and the autumn foliage joins the maples in a display of color. The plump, juicy fruits contribute to nature's wild harvest, to be preserved in jams, jellies, and sauces.

Aside from their need for full sunlight, plums are not highly demanding. They do prefer moist well-drained soils which are pH neutral or slightly alkaline. The shallow roots make transplanting a cinch. If planted as soon as the frost is out of the ground, success rates are high. Like staghorn sumach, plums spread rapidly by suckers from their shallow roots. Plant one and you get a dozen more as a bonus. If only one tree is desired, suckers should be mowed or removed; if space is available, they may be allowed to spread into a plum thicket. Like commercial fruit trees, wild plums can be pruned (the pun is unavoidable) to encourage more fruit, or left *au naturel.*

Seeds should be sown as soon as the plums ripen. Remove the flesh and bury the stones 3–5 centimeters (1–2") deep in the seedbed. Mulch for the winter. Normally less than half the seeds will germinate, so plant twice what is required. Protect from rodents. If the soil is acidic, add dolomitic lime before sowing; fertilizer is not required. Seedlings will be ready to outplant in the spring following the first growing season.

Native plums do not require a lot of space and will share the beauty of their spring blossoms and the bounty of their fall fruit within a few years. In northern climates, try Canada plum; further south, wild plum. In the Great Lakes region, plant both.

plum forgotten

The wide heartwood of the plums has a rich reddish brown color, and is hard, strong, and heavy. But because of its diminutive size, it has thus far been overlooked for commercial use. There may be a small business opportunity out there for some entrepreneurial woodworker or artisan.

the physical and the spiritual

It is not clear whether Native people cultivated plum trees or simply gathered fruit from nearby groves of wild trees. Plums were an important item in their diet, fresh or dried into prunes for winter sustenance. When the Pawnee were relocated from Nebraska to Oklahoma, they carried with them dried, unpitted wild plums. Plum thickets arose wherever they built lodges in their new territory.

Aside from being a food staple, plum trees yielded both medicines and dyes. The Cheyenne and Ojibway crushed and boiled rootlets and root bark with the roots and fruit of other shrubs as a cure for diarrhea and worms. Iroquois chose the fruit as their diarrhea remedy. The Meskwaki used wild plum root bark as an astringent, and steeped a Canada plum bark tea to settle upset stomachs. The Omaha applied boiled root bark to soothe and heal skin scrapes and abrasions.

Ojibway included wild plum inner bark and roots in their dye recipes, to "fix" the colors derived from the bark and roots of other plants such as bloodroot, red osier dogwood, and sumach.

Iroquois brewed a coffee-like beverage by adding boiling water to dried plums. The Meskwaki made a plum butter from both varieties of plums, while other tribes produced a plum sauce — long before the eggroll was introduced to North America.

The Teton Dakota fashioned religious wands from young plum trees and root suckers, to which they attached offerings of tobacco to the spirits for relief of the ill.

Like cherries, also members of the rose family, various parts of plum trees contain cyanogenic compounds and are poisonous. Of course, the fruit is not only harmless, it is healthful.

just desserts for omnivores

Bees and other insects tap into a spring source of pollen and nectar from wild plum flowers. Plum trees in hedges, thickets, windbreaks, and fencerows provide both food and shelter for game birds such as pheasants, bobwhite quail, and prairie chickens.

The fruit is a favorite of deer, muskrats, and gray and red foxes. Mice and rabbits comprise over half the fall and winter dinners of red foxes, but fruit is their dessert. Plums, fresh or frozen, round out their well-balanced diet.

Heavy and habitually hungry black bears, omnivores as well, often shatter the stiff branches by clambering up the small trees to gorge themselves on ripe and juicy plums.

Pin Cherry

(*Prunus pensylvanica*)

fire cherry
bird cherry
wild red cherry
hay cherry

cerisier de Pennsylvanie
merisier
cerisier d'été
petit merisier

Oneida: *ganadjie'gwa*

Leaf
- simple, alternate; narrow; pointed at the tip; 6–12 cm (2½–5") long;
- bright shiny green on top; underside slightly paler;
- tiny, uneven, incurved teeth; thin and fragile;
- often bright scarlet in autumn, or half-green, half-red;
- least poisonous of the native cherry leaves.

Flower
- white, with 5 petals, 8–12 mm (¼–½") wide; in clusters;
- on slender stems 2–3 cm (1") long, emanating from a central point;
- showy; appear with unfolding of leaves in spring.

Fruit
- bright red, 5–8 mm (¼") round; thin, edible, but sour pulp;
- borne on long stems; ripen late August; pits poisonous;
- begin bearing fruit at age 5–10; bumper crop every 3 years.

Twig
- very slender, wine red, shiny, often coated with thin gray film;
- almond odor when crushed; bitter-tasting;
- buds reddish brown, tiny, roundish; cluster at tip of twig.

Bark
- on younger trees, smooth, shiny, dark red brown; with raised orange lenticels;
- on older trees, cracking into papery horizontal strips.

Wood
- moderately soft, light, weak, close-grained, porous; aromatic;
- heartwood variable — light reddish brown, pink, greenish; sapwood narrow, yellowish;
- annual growth rings fairly distinct.

Height
8–12 m (25–40')

Diameter
10–35 cm (4–14")

Longevity
30–40 years

Each spring, five-petaled white flowers blossom in clusters at the end of the twigs.

the pioneering pin cherry

Pin cherry is a pioneer. It colonizes forest sites denuded by wildfire, clearcuts, insect infestations, or other major disturbances. Cherry seeds can lie buried and dormant in cool, shaded soil for 50 years, fallen from some long-deceased tree or dropped by birds who ate the fruit and passed the pits. In either case, the seeds await the opportunity to germinate. With the tree overstory gone, full sunlight and high soil temperatures trigger germination. A forest begins anew.

Pin cherry seedlings, with other early succession species such as raspberry, aspen, or gray birch, reclaim the site. Their shallow roots penetrate and bind the soil, preventing erosion and nutrient loss. Their rich leaves

When ripe, pin cherries disappear quickly, consumed by a wide variety of songbirds, gamebirds, and mammals.

add minerals and organic matter. They grow rapidly to provide shade and shelter for later-succession trees such as yellow birch, balsam fir, or sugar maple, whose light seeds are blown onto the site.

During their short lifespan of 30 to 40 years, pin cherries nurse the seedlings of longer-lived trees beneath them. By the time they reach maturity, their ecological mission is complete, and they gradually die off. Whether the forest that succeeds them evolves to a climax stage, or is in turn destroyed by a disturbance, is not predictable. But if a disturbance does occur, pin cherry seeds, as always, lie buried and dormant, ready to start the cycle anew.

The most dramatic disturbances followed by early succession species such as pin cherry are abandoned gravel pits and quarries, strip mines, and paved roads. On all of these sites one may find pin cherry, virtually without soil, struggling to reinstate the forest — stunning examples of the resilience of nature, and its relentless determination to return to its former state.

Pin cherries are not necessarily restricted to post-disturbance sites, however. Wherever there is full sunlight — roadsides, forest edges, abandoned fields, and fencerows — pin cherries will flourish.

cherry delight

The diminutive pin cherry adds a delightful accent to the home landscape year round — clusters of white blossoms in spring, light and graceful foliage throughout summer, bright red fruit in August, crimson leaves in autumn, and the burgundy red bark and boughs throughout winter. The tiny ripe cherries are an open invitation to dozens of species of songbirds to visit one's property.

To plant from seed, gather the fruit when ripe in late summer, remove the flesh, bury the pits 1 centimeter (½") deep, and cover with light mulch. Be sure it is a sunny location. Remove the mulch in spring to allow the soil to warm up, and the seeds will germinate. One may wish to plant half a dozen or more, about 30 centimeters (1') apart. Later the best trees may be selected and the others removed, or all may be left as a cluster.

Black knot, a fungus common to all native cherries and plums, can be a problem, but not an insurmountable one. Unsightly black masses, descriptively nicknamed *crottes de chien* in French, grow on the twigs and branches, and may kill a whole branch. Simply cut off the branch about 15 centimeters (6") below the knot, and burn it so the spores can not re-infect the tree.

different strokes

The diversity of our forests provides habitat for an equal diversity of wildlife. While some animals are generalists, most have a niche. Some require old growth; some need wetlands; some prefer mature hardwoods, some young softwoods, some mixed woods. "Edge species" depend on a mix of forest and clearing. In late summer, at least 17 species of songbirds prefer the habitat of the early successional forests of pin cherry. Pin cherries comprise one quarter of the fall diet of cedar waxwings, robins, evening grosbeaks, thrushes, and eastern bluebirds.

The tart cherries are also consumed by deer, red foxes, bears, skunks, raccoons, and red squirrels. Ruffed and sharp-tailed grouse eat both the fruit in the fall and the buds in winter. Snowshoe hares, sometimes called varying hares, love to gnaw on the thin red bark; when their cyclical populations peak, they can girdle and kill young trees.

Native knowledge of herbs

They were not subject to diseases, and knew nothing of fevers. If any accident happened to them by falling, by burning, or in cutting wood . . . they did not need a physician. They had knowledge of herbs, of which they made use and straightaway grew well.
Nicolas Denys, 1672

The fruit of the poor pin cherry may be impossible to eat, but somehow word spread among distant Native peoples that other parts of the tree had great possibilities as medicine. Quebec Mohawk and Michigan Potawatomi both prescribed a cough remedy made from the inner bark. Likewise the Iroquois of northern New York and the Ojibway of Minnesota each brewed decoctions of crushed pin cherry roots for stomach pain and disorders. The Maliseet of New Brunswick ground the inner bark into a fine baby powder and talc; the nomadic Tête de Boule of western Quebec grated it and applied it to babies' umbilical cords for prompt healing.

Prairie Cree used the inner bark as a cure for sore eyes, a common affliction among Native people, whose food and warmth depended on open fires, often with inadequate smoke ventilation, in their winter dwellings.

Facing page: In autumn, diminutive pin cherries contribute more than their share of color to the landscape. Leaves are often half red, half green. Soon the leaves drop, contributing minerals and organic matter to the soil, just part of their job as pioneers.

Black Cherry
(*Prunus serotina*)

rum cherry
cabinet cherry
black wild cherry
wild cherry
mountain black cherry

cerisier noir
cerisier tardif
cerisier d'automne

Forest Potawatomi: *okwe'minum*

Leaf
- simple, alternate; long narrow oval; tapered at both ends; tip pointed; 6–14 cm (2½–5½") long; poisonous;
- upper side shiny dark green; underside paler, with cork-coloured fuzz along midvein;
- thick, somewhat leathery texture; incurved teeth;
- stalk 2 cm (⅔") long, with 1 or more red glands at leaf base;
- turn yellow, orange, or red in the fall.

Flower
- tiny; 5-petalled; in loose clusters 9–14 cm (4–6") long, at end of new shoots;
- after leaves fully grown; contain both male and female parts (perfect);
- insect pollinated.

Fruit
- in hanging clusters, on yellow central stem; round, 8–10 mm (¼–½") in diameter;
- turn from green to red to black at maturity in late summer or early fall;
- cherries thick-skinned, with bittersweet pulp; wine-like flavor; contain 1 pit;
- good crop every 3–4 years.

Twig
- slender, reddish brown, with gray film and lenticels;
- bitter almond odor when broken;
- buds slightly flattened, lower half hugging the twig; reddish or greenish brown;
- spiraling around twig;

Bark
- on younger trees, smooth, dark reddish brown, with grayish horizontal lenticels;
- on older trees, charcoal black, with large flaky scales loose at the edges.

Wood
- moderately heavy, hard, strong, stiff; straight-grained; fine-textured;
- heartwood rich deep red to reddish brown, durable; thin sapwood yellowish white;
- annual growth rings distinct.

Height	Diameter	Longevity
15–30 m (50–100')	40–100 cm (16–40")	150–200 years

at home in the Alleghenies

Black cherry is at home in the deciduous forest region, with its heart in the Allegheny mountains. There its slender black trunk towers, straight and limbless, 20 meters (60') or more, before it unfolds into a dominant crown. It is a woodsman's delight. The further north black cherry roams, the smaller its stature. At its most northerly limit in Ontario, Quebec and the Maritimes, it may shrink to little more than a small tree or tall shrub.

Black cherry ranges from Nova Scotia to North Dakota, and south to Texas and Florida. A variety grows in Mexico, Guatemala, and parts of South America.

cherry blossoms

> *Loveliest of trees, the cherry now*
> *Is hung with bloom along the bough*
> *And stands about the woodland ride*
> *Wearing white for Eastertide.*
>
> A. E. Housman,
> 1859–1936

The loose clusters of white flowers are pollinated by insects.

Despite its white blossoms, lustrous dark green foliage and colorful and prolific fruit, black cherry is a rather unpredictable ornamental. While the crown is generally oval in shape, the sparse, heavy, and irregular limbs can give it a straggly appearance. Ornamentally, it is no match for the Japanese Yoshino cherries of Washington, D.C., whose spectacular blossoms give the capital cityscape a unique charm each spring.

Black cherry seedlings commonly develop a tap root, a point to keep in mind if digging up a wildling for transplanting. By the sapling stage the tap root is replaced by a shallow root system. Cherry roots are lazy. If they can soak up the moisture they need near the soil surface, they won't dig deeper. Cherries on wet, poorly drained sites are prone to toppling over in heavy winds.

In the wild, fruit drop at maturity, and are buried beneath the autumn leaves, so that they are insulated over the winter. To plant from seed, gather ripe cherries, remove the flesh, and dry at 32° C (90° F) for three hours. Immediately sow the seeds 2–3 cm (1") deep in moist, well-drained prepared soil, and mulch for the winter. Protect against mice. Leave in the nursery bed for one growing season, and transplant the seedlings to a permanent sunny home early the following spring.

As with all tree seeds, 100 percent germination is rare; so plant more than needed. If more survive than required, they can be potted as gifts to children that will last a lifetime and more.

world-class wood

Black cherry is one of the finest cabinet woods in the world. Like fine wine, it mellows with age. Freshly sawn, the mildly aromatic heartwood has a warm reddish tone; with exposure to light over time, it darkens into a deep rich amber.

In the region of its best development [black cherry] does not hold a high place, because of the presence of more valuable species . . . it is too short lived and of too limited economic value to be recommended for extensive planting.

USDA Forest Service
Circular, 1907

The times have changed. Once considered a poor man's substitute for mahogany, black cherry came into its own in the twentieth century, and is now one of the most sought-after and prestigious native woods for furniture, flooring, doors, stair posts, handrails, gun stocks, piano actions, wall paneling, and caskets. Because of its strength, hardness, and low shrinkage, it was traditionally the wood of choice for printing and engraving blocks.

It is not surprising that cabinetmakers find cherry a pleasure to work with. Once seasoned, it does not shrink, warp, or check. It saws cleanly, planes to perfection, and has little blunting effect on tools. It glues readily, takes nails and screws firmly, turns well on a lathe, and finishes with a beautiful luster. When the project is completed, cherry's hardness withstands normal household abuse without marring.

Supply and price are black cherry's limiting factors. Environmental concerns over the status of the endangered Indiana bat in Pennsylvania's Allegheny National Forest, the prime growth region of cherry, have reduced its availability. It is now the most expensive wood in North America.

black cherry cough and cold medicine

The benefits of black cherry are not limited to its wood. Native people valued it as one of their most important medicines to relieve the symptoms of colds, consumption, and related respiratory ailments. The Ojibway, Onondaga, Seneca, Mohawk, Mi'kmaq and Maliseet boiled or steeped the inner bark into an expectorant cough syrup, inhalant for head colds, poultice for headaches, or steam treatment for bronchitis and chest pains. Cherry bark extracts are still used today in commercial cough syrups.

The Shinnecook of Long Island and Mohegan of Connecticut fermented the cherries for relief from dysentery. The juice from the boiled bark yielded a bitter but healthful tonic, and the bark itself was applied to cuts, sores, and wounds to speed healing.

Early settlers blended black cherries with rum or brandy for a drink they called "cherry bounce," the root of the local name "rum cherry."

fruit for all

Warbling vireos and yellow-throated vireos build their nests among branch forks high in the crowns of black cherries. Robins and starlings eat the ripe cherries and regurgitate the pits, helping to propagate new trees. They are among the 46 bird species that eat the high-fiber, high-protein, and high-fat fruit. Mice, chipmunks, squirrels, red foxes, and white-tailed deer eat all the fruit they can muster. Black bears stand on their hind legs to strip cherry clusters from the branch tips, and whole families of raccoons clamber among the limbs to gorge themselves on cherries.

Black cherry leaves, twigs, and fruit pits contain prussic acid, a cyanide compound, and can be fatal to browsing livestock. Deer, however, appear immune to it; where black cherry grows, the twigs and leaves of young seedlings and sprouts are one of their favorite foods. Black cherry is also host to over 200 species of butterflies and moths. Honey bees pollinate the flowers in their pursuit of nectar.

Choke Cherry
(*Prunus virginiana*)

cabinet cherry
rum cherry
wild cherry

cerisier à grappes
cerisier sauvage
cerisier de Virginie

Assiniboin: *champah*

Leaf
- simple, alternate; inversely egg-shaped; thin; 6–10 cm (2¼–4") long;
- base tapered or slightly rounded; abruptly tapering to a short pointed tip;
- edges finely and sharply toothed; short stalk with glands near base of leaf;
- upper side dull dark green; underside paler, with tufts of fuzz at vein junctions;
- turn orange or yellow in the fall.

Flower
- 5-petaled small white flowers, with prominent yellow stamens; after leaves unfold;
- in dense bottlebrush clusters 8–14 cm (3–5½") long, on a central stem; at end of new shoots;
- contain both male and female parts; noticeable bitter almond smell.

Fruit
- round, fleshy, edible, astringent; pea-sized; with one large round pit;
- in nodding clusters, on a red central stem;
- when ripe, amber to crimson to black.

Twig
- somewhat thick, gray brown, smooth; rank odor when crushed;
- buds pointed, chocolate brown, angling away from the twig.

Bark
- on younger trees, thin, smooth, dull gray-brown;
- lenticels not elongated, but noticeable; hard, heavy, weak; fine-textured;
- on older trees, scaly, almost black.

Wood
- heartwood light brown; thick sapwood paler.

Height	Diameter	Longevity
4–9 m (15–30')	8–15 cm (3–6")	20–40 years

the ubiquitous choke cherry

Under ideal conditions, choke cherry develops into a small tree, but frequently it is not much more than a tall shrub. From Newfoundland to the Yukon, to California and to Texas, its varieties comprise the widest-ranging woody plant on the continent. It is equally at home as a pioneer on shifting sand dunes, rocky escarpments, or the borders of wetlands. Choke cherry thrives under just about any condition imaginable, except heavy shade.

East of the Rockies, choke cherry commonly lines farm fencerows, roadside ditches, stream banks, and forest edges, or creeps onto idle pastures. Along with pin cherry, it has been planted extensively for wildlife habitat in farm shelterbelts on the prairies.

pretty dangerous

Choke cherry adds charm to the home landscape from spring to fall. The arching tubular clusters of tiny white blossoms are among the most attractive the forest has to offer. In late summer, the colorful little cherries invite a host of birds, and in autumn the foliage turns pleasant shades of yellow and orange.

Young choke cherries transplant well, if care is taken to dig up all the roots, along with as much of its home soil as possible. Any site with adequate sunlight will do, but they flourish on moist well-drained soil. In time, the roots will likely sucker, generating a little cherry thicket.

A word of warning: the twigs, leaves, bark and pits all contain prussic acid, and in sufficient quantities can be fatal to humans and browsing animals alike. If you have a pet goat or llama, scratch choke cherry off your tree planting list.

harvest time

If you plan to make choke cherry jelly, be prepared to beat the throngs of wild critters to the ripe fruit. Gamebirds, songbirds, and mammals of all sizes may not wait for the crop to totally ripen. Robins, whom we normally envisage tugging at earthworms in the spring, actually depend on fruit for 60 percent of their diet. Before their fall migration, they gorge themselves on choke cherries. They regurgitate the pits, "planting" new trees, ensuring that they and future generations will have a sustained supply of the fruit.

Robins are not alone. Over 70 species of songbirds consume choke cherries — among them thrushes, grosbeaks, woodpeckers, jays, bluebirds, catbirds, and kingbirds. Ruffed grouse and ring-necked pheasants also harvest the purple fruit as a late summer delicacy.

What the feathered set don't devour, their furry friends finish off — from lowly mice and voles, on up to chipmunks, squirrels, skunks, foxes, deer, black bear, and moose.

pucker up

> . . . *if they be not very ripe, they so furre the mouth that the tongue will cleave to the roofe, and the throat wax horse with swallowing those red Bullies . . .*
>
> William Wood, 1634
> *New-England's Prospect*

Choke cherry's bitter, but not altogether unpleasant taste, and its puckering effect on the mouth is reflected in its Penobscot name *ebi'mi'nuzi*, "bitter berry wood," and the Maliseet *ul-wi-min-ul*, "berries that draw together (the lips)." (This translation appeared in a 1944 paper in the *Acadian Naturalist* journal. While researching my first book, *Weeds of the Woods*, in 1983, I related this to Peter Paul, a Maliseet elder, at his home in Woodstock, NB. He laughed, and said: "The real meaning of the word is 'can't shit.' Those academics can never get it right." Choke cherry apparently draws together both the lips and the bowels.)

First Nations people took full advantage of the little tree's diverse therapeutic

At blossom time, dense clusters of white flowers adorn the branch tips.

properties. They created a healthful blood tonic by boiling the fruit, and sweetened the juice with honey or maple sugar. They boiled the inner bark, roots, and fruit to relieve cough and cold symptoms. It was used as a tea for stomach cramps and indigestion, as an appetite stimulant, a medicinal herb in sweat baths, a pre-natal blood purifier, a sedative, an eye wash, and a douche for hemorrhoids.

Wherever choke cherry grew, it was universally prescribed to treat diarrhea. Maritime Mi'kmaq, Maine Penobscot, Seneca in upstate New York, Hudson Bay Cree, Wisconsin Menominee, and Ponca of Nebraska all boiled the inner bark as an organic precursor to today's chemical concoctions.

camping caterpillars

Three different species of tent caterpillars — northern, eastern, and prairie — pitch their tents in choke cherry, and devour every leaf within reach. Colonies of the unrelated uglynest caterpillar do the same. All four can be controlled without chemicals. On a cold cloudy day when the caterpillars are not too venturesome, remove the nest and incinerate it, along with its contents. An effective alternative is to poke a hole in the nest and spray a bacterial insecticide (Bt) inside.

Choke cherry, like all cherries and plums, is susceptible to black knot fungus; for a description and treatment, see page 209. In severe cases, black knot can girdle and kill a tree.

White Oak
(*Quercus alba*)

stave oak

chêne blanc

Mohegan: *anaske'mezi*

Leaf
- simple, alternate; 5–9 rounded, toothless lobes, variable in shape and depth of notches; base tapered;
- upper side bright green; lower side paler; midrib yellow; 10–20 cm (4–8") long;
- when unfurling, dusty rose and velvety;
- turn russet brown or burgundy in autumn; some faded leaves persist all winter.

Flower
- while leaves unfolding; males and females on same tree;
- males yellowish green; in clusters of hanging delicate catkins 6–8 cm (2–3") long;
- females greenish red; at base of leaves; inconspicuous; wind pollinated.

Fruit
- acorns shiny brown at maturity in autumn; 1.5–2.5 cm (⅔–1") in diameter;
- quarter-covered by bowl-shaped cap with knobby scales; tip pointed;
- solitary, sometimes in pairs, occasionally in clusters; mature in one growing season;
- begin bearing acorns at age 20–25; good crop irregular, every 4–10 years.

Twig
- smooth, somewhat thick; reddish green, later becoming gray;
- terminal bud round, reddish brown, clustered with lateral buds;
- lateral buds slightly angled away from twig.

Bark
- on younger trees, smooth or slightly scaly; ash gray;
- on older trees, light gray, with shallow or deep fissures, and irregular thin scales.

Wood
- very heavy, hard, strong, stiff, straight-grained; durable; flexible;
- heartwood pale brown, rot-resistant; thin sapwood nearly white;
- annual growth rings distinct.

Height	Diameter	Longevity
20–35 m (65–115')	80–120 cm (30–48")	300–500 years

grandpappy of the oaks

The 60-plus species of oak in North America are members of the worldwide beech family. Botanists divide our oaks into two general groups: white oaks and red oaks. White oak leaves have rounded lobes, and their acorns mature in one growing season. Lobes of the red oak group have pointed tips, and their acorns take two years to ripen.

White oak is the grandpappy of the white oak group. It grows the largest, lives the longest, and ranges the furthest. Adaptable to a wide range of soils, it draws the line only where the soil is alkaline or wet. It thrives on bottomlands, where the soil is deep, fertile, and well-drained. In the Ohio River basin, white oaks routinely reach heights of 45 meters (150').

The U.S. Big Tree champion, in Wye Mills State Park in Maryland, sports a trunk over 3 meters (10') wide. A little long in the tooth, it is currently on an artificial life-support system — cables have been attached to the massive limbs to reinforce them against storm damage.

The range of white oak is roughly square, beginning in lower Maine, and extending down to the Florida panhandle, over to eastern Texas, and up to Minnesota. In Canada it is limited to the southwest corner of Quebec, the region north of Lakes Ontario and Erie as far as Georgian Bay, and the bottom of Lake Huron. The largest recorded white oak in Ontario, near Peterborough, is a respectable 27 meters (90') tall and just under 2 meters (7') in diameter.

White oak enjoys the triple distinction as the state tree of Connecticut, Maryland and Illinois.

not a trailer park tree

To plant a white oak, one requires three things — selflessness, lots of space, and an acorn. Slow-growing and long-lived, its benefits are bestowed upon future generations.

The planter, no matter how young, will never fully enjoy the fruits of his or her toils. White oak will flourish into a magnificent, tall, wide-spreading shade tree, but not within one's lifetime.

It is usually recommended that those who wish to plant a tree from seed nurture it in a nursery bed for a year or two, and then transplant it to its permanent site. Not so with white oak. As soon as an acorn is sown, it germinates, and the tap root is off and running, penetrating deeper and deeper into the soil. Transplanting, even as little as a year later, becomes a difficult chore.

Acorns are best sown directly onto their permanent site, in a sunny location, with the soil loosened as deeply as possible in a 1-meter (3') radius. As soon as they fall from the tree, plant six to eight sound (no insect holes) acorns in the middle of the site, about 20–30 centimeters (8–12") apart, cover with 2–3 centimeters (1") of tamped soil, mulch for the winter, and cover tightly to keep out rodents. If planting more than one tree, leave at least 10 meters (30') between planting sites, to allow each tree the space it will eventually need.

In early August of the following year, select the hardiest specimen, and snip off the rest at ground level. Fertilize annually, but do not add lime to the soil. White oaks, like white birch, are sensitive to ground disturbance and soil compaction, so minimize landscaping or construction activity above the wide-spreading roots.

tall ships and booze barrels

In the era of wooden ships, white oak was as invaluable as white pine. The pines created the tall masts and spars of the vessels, and the oaks the timbers, hulls, and decks. Impervious to water and resistant to rot, white oak was instrumental in the flourishing shipbuilding industry, a keystone in the fledgling North American economy. Shipyards, large and small, spawned scores of

Leaves can vary greatly in shape, but all white oaks have rounded, rather than pointed, edges.

villages, towns, and cities all along the Atlantic coast and inland waterways.

The same inherent qualities made white oak the cooper's choice for the staves of casks, barrels, and kegs for molasses and liquor. Today, rum and whiskey aged in white oak casks are still the hallmark of a premium product. Newfoundlanders originally produced their screech by "swishing" the dregs of West Indies rum from oak barrels. Tabasco sauce, made in Louisiana, is still aged in white oak barrels.

Today, used oak barrels sawn in two are popular flower planters for home and cottage. Eventually, of course, even white oak decays, but not until after many years of solid

service as liquid and landscape containers.

White oak's high resistance to impact, its waterproof properties, and attractive figure make it ideal for tongue-and-groove and parquet flooring. In North America it is not the first choice of furniture and cabinetmakers, but ironically, top-grade white oak lumber exported to Germany and Japan is very popular with furniture makers and architects in those countries.

White oak has a reputation as a difficult wood to work with. It shrinks considerably in drying, tends to crack or check in the process, doesn't take most glues well, and often splits when nailed. However, it shapes, planes, and mortises admirably, finishes nice-

Like all oaks, the leaves are alternate on the twig, with a cluster at the tip.

ly, and is less expensive than the hardwoods in greater demand, such as cherry and maple.

It is commonly used for doors, sashes, trim, and wainscotting. Its strength and durability, even without preservatives, accounts for its wide use in the south for railway ties. White oak veneer and decorative plywood are also some of its more common applications. Finally, white oak is among the

hottest burning fuelwoods, exceeded in Canada only by shagbark hickory and rock elm. A cord of white oak generates twice the heat value, for example, as balsam fir.

Not surprisingly, three-quarters of the white oak in the lumber yard comes from white oak itself; the rest is made up of bur oak, overcup oak, post oak, chestnut oak, swamp chestnut oak, swamp white oak,

Chinquapin oak, and west coast Garry oak. All are marketed simply as "white oak."

acorn energy

White oak acorns are low in protein and crude fiber, but high in carbohydrates. Mammals who need an energy boost to cope with winter consume whatever they can get their paws on in the fall. Raccoons, before denning in hollow trees; chipmunks, before hibernating in underground nests; black bears, whose heart rates drop when they curl up and snooze for the winter (they are not true hibernators); and white-tailed deer, who eat well before deep snow curtails their travels and they congregate in sheltered deer yards. Gray squirrels eat the nuts on the spot, and stash red oak acorns for winter. Porcupines, red foxes, and constantly craving red squirrels are other furry folk who rely on acorns.

There are at least 36 species of birds who consume white oak acorns. Blue jays are perhaps the most reliant — they carry them off by the scores and stash them in leaves, grass, and tree cavities, hopefully remembering where they hid them. Gamebirds such as wild turkeys, bobwhite quail, and ruffed grouse need the extra energy in their fall diet before winter sets in and the pickings get slimmer. Wood ducks are also acorn aficionados, as are almost all woodpeckers.

White oak crowns are choice nesting sites for robins, orioles, scarlet tanagers, red-eyed vireos, and Cerulean warblers; their eggs and nestlings are well hidden amid the thick limbs and dense foliage. Cerulean warblers are listed as "vulnerable" on Canada's endangered species list.

for an assortment of afflictions

Oaks have been part of the eastern North American forest ecosystem for millennia. Archeologists have unearthed acorns 5,000 years old. Oaks became both food and medicine as soon as the first Americans migrated southward into their range. Digs at Iroquois sites in Ontario, New York, Ohio, and Michigan revealed that Iroquois consumed acorns from uncultivated oaks as far back as AD 1000.

While white oak acorns were food, the inner bark was medicine. The Ojibway capitalized on its astringent properties by drinking a bark tea to treat diarrhea. The Penobscot and Menominee administered the decoction orally, or with enemas, to relieve hemorrhoids. The Mohegan and the Shinnecook steeped the tannin-rich bark into a liniment for sore muscles. The Illinois-Miami used the bark decoction to soothe sore eyes and to help heal wounds. Meskwakis prepared a bark tea for congestion; when taken in copious quantities, it induced vomiting and discharge of phlegm from the lungs.

White oak inner bark was classified as an official drug in the *U.S. Pharmacopoeia* for almost a century, and was likewise recognized in the *National Formulary* as recently as 1936.

White oak acorns contain less tannin than the red oaks, and are sweet and edible. Boiling further reduces the tannin level. In the nineteenth century, white settlers browned and pulverized the nuts into a coffee substitute; Native people boiled, dried, and ground them into meal for baking bread.

Bur Oak
(*Quercus macrocarpa*)

burr oak
mossycup oak
blue oak
scrub oak

chêne à gros fruits
chêne blanc frisé

Dakota: *uskuyecha-hu*

Leaf
- simple, alternate; shape very inconsistent; oblong, wider above the middle; 10–25 cm (4–10") long;
- lobes rounded and wavy; deeply indented near middle, almost to the midrib;
- base tapering to stalk 2–5 cm (1–2") long; grooved on top, rounded on bottom;
- upper side dark green, glossy; underside grayish green, downy;
- turn dull yellow or brown in autumn.

Flower
- males in clusters of slender, dangling, yellowish green catkins, 10–15 cm (4–6") long;
- females red, hairy, inconspicuous, usually solitary;
- male and female on same tree; before leaves fully formed.

Fruit
- large acorn 2–3 cm (approx. 1") diameter; half or more enclosed in deep knobby cup with fringed rim;
- matures in one growing season; edible, somewhat sweet;
- begin bearing acorns at age 30–40; good crop every 2–3 years.

Twig
- thick, yellowish brown, fuzzy; on branchlets with corky ridges;
- terminal bud reddish brown; clustered with several lateral buds and loose curly scales; lateral buds pressed against twig.

Bark
- on younger trees, grayish brown, becoming rough;
- on older trees, dark gray brown; thick; with deep furrows and scaly ridges.

Wood
- hard, heavy, strong, straight-grained;
- heartwood light to medium brown; thin sapwood nearly white;
- annual growth rings distinct.

Height
15–25 m (50–80')

Diameter
60–120 cm (24–48")

Longevity
200–300 years

The indentations of the variable-shaped leaves often extend almost to the midrib.

Bur oaks were the shock troops sent by the invading forest to storm the prairie. Each April, before the new grasses had covered the prairie with unburnable greenery, fires ran at will over the land, sparing only such old oaks as had grown bark too thick to scorch.

Aldo Leopold, 1949
A Sand County Almanac

Bur oaks in the Qu'Appelle River valley in Saskatchewan shrink in stature to that of a humble shrub. Hence the common name "scrub oak." In Manitoba, it joins with trembling aspen in the aspen parkland, the transition zone from prairie to boreal forest. In the American midwest, bur oak is the common oak found in savannas. Hardy and drought-resistant, it is also one of the more popular trees planted in prairie windbreaks and shelterbelts on both sides of the border.

from giant to dwarf

Bur oak's range is a little unusual. Its outline is an inverted equilateral triangle, starting in southeast Saskatchewan, extending south to the Gulf of Mexico in Texas, then northeast to the Montreal area, and back through Ontario across southern Manitoba. Outside the triangle, isolated pockets occur here and there, such as the Grand Lake area of New Brunswick, lower Maine, the shores of Lake Champlain dividing New York from Vermont, and in river valleys in Kansas and Nebraska. Otherwise it is virtually absent in almost all of Atlantic Canada, New England, the Atlantic seaboard, and the southern states.

Two-hundred-year-old bur oaks reach massive proportions on the rich bottomlands of the Ohio River valley and the basin of the Wabash River, the border between southern Illinois and Indiana. Even the acorns are large — up to 5 centimeters (2") long. South of the Ohio River, in Paris, Kentucky, resides the American Forests record tree, whose diameter measures 2.6 meters (8½').

a tree with character

If space provides, and with the right climate and soil, bur oak slowly develops into a truly magnificent shade tree. In the open, its massive trunk divides into thick, wide-spreading horizontal lower limbs, its upper branches ascending into a full, round, but rugged, crown. Not at all delicate, it has all the characteristics one associates with a mighty oak.

The ideal time to plant is in the fall, as soon as the acorns drop. Sow the acorns in a prepared seedbed, and cover with 2–3 centimeters (1") of tamped soil. Mulch, and cover with a screen or tarp to keep the squirrels and other pesky rodents away. When the risk of frost is gone in the spring, remove the cover and mulch, and partially shade the emerging seedlings.

Seedlings should be transplanted the following spring before the leaves unfold, ideally on moist, fertile, well-drained soil. Above ground, the little trees may not be all that impressive, but underground the tap root can penetrate a meter (3') or more in the first growing season. When transplanting, be sure to dig up the entire tap root and laterals, and ensure that the planting hole is deep and wide enough to spread them without curling.

Bur oak tolerates most city pollutants such as vehicle exhausts, smoke, soot, and ozone. It is an ideal city tree. But its size at maturity requires a large lot such as parks, school grounds, suburban office building sites, industrial parks, estates, or golf courses can provide.

at the lumberyard

When you shop for white oak at the lumber yard, you may get bur oak, swamp white oak, white oak itself, or any number of oaks that fall into the broad white oak grouping. Even expert wood technologists have difficulty differentiating among the various white oak species. Bur oak is not quite as heavy or as strong as white oak, but otherwise it has essentially the same characteristics. It is and has been used interchangeably for all the same purposes, such as flooring, furniture, boats, and liquid-bearing barrels and vats.

food, medicine, and dyestuff

To Native children, bur oak acorns were a natural fall treat. They gathered handfuls as the nuts fell from the trees, cracked them open, and ate the kernels raw. Not too many, mind you, for the tannin in the acorns can produce a serious bellyache. Native women buried the acorns in moist soil to mellow the flavor for later use, and then ground them into a meal for thickening soups or shaping into loaves. The Ojibway boiled the acorns or roasted them in hot ashes, to eat them whole or mashed, more or less as a vegetable side dish.

The Seneca and Pawnee stripped the inner bark off young trees, boiled it, and drank the decoction to relieve diarrhea. Some western tribes simply chewed the raw inner bark for the same purpose. The Meskwaki boiled the bark with staghorn sumac fruit and spurge roots to expel pinworms. The Ojibway boiled the bark with blackberry roots, and drank the mixture for lung problems.

The Ojibway recipe for a durable black dye contained bur oak inner bark and butternut bark and roots, which were combined with black earth, water. and the green husks of hazelnuts.

acorns for all

Acorns of the 60 to 70 oak species in North America are extremely valuable fall and winter food for songbirds, gamebirds, and large and small mammals. Generally low in protein, but high in carbohydrates, they supply the energy needed to survive winter.

Bur oak is no exception. Its large acorns contain about half the tannin of the red oaks, and are more palatable to a wider range of wildlife. Among acorn aficionados are black bears, wood ducks, squirrels of all kinds, wild turkeys, prairie chickens, woodpeckers of all sizes and descriptions, white-tailed deer, ruffed grouse, and raccoons.

Bur oak is particularly important on the prairies, where it is the only native oak. Not only are the acorns a source of food, but the tree provides cover and valuable nesting habitat for wildlife, including mourning doves.

not to worry

Bur oak, like most trees, hosts its share of caterpillars, loopers, sawflies, lace bugs, and galls. But most outbreaks are localized, and damage is rarely serious or extensive. Its very long taproot and wide spreading laterals render the tree sturdy in the heaviest of winds, and its thick bark protects it from fire. Bur oak is susceptible to soil compaction, and will not tolerate prolonged flooding. It is very drought resistant.

Red Oak
(*Quercus rubra*)

northern red oak
gray oak

chêne rouge
chêne boréal

Pawnee: *nahata-pahat*

Leaf
- simple, alternate; with 7–9 sharp pointed lobes; teeth with bristle tips;
- dull dark green above, apple green below; variable in shape; papery texture;
- pale yellow midrib and veins, raised on underside, lead to lobe tips;
- stalk round, grooved on top, yellow/green brown, about 3 cm (1") long;
- somewhat later than other hardwoods to reach full leaf in spring;
- turn deep scarlet in fall; one of last trees to shed; some dead leaves persist most of winter.

Flower
- male and female on same tree, while or after leaves unfold;
- females small and inconspicuous, in axils of current year's leaves;
- males in clusters of hanging catkins, in axils of last year's leaves.

Fruit
- acorn round, flat-topped, with sharply pointed tip, thin-shelled, shiny, reddish brown when ripe; bitter; 2–3 cm (about 1") diameter;
- beige saucer-shaped cap covers a quarter of acorn; attached to twig on a very short stem;
- takes 2 growing seasons to mature; ripens in autumn;
- begin bearing acorns at age 20–25; good seed crop every 2–5 years.

Twig
- fairly stout, reddish brown, hairless, grooved; pentagon-shaped; often with gray film;
- buds, shiny, hairless, reddish brown;
- larger terminal bud surrounded by cluster of smaller lateral buds.

Bark
- on younger trees, smooth, slate gray or greenish;
- on older trees, vertically grooved, with wide flat ridges;
- inner bark salmon pink.

Wood
- heavy, stiff, hard, strong, porous;
- heartwood reddish brown; thin sapwood almost white;
- pungent odor when freshly cut; later odorless and tasteless;
- annual growth rings distinct.

Height
20–25 m (65–80')

Diameter
40–90 cm (16–36")

Longevity
150 years

228

In autumn, leaves turn a variety of shades of red, magenta, and purple — part of the fall splendor.

the range of red oak

Those green-robed senators of mighty woods,
Tall oaks, branch-charmed by the earnest
stars,
Dream, and so dream all night without
a stir.

John Keats, 1795–1821

The British oaks of Sherwood Forest, some still living today that were saplings in the days of Robin Hood, the white oaks of North America, whose watertight wood built the brigantines that sailed the seas to defeat Napoleon, and the cork oaks of the Mediterranean region, without which there would be no vintage wines, are but some of the 500 to 600 oak trees and shrubs world-wide. There are 60 to 70 species of oak native to North America.

In 1535, Jacques Cartier, recollecting his first encounter with the mountain that is now surrounded by the city of Montreal, described the setting as: *the most beautiful country, and even better, full of oaks, as fine as those in the forests of France, and the earth beneath them was covered in acorns.* He was so impressed that he took acorns back to plant in France.

Red oaks range from Nova Scotia to southern Ontario, and as far south as the Carolinas and eastern Oklahoma. The further north, the smaller the trees. But their ideal growing region is the Ohio River valley, where they reach heights of 50 meters (160'). Occasionally found in pure stands, red oaks normally form part of mixed broadleaf ecosystems. Because of their intolerance of shade and their rapid growth, they are usually the dominant trees in such stands.

They prefer moist, well-drained, fertile sites, but often regenerate on drier sites where competition from other trees is less severe.

There is little doubt that oaks were far more plentiful before the arrival of the settlers. The prime farming zones of eastern North America coincide with the range and soil preferences of red oak. Upon arriving in the Niagara region in 1807, adventurer George Heriot lamented, *A stranger is here struck with sentiments of regret on viewing the numbers of fine oak-trees which are daily consumed by fire, in preparing the land for cultivation.*

Red oak is officially honored as the state tree of New Jersey and the arboreal emblem of Prince Edward Island.

the (in)edible acorn

Acorns of red oaks, unlike those of their cousins the white oaks, are bitter and unpalatable. They contain 5 to 6 percent tannin, an acrid water soluble compound used to tan animal hides. Squirrels and other forest critters don't seem to mind the taste, but humans will have to leach out the yellow compound to produce an edible acorn. Two boilings should do the trick. Natives would boil them in lye from wood ashes to get the same result. When dried, they were ready to be used in soups, or to be ground up into flour or meal for bread.

the ultimate ornamental

Forest-grown red oaks are tall and straight, often without a limb for the first 10 or 12 meters or so (30–40'). Open-grown trees are a different story. Large at the stump, they quickly branch out in all directions, with no particular pattern. If one has the space, these are the trees whose sturdy spreading branches are perfect for hanging a swing or building a tree house.

Picturesque throughout the year, they come into their own in the autumn, when their foliage turns a deep scarlet. Unlike the live oaks of the south, which hold their leaves all year long, red oaks shed most of their leaves, but always hold on to a few well into winter, a characteristic they share with their distant cousin the beech. This is an easy way to identify them in winter.

Red oaks are easily planted from acorns — in fact nature will do that for you, if there is a nearby seed source. Any place where there is fertile moist soil and litter in which the acorns can hide provides a potential birthplace for a young oak. Acorns that drop in the fall lie dormant all winter and germinate the next spring. For best results in home planting, do what nature does. Plant the acorns in the fall about 1–2 centimeters (½–1") deep and cover with leaves or dried grasses. In the spring, remove the mulch, and the acorns will begin germinating. Don't be surprised if the first leaves don't look exactly like red oak; the ones that follow will.

If you prefer to transplant a young tree, you will have to dig deep to get the whole tap root. They do respond well to transplanting, if it is carried out before the leaves unfold.

The only drawback to red oaks as ornamentals is the need to rake the leaves and acorns in the fall — squirrels will be happy to help with the latter. Oaks shed their leaves later than most hardwoods, so more than one raking is necessary. Because of their high lignin content, they do not decompose quickly, and are not recommended for composting.

Red oaks are beautiful, fast-growing, hardy, provide plenty of shade, are somewhat salt resistant — they make the ultimate ornamental . . . and excellent firewood.

food for forest critters

Throughout its range, red oak is one of the most important wildlife trees.

Wild turkeys, today recovering nicely after a near brush with extinction, depend upon a mix of mature oaks and clearings for

their habitat. Acorns, which they gobble whole, are vital to their winter survival. In early winter dominant males gorge themselves on acorns, amassing a two-pound layer of fat called a breast sponge. In spring, when they are too preoccupied with courtship and mating to eat, they draw energy from the sponge.

A bird of a different feather whose dietary staple is the acorn is the handsome but pesky blue jay, who helps to spread seeds far and wide. A host of other birds feed on acorns, including grackles, thrashers, bobwhites, flickers, vireos, nuthatches, and towhees. Red oak acorns are fairly rich in fats that help birds survive a cold winter or a migration south. They are the preferred food of wood ducks.

Scarlet tanagers build their nests high up in the oak's crown, and further below, blue-gray gnatcatchers saddle their beautifully constructed nests on the forks of lower limbs. The yellow throated vireo suspends her nest from forked branches near the lower trunk, close to the family food supply.

Among the mammals who find nourishment in red oak acorns are deer, bear, raccoons, and of course, the various species of squirrels. Gray squirrels eat most white oak acorns as they gather them, but cache red oak acorns for later consumption.

stinky feet and the Round Table

Perhaps the most famous piece of oak furniture is the legendary Round Table of King Arthur, crafted from a single slice of a giant British oak. A thirteenth-century reproduction can still be viewed today in the Great Hall in Winchester. It is 5.5 meters (18') wide.

Oak has been prized for centuries for the finest of furniture. Today in North America, red oak, sugar maple, and black cherry vie for supremacy among our native hardwoods. Red oak's flesh-toned heartwood, silvery grain, and solid strength make it a favorite of both professional and amateur woodworkers. It lends a touch of richness to kitchen cabinets, tongue-and-groove flooring, doors, mantelpieces, table legs, and wainscotting. Its characteristic grain produces a unique veneer. In days gone by, red oak was the wood of choice for wooden ice-boxes and sewing machines, both in demand today as antiques. Red oak still produces one of the most elegant funeral caskets.

Nova Scotia red oak was used for the keel, bow, ribs, and planking of the original *Bluenose* schooner.

Its heavy wood seasons slowly, shrinks considerably, and has a tendency to split at the ends when drying. When green, it emits an odor slightly reminiscent of stinky feet; when dry, fortunately, its smell disappears. It holds nails and screws well, but may split if not predrilled. It is easy to glue, stains beautifully, and has good bending properties when steamed. It can be a little hard on cutting tools.

It is believed that the wood of northern-grown red oak has a better color than that of trees grown further south. Some suggest rubbing the wood with wet steel wool will highlight the grain.

Among the more mundane uses of red oak are wood products calling for decay resistance. Its high porosity allows preservatives to soak in thoroughly, so lower grades of red oak lumber are used for railway ties, mine props, piles, and pallets — where hardness, strength, durability, and resistance to impact are key. In the past it was extensively used in "slack cooperage" — barrels not required to be watertight, in which nails, nuts and bolts, and the like were shipped, before metal and plastic barrels.

Facing page: When cut down, oaks are prolific sprouters from the stump. Using the root system of the parent tree, the sprouts develop fairly rapidly into clumps of trees, with the smooth, slate gray bark that is characteristic of young red oaks.

Male flowers hang in delicate catkins, singly or in clusters.

oak attackers

The high tannin content of red oak leaves makes them unattractive to many insects. But some, like the introduced gypsy moth, prefer red oak. In a Massachusetts experiment that went awry, these European insects were accidentally released in 1869, and have been multiplying and spreading ever since. The female moth, who can't fly, lays 200 to 300 eggs in yellow masses on bark, rocks, old logs, sheds, houses, fences . . . and vehicles. The egg mass hitchhikes to the vehicle's destination, and in spring the eggs hatch and the infestation spreads.

When at epidemic levels, gypsy moth larvae can devour all the leaves on a full-grown tree in a matter of days, leaving a leafless skeleton. If this devastation is repeated for another year or so, the tree may die or become susceptible to any number of secondary damaging agents.

A particularly troublesome disease in the Great Lakes region is oak wilt, which is capable of causing mortality to a tree within a few weeks. The disease is carried by a sap-sucking insect; trees that have recent wounds or have been pruned are the most susceptible.

Galls, a common occurrence on oak leaves, are created by a variety of mites, midges, aphids, and some 700 species of wasps. While they may produce abnormal growth, they rarely cause mortality, and are considered one of nature's curiosities. Some people call them "oak apples."

Anyone who has gathered acorns has come across the damage caused by the acorn weevil. It lays its eggs in young acorns, and its larvae eventually destroy the embryo within. Squirrels eat the acorns, worms and all, perhaps for a little protein boost. But they are not recommended for people, especially the squeamish.

from soup to nuts

The leaves of the tree were the healing of nations.

Revelation 22:2

From the territory of the Potawatomi in the Great Lakes to the land of the Maliseet in the Maritimes, the astringent property of red oak was common knowledge to Native people. Red oak leaves bound over a cut promoted rapid healing. They steeped a tea of the inner bark to relieve the symptoms of diarrhea. The Ojibway used the inner bark for heart disorders and bronchitis.

Native people viewed acorns as a reliable source of food, particularly during difficult winters. Acorns found their way into soups, stews, breads, and other staple rations. The Iroquois are reported to have eaten the inner bark of young oaks as an emergency food.

Tannin extracted from the bark was used extensively to tan animal hides required for clothing, bedding, and shelter. Various parts of the red oaks were used to produce dyes; leaf galls, or oak apples, for example, were selected to create a black dye.

home of the shiitake

Oaks, especially red oak, are the prime medium for growing shiitake mushrooms. Small diameter logs, branches, or sawdust are inoculated with mushroom spawn and left in a moist, shaded area. Nature does the rest. In early summer the next year, succulent — and expensive — shiitakes sprout, and will continue for four or five years.

black oak

Close kin to red oak is the somewhat smaller and shorter-lived black oak. A tree of poor sandy or heavy clay soils, it would thrive on better sites, but it is intolerant of shade and

Bark on mature trees is thick, with deep vertical fissures.

cannot compete with other oaks. Its U.S. distribution runs from southern New England west to Wisconsin, and south to northeast Texas and Georgia. In Canada, it is confined to the Carolinian forest and the region around Belleville on Lake Ontario's north shore.

Black oak leaves are a very shiny, dark green, with deep U-shaped notches between the lobes; but, like all oaks, their shape is inconsistent, even on the same tree. The bark on mature trees is thick and black, the ridges broken into rough rectangles. Its acorns are tannin-rich and bitter, as is the yellow, orange inner bark. At one time, quercitron, a commercial yellow dye, was manufactured from the inner bark. Black oak lumber is marketed as red oak, and is used for the same purposes.

The Willows
(*Salix genus*)

Saule

Montagnais: *vapineu-mitshima*

Leaf
- simple, alternate; long, narrow, tapering at both ends, often to a pointed tip;
- finely toothed or untoothed; stalk short, with 2 miniature leaves, called stipules, where leaf joins twig;
- unfold early in spring; shed late in autumn.

Flower
- male catkins green or yellow; semi-erect, angling away from twig;
- female catkins green or yellow; usually erect;
- males and females on separate trees; before leaves unfold, or with new leaves.

Fruit
- catkins of many small, green to brownish, pointed pods, swollen at the base;
- capsules split in 2 to release seeds; surrounded by long white silky hairs;
- mature in early summer; dispersed by wind and flowing water;
- seeds can germinate within hours on moist site, but lose viability in a few days;
- good seed crop most years.

Twig
- slender; color varies with species, frequently yellowish brown, sometimes red;
- buds pointed, pressed against twig, with one scale; no real terminal bud.

Bark
- on shrubs and younger trees, green, yellow, or red, smooth, with lenticels;
- bitter taste; on older trees, grayish brown, with interlaced ridges.

Wood
- soft, light, straight-grained; tough and impact resistant;
- heartwood light brown; sapwood pale creamy brown;
- annual growth rings indistinct.

Note There is such a range of sizes and life expectancies among the many species of willow that any attempt to generalize here would be meaningless. Black willow, the largest North American species in the *Salix* genus, commonly lives to 60–75 years; the lifespan of most of the willow shrubs is considerably shorter.

Leaves of the myriad willow species vary in shape and size, but most are narrow and pointed.

mission impossible

Looking for a lifelong career that is challenging, frustrating, unrewarding? One that is fraught with hair-splitting minutiae? One that requires post-doctoral degrees in genetics, microbiology, psychology, and diplomacy? And one that 99.9 percent of the population couldn't care less about, but will earn you persona non grata status with the 0.1 percent who do? Then consider a career in taxonomy, specializing in willows of the world.

Willows are another of those genera, like the serviceberries, which baffle even the best of botanists. First, there are so many species in the genus, with so many similarities, that authorities cannot concur on how many species there actually are. Second, there is such variation within species, that a large tree on a Manitoba lakeshore may be the same species as a small shrub in the mountains of New York. Finally, willows are promiscuous — they interbreed and hybridize at will, making positive identification a mission impossible.

conservation roots

A hollow vale where watery torrents rush.
Sinks in the plain the osier and the rush.
The marshy sedge and bending willow, nod
Their trailing foliage o'er the oozy sod.

Ovid, 43 BC – AD 17
Metamorphoses, Book VII

The name *Salix* is derived directly from the Celtic *sal*, meaning near, and *lis*, meaning water. Of the 70 to 90 species of willow in North America, almost all are at home on moist alluvial soils along brooks, rivers and lakeshores, and surrounding wetlands and prairie sloughs. Here they fill their ecological niche. Their shallow, wide-spreading, and fibrous roots control erosion by stabilizing soils on stream banks, islands, and sand bars. Throughout the twentieth century, forest and farm conservationists planted millions of willows to combat shoreline erosion. They employed both native willows and European imports such as purple osier and white willow. Some operations were simple — sticking willow cuttings into the soft soil on watercourse edges, and letting them grow. Others were far more elaborate. On the lower Mississippi, willow "mats," the size of six football fields, were fabricated and submerged to anchor riverside soils.

go native

Visualize "willow" and one of two images comes to mind — native pussy willows, every child's gift to Grandma, or introduced weeping willows, arguably the most easily recognized ornamental tree on the continent. Today, commercial nurseries carry weeping everythings, inspired by the popularity of the willow.

With 70-plus species of native willow trees and shrubs to choose from, there is something to complement any landscape design. Of the smaller trees, the most striking are the shining willows (*S. lucida*). Their bright green polished foliage, dense crown of golden branches, and yellow spring flowers offer aesthetic appeal year round. Like most willows, they require full sun and moist soil, and are adaptable to a wide pH range from 5.5 to 7.5. They grow fast and require minimal maintenance, but are short-lived. Avoid planting where their thirsty roots can contact sewage and water lines.

There are four prime choices for large shade trees, other than the weeping willow. Two were introduced from Europe and have become naturalized here — white willow (*S. alba*) and crack willow (*S. fragilis*). The other two are native — black willow (*S. nigra*) and peachleaf willow (*S. amygdaloides*). All are easily planted and fast growing, but are a wee bit messy. Willow's brittle branches, especially those of crack willow, are susceptible to wind damage; keep the grass rake handy. With all ornamental willows, males are preferable — the flowers are a little more showy, and there are no windborne seeds.

Willows are the easiest of trees to plant. Forget the seeds — they are viable only for a few days. In the spring, while the tree is still dormant, cut a few vigorous shoots 20 to 30 centimeters (8–12") long. Make planting holes slightly shorter, with a metal rod the diameter of the shoots. Insert the cuttings, leaving two buds above the surface. Tamp around them to ensure there are no air pockets, and water daily until it rains. (Oh, yes . . . plant right side up, with the buds pointing skyward.) The salicylic acid in willows is a natural rooting compound; they will begin to root within days.

willows of the Arctic

Willows have the distinction of being the most northern trees in North America. On the western side of Victoria Island, hundreds of miles north of the treeline and deep into Arctic tundra, isolated oases of willow line the sheltered ravines and river valleys. On coarse sandy gravels of the floodplains, where summer temperatures may be as much as 18° F (10° C) warmer than the surrounding region, feltleaf willows (*S. alaxensis*) reach heights of 8 meters (25') and 80 years of age, an anomaly in an otherwise treeless landscape.

the willow feedfest

Willows existed on this continent at the end of the Cretaceous period 70 million years ago. Just prior to their extinction, brontosauruses (brontosauri?) were nibbling on willow shoots, much as moose, deer, and a host of other wildlife do in this millennium.

From Newfoundland to James Bay to Alaska, at and well beyond the treeline, ptarmigans rely on willow twigs, buds, and seeds to survive the long harsh winters. On the Arctic tundra, where food is at a premium, muskoxen — stocky, hairy relics of the woolly mammoth era — dig craters in the snow to feed on shrub willows.

Along the streamsides and valleys of the boreal forest, willow twigs and buds supply moose with 10 to 25 percent of their winter food — adult moose consume 1.5 to 4 kilograms (3–9 lbs.) of willow browse a day.

White-tailed deer browse willows year round, contributing to about 5 percent of their diet. Beavers stock their underwater food caches with willow branches each fall before the ice sets in, while rabbits and hares bound on the snow from willow to willow, nipping off the twigs. In spring, porcupines consume the catkins, a break from their winter diet of tree bark.

Feathered fauna join in the willow feedfest as well. Ruffed and sharp-tailed grouse, like their northern cousins the ptarmigans, are big fans of willow buds, especially pussy willows. So too are grosbeaks and redpolls. Wood ducks and mallards, after their spring migration north, replenish their energy on willow catkins, while preparing to settle in for the summer.

With all this winter feeding, one might wonder how willows survive the onslaught. But they are amazingly resistant to heavy browsing, and each spring bounce back by sprouting, suckering, and reseeding, often in greater numbers than before.

The early spring flowering of willows provides an important source of nectar for honeybees when little else is flowering, producing an excellent grade of honey in the process. Bees, as well as other insects, pollinate the flowers, helping proliferate the species. Several songbirds, including alder flycatchers, redpolls, goldfinches, and Lincoln's sparrows, prefer the cover of willows for nesting.

Like alders, willows overhanging streams keep waters cool for freshwater fish such as speckled or brook trout, while providing insects for food. They furnish shoreline cover for a variety of waterfowl, and larger hollow trees attract cavity-nesting wood ducks, golden eyes, and buffleheads.

a cornucopia of cures

Salix is a tree knowne to all whose fruit and leaves have an astringent qualitie . . . the juice out of ye leaves & barck . . . doth help ye griefs of the eares, and the decoction of them is an excellent fomentation for ye Gout. It doth also cleanse away scurfe.

Pedanius Dioscorides,
1st century AD,
De Materia Medica, Book I

All species of *Salix* contain both tannin and the natural chemical salicin, now synthesized and processed into salicylic acid, a common corn-remover, and acetylsalicylic acid, known familiarly as ASA or aspirin. The Greeks discovered willow's medicinal benefits about the same time as did North American Indians. Salicin was officially recognized in the *U.S. Pharmacopoeia* until 1926, and in the *National Formulary* until 1955.

Every North American nation included some species of willow in their medicinal potpourri. The Montagnais of Quebec and Chickasaw of Oklahoma both used red willow inner bark for headaches. For fever, the Alabama, Natchez, Creek, and Pima drank infusions of the inner bark. The Cree, Potawatomi, Ojibway, and Mi'kmaq applied the bark to arrest excessive bleeding from wounds. The Tête de Boule and Seneca used the inner bark or roots as a sore throat remedy. The Dene and Ojibway applied it externally to heal persistent sores. The Penobscot and Ojibway drank a root decoction for coughs and colds. The Menominee, Meskwaki, Woods Cree, and Northern Saulteaux all steeped a bark or root tea for relief of diarrhea.

Toasted willow bark, called kinnikinnick, was smoked, both for pleasure and for ceremony, by the Montagnais, Ojibway, Dene, and Maliseet. The Penobscot smoked it to relieve the symptoms of asthma. Pipe stems were also commonly made of hollow willow twigs.

Prairie Athapascans fashioned their bows from willow. The Ottawa, Woods Cree, and Winnebago wove pouches, nets, and rope from the bark fibers. Young willow shoots, peeled and soaked in hot water to make them tough and flexible, supplied the raw materials for baskets. Maritime and Gaspé Mi'kmaq produced a black dye from the roots, and the Saulteaux north of Lake Superior extracted a dark orange dye from the bark.

Indigenous people, as was their custom, shared their panoply of cures with the colonists. But somewhere along the line there must have been a slight communication breakdown. A 1920s encyclopedia of health suggested a tea of willow buds and twigs would suppress sexual desire; another herbal, published a few years later, described willow as an aphrodisiac.

wicker and the sticky wicket

Willow wood is no longer used to the extent it once was. One reason is that there is less of it. For a so-called hardwood, it is quite soft and light. But it is tough, withstands abuse, dries well, is straight-grained, and doesn't splinter. It takes nails and screws well, and glues and finishes superbly. As it is soft like basswood, some wood sculptors and toy carvers love working with willow.

In the past it has had a rather eclectic history of utilization: artificial limbs, gunpowder, charcoal, water wheels, excelsior packing material, whistles, ironing boards, wicker furniture, barrel staves, cricket bats, fence posts, and polo balls. Two thousand years ago, the shields of the Roman legions were made of lightweight willow covered with rawhide and brass.

The pointed winter buds are pressed against the twig.

Today willows are being experimented with as agroforestry short-rotation crops for fuel, wood fiber, and chemicals.

willow cones?

Willows are subject to a motley crew of insects — sawflies, loopers, caterpillars, and lace bugs, as well as leaf beetles, rollers, tiers, and miners. Perhaps the most curious is a gall-forming midge that lays its eggs on new growth in the spring; its larvae develop a golf ball-sized gall at the end of the twig. In summer the gall looks like a miniature green cabbage, but by winter it takes on the appearance of a woody jack pine cone. Yes, only conifers bear real cones.

The Mountain-Ashes
(*Sorbus* genus)

Leaf
- compound, alternate; 11–17 narrow, toothed, leaflets in pairs along central stalk;
- end leaflet wider; leaflets 5–10 cm (2–4") long; leaf 12–25 cm (5–10") long;
- bright green above; underside paler;
- turn yellow, orange, red or purple in autumn.

Flower
- tiny; creamy white, 5-petalled; in dense, flat-topped clusters 6–15 cm (2½–6") wide;
- at ends of shoots; after leaves fully grown;
- individual flowers bearing both male and female parts (perfect).

Fruit
- bright orange or scarlet, pea-sized berries in dense hanging clusters;
- berries mealy, bitter; less sour after frost; containing 2–10 tiny brown seeds;
- may persist on tree much of winter; good crop every year.

Twig
- slightly thick, grayish or reddish brown; smooth; with gray film that weathers off;
- plump lateral buds pressed against twig; longer terminal bud dark purple, sticky, slightly curved.

Bark
- on younger trees, thin, smooth, grayish or greenish brown, with sporadic oval lenticels;
- on older trees, gray, sometimes scaly.

Wood
- weak, soft, light;
- heartwood pale brown; sapwood white.

Height	Diameter	Longevity
6–10 m (20–35')	10–30 cm (4–12")	30–50 years

same difference

There are two tree species of mountain-ash native to eastern North America. American mountain-ash (*Sorbus americana*) ranges from Newfoundland to Minnesota, south to the mountains of Georgia, and back up to the Maritimes. The hardier showy mountain-ash (*S. decora*) grows from Newfoundland and Labrador, through northern Quebec to James Bay, and west past Lake Winnipeg, but extends south only to isolated areas in the Lakes states.

A smaller, shrubby variety grows in Labrador, and western mountain-ash, a multi-stemmed shrub, ranges from Saskatchewan to Alaska.

The introduced and widely planted European mountain-ash, or rowan tree (*S. aucuparia*) has escaped, courtesy of the bird community, to roadsides and forest edges throughout the countryside. In some locales, it has hybridized with our two native species.

The differences among the three — American, showy, and European — are subtle: the shape of the leaflets and flower clusters, the stickiness or hairiness of the buds, and the size and color of the berries. In stature and appearance, site requirements, ornamental value, wildlife use, edible and medicinal properties, and susceptibility to insects and disease, the three are essentially similar, and are treated here collectively.

little apples, not ashes

Despite the name, mountain-ashes are not related to the ash genus. The misnomer arose when pioneers confused their compound leaves with those of the ashes. They are members of the rose family, which includes apples, pears, peaches, plums, cherries, hawthorns, serviceberries, and some 1,500 other species worldwide. Not long ago, the scientific name for mountain-ash was *pyrus*, the same as apple. The berries — correctly considered "pomes" — do resemble tiny apples.

jewels on the landscape

Why nurseries and garden centers have traditionally promoted European mountain-ash, rather than our native trees, is baffling. The natives, particularly showy mountain-ash, are as attractive as the imported model, and are naturally acclimatized to our growing conditions.

Beautiful large clusters of creamy white blossoms in late spring, light feathery foliage throughout summer, and striking orange or scarlet fruit in autumn make the little trees living jewels on the home landscape.

To plant from seed, pick the ripe berries, dry, and remove the tiny seeds. Sow them in a nursery bed immediately, and lightly cover with 15–20 mm (½–¾") of soil. Some may take two years to germinate. Seedlings are ready to transplant after their second growing season. Faster results can be achieved by digging up young wildlings beneath older trees, and transplanting directly to their new home. Or ask your local garden center if they carry native mountain-ashes.

search and destroy

Good detective work is the key to minimizing insect and disease damage to ornamentals. Dark brown egg masses wrapped around twigs spell forest tent caterpillar, the most widespread tree pest on the continent. Pick them off in fall or winter, and destroy them. Or give them to your kids — they make a great show-'n-tell item at school.

Shredded wood fibers at the base of the tree are a clue that round-headed apple borers are tunneling into the wood. To prevent the beetles from laying eggs in the bark, wrap the lower stem of new transplants loosely with tar paper for the first few years.

Tiny swellings on the teeth in June mean eggs of the mountain-ash sawfly. If you detect the swellings, simply squish the leaflet edges between your fingers to destroy the eggs within. If you miss the eggs, green or yellow caterpillars with black spots will begin feeding on the edge of the leaflets, until all that remains is the midrib. Remove affected leaflets, or the whole leaf, and destroy. Check again in September — there may be two generations in the same year.

Of the various rusts, cankers, leaf spots and scabs that infect mountain-ash, fire blight is the most threatening. The bacteria can kill trees in weeks. Leaves suddenly wilt and collapse, appearing scorched. Cut infected branchlets 30 cm (12") below the blight and destroy them.

panacea or poison?

The medicinal uses of mountain-ash by native people was, to say the least, varied. In Quebec, Montagnais in Lac St. Jean drank a decoction of the bitter inner bark to stimulate the appetite and purify the blood. In *la Mauricie* region, Tête de Boule drank it to relieve depression. Hudson Bay Cree boiled the scrapings from young branches for pleurisy and inflammatory diseases. New England's Penobscot used it to induce vomiting, to alleviate a variety of internal ills.

Mi'kmaq in La Gaspésie and the Maritimes chewed the bark raw to alleviate stomach pains, while their Maliseet neighbors applied the burnt bark as a poultice to boils. They also steeped a bark tea to relieve mothers' pains after childbirth. The Potawatomi around Lake Huron steeped the leaves into a tea for colds, pneumonia, and croup. Patients would vomit, expelling excess mucous symptomatic of the illness.

Mountain-ash berries contain citric, parasorbic, and malic acids, as well as iron, tannin, and pectin. One of the two fruit sugars in the berries reportedly relieves eye pressure in patients suffering from glaucoma.

Like that of its cousins the cherries, mountain-ash bark contains hydrocyanic acid and is poisonous. None of the above remedies should be contemplated without consulting a doctor.

Mountain-ash fruit clusters — both beauty and bounty.

pretty attractive to wildlife

The bright orange and red berries are not just decorative. In the forest, sharp-tailed, ruffed, and spruce grouse are great gobblers of the fruit. Deer and moose snack on the leaves in summer, and browse the twigs and buds in winter. And the berries are a favorite of black bears; the Potawatomi name for mountain-ash is *mukwo'mic*, or "bear tree."

Closer to home, 20 species of birds, including bluebirds, orioles, and woodpeckers, brighten the landscape when they visit the lawn ornamental for a fall feast. Robins fatten up on the berries before their migration south.

If the autumn avian set don't clean out the supply, the berries present a scarce source of nutritious fruit for year-round residents such as pine grosbeaks and cedar waxwings. Evening grosbeaks are not thrilled with the fruit; they pick out the seeds and reject the pulp. Blue jays attracted by the fruit stick around in spring, and return the favor by helping control tent caterpillars. They feed the pupae to their nestlings.

Eastern White Cedar
(*Thuja occidentalis*)

northern arbor vitae
northern white cedar
swamp cedar
tree of life
eastern thuja

cèdre
balai
thuya occidental
arborvitae
cèdre blanc
cèdre de l'est

Penobscot: *kanksku'zi*

Leaf
- yellowish green, scale-like, aromatic; in 4 rows around twig;
- top and bottom scales pressed flat to twig, with tiny glandular dots;
- side scales overlapping; glandless;
- flat, fan-shaped leaf sprays; smooth to the touch;
- turn slightly brownish in late fall and winter.

Flower
- male flower yellow; female pink; in April or May;
- solitary, at tips of different branchlets, on same tree.

Fruit
- cones green, egg-shaped; 6–12 mm (¼– ½") long; in upright clusters on short curved stems;
- mature in 1 season; turn reddish brown at maturity in late summer,
- open and release seeds in early autumn; may remain open on twig all winter;
- tiny oblong brown seeds winged on both sides; wings same width as seeds;
- begin to bear cones at age 15–20; good seed crop every 3–5 years.

Twig
- young twigs thin, flat, completely concealed by leaves;
- older twigs leafless, orange-brown; buds tiny.

Bark
- on younger trees, smooth, shiny, cinnamon-colored; cracking into papery scales;
- on older trees, gray, fibrous and shreddy; in long narrow flat ridges;
- ridges often intersecting; occasionally spiraling around trunk; easily peeled off.

Wood
- aromatic, very light, soft, weak, brittle; easily split; usually knotty;
- heartwood straw-brown, rot resistant; narrow sapwood nearly white, less resistant;
- annual growth rings fairly distinct.

Height	Diameter	Longevity
12–18 m (40–60')	50–80 cm (20–30")	200–300 years

When mature in autumn, clusters of tiny cedar cones open to release their winged seeds.

the tree of life

The name "cedar" (*cèdre, en français*) is actually a misnomer. *Thuja occidentalis* is a member of the cypress family. It may closely resemble the Old Testament's cedars of Lebanon, with which Solomon built the temple that housed the Ark of the Covenant, but it is not related.

One of cedar's other common names, arbor vitae — Latin for tree of life — harkens back to the cure of Jacques Cartier's crew by the Iroquois, who brought boughs of a medicinal tree to his icebound ship in the winter of 1535. On his return to France, Cartier gave arbor vitae seeds to King François I. Sown in the king's royal gardens at Fontainebleau, they were the first recorded North American trees planted in Europe. Almost 500 years later, there is still debate as to which tree saved Cartier's crew from scurvy: cedar, spruce, hemlock, or pine. All are rich in vitamin C.

The other common French name of white cedar is *balai* (broom), stemming from the use of its boughs by early French settlers as a sweeping and deodorizing broom. A broom that doubles as a deodorizer might have considerable marketing potential today.

Eastern white cedar, diminutive cousin of the giant western redcedar, *Thuja plicata*, ranges from the Gaspé peninsula to the foot of James Bay, down to the southeast corner of Manitoba, and from Minnesota east to Maine and New Brunswick. Isolated pockets occur in western Nova Scotia and Prince Edward Island, at the top of Lake Winnipeg, and in the Appalachians of Virginia, West Virginia, and North Carolina.

the ultimate ornamental

Ah, happy, happy boughs! That cannot shed
Your leaves, nor ever bid the spring adieu;
John Keats, 1795–1821
"Ode to a Grecian Urn"

White cedars are unquestionably the most widely planted ornamental conifers on the continent. They grow slowly and naturally into steeples of dense foliage that extend to the ground, with all the appearances of having been pruned and sheared. At close spacing, they develop into thick evergreen hedges that can be molded into any size or shape. If one should be so fortunate as to be heir to a sprawling estate, a cedar maze is a fascinating prospect.

Cedars are very easily transplanted. If the soil is acidic, incorporating lime before planting will make young cedars feel more at home. Once established, balanced fertilizers will accelerate their growth rate and enhance the foliage color.

Cedars are not prey to many insects or diseases, but they are susceptible to damage from road salt or ocean spray. Severe ice storms can break both leader and limbs. Cedar's metabolism is immune to city pollutants such as sulfur dioxide and ozone.

Throughout late autumn and winter, cedar foliage takes on a somber bronze tone, but the leaves always green up again in the spring.

Countless cedar cultivars are available from commercial nurseries in a host of sizes and shapes, from dwarf trees, to round, conical and columnar forms, as well as foliage colors from deep greens to yellow golds.

don't fence me out

One of the more charming man-made structures adorning our countryside is the weathered and gray split rail fence. Although the fences are simple and ingenious in design, one has to appreciate that years ago it took some farmer months to harvest the trees, haul them home, peel the bark, saw up the posts, split the long rails, dig the post holes, and erect the fence, all without the aid of modern machinery. The wood, of course, was cedar, whose heartwood is one of the most decay- and termite-resistant woods on the continent.

Fences built 150 years ago are still in place, without the benefit of wood preservatives. It did not take settlers long to discover that this tree, unknown in their homes in Europe, could withstand the elements. Aside from fence posts and rails, cedar was used for poles, roof and siding shingles on houses and barns alike, for docks and piers, and eventually for railway ties. With the introduction of creosote, chemical wood preservatives, and pressuretreating, stronger and less tapered woods have replaced cedar for ties, docks, and piers, but it is still the wood of choice of most farmers for fence posts.

Cedar does not grow in Newfoundland. Might this be one of the reasons Newfoundlanders traditionally did not build fences to contain livestock, but only to prevent free-ranging horses, cattle, and sheep from invading home, lawn, and garden? Perhaps.

White cedar is very light, aromatic, and decay resistant. Very easily peeled of its bark, it was the wood of choice for pioneer log cabins. It still has many applications in and around the home — interior and exterior shingles, siding, patio furniture, picnic tables, trellises, closet and chest lining, and saunas.

knotty but nice

The aroma of cedar creates a pleasant environment in the workshop. The wood shrinks very little in drying, is very light and easy to handle, has nice straight grain, takes paint, stain and a variety of glues well, and does not dull tools. Its ability to hold nails, however, is weak, and its chemical makeup corrodes non-finished nails and screws. Its knottiness can be an aesthetic asset, but a sawing and planing liability. The decay resistance of the heartwood makes cedar ideal for any outdoor project, from patio decks to duck decoys.

cedar au naturel

Forest cedars have a different form from open-grown trees. The base of the trunk is often bent just above ground level, lower limbs are bare or sparsely leafed, and only the upper half bears a live crown. Some trees grow perfectly straight; others maintain a bow shape, called sweep, throughout their lives. On very old trees the butt often flares above the roots, or is occasionally buttressed, a common trait of its western redcedar cousin.

Seedlings germinate on bare mineral soil or on old logs on the forest floor. Where

The bark is thin, gray, fibrous, and shreddy.

lower branches contact the soil, they take root and reproduce by layering. Even branches of fallen trees will root and grow upright, creating cedar clumps.

Almost everywhere cedar grows, calcium is present: in cedar swamps — usually near a spring — with underlying limestone, on moist, well-drained abandoned farmland, on sand dunes, on dry shallow upland soils, and along river banks and terraces where calcium is deposited from the flowing water. Cedar grows best where the soil pH is neutral to high; it is definitely not a tree of acidic soils. Contrary to popular belief, the chemistry of the soil and its underlying rock are more critical to cedar growth than the abundance of water.

Older white cedars are prone to heart rot, making the task of determining a tree's

The bark peels off easily, a boon to those who need fence posts or rails.

age by counting the annual growth rings impossible. But cedars 250 to 300 years old are not at all uncommon.

hydroponic old growth?

Cedar's affinity to limestone is exemplified on the Niagara Escarpment, the 750-kilometer (500 mile) stretch of cliffs from Niagara Falls north to Lake Huron. Throughout the Escarpment, cedars of all ages cling to the cracks, crevices, and hollows in the limestone cliffs. Virtually without soil, their roots derive moisture and nutrients leached from the rocks themselves.

The oldest Escarpment cedar dated thus far took root 1890 years ago, long before Europeans first explored North America. They comprise the oldest, longest-ranging, and most undisturbed old-growth forest eco-system in eastern North America. Gnarled, deformed, and severely stunted, they cling tenaciously to the vertical face of the rock, growing 1,000 times more slowly than cedars in their usual habitat. The cedar limestone cliff ecosystem is a wealth of biodiversity — small mammals, songbirds, bats, spiders, snails, and insects abound. The Escarpment has been declared a World Biosphere Reserve by UNESCO.

Similar ancient cedars have been found on the cliffs of the Ottawa River, not far from the Parliament Buildings, and in the Abitibi region of northwestern Quebec, at the fringe of the boreal forest.

Remarkable similarilities exist between these cedar veterans and the bristlecone pines in the White Mountains of California. Both are ancient, stunted, windswept, and slightly grotesque. These living relics cling to life

Open cones, having dispersed their seeds, remain on the branches over the winter.

under extremely adverse conditions, and are rooted in thin rocky soils or virtually soil-less limestone. But the bristlecone pines are much older — some over 4,600 years — and are among the oldest living beings on Earth. Curiously, the oldest specimens of many tree species investigated worldwide are not found in their ideal habitat, but where nature has dealt them a most difficult hand to play. It would appear that, at least with some species, hardship breeds longevity.

waste not

Throughout cedar's range, Native medicine people prescribed some part of the tree to relieve the pain of rheumatism and related disorders. They concocted more ways to administer it than there are rheumatism remedies on the drugstore shelf today.

The Mohawk, Maliseet, and Pillager Ojibway steamed the boughs in their sweat baths. Montagnais pounded the twigs into a pulp, steeped it in boiling water, and applied it directly to the affected part of the body. The Penobscot applied leaf poultices to reduce swelling. The Mide'wewin inhaled the fumes of cedar leaves placed on hot stones. This is not surprising, for cedar leaves contain the same ingredient — camphor — as the Vicks line of commercial products.

Two tribes burned the bark, mixed the

ashes with lambskill (Penobscot), or the gall of a bear (Ojibway), and practiced a treatment suggestive of acupuncture. They pierced the patient's skin with a needle or sharp quill, either on the area in pain or on the temple, and rubbed the mixture under the skin, leaving a permanent black tattoo.

Taking a clue from the Indians, settlers boiled calcium-rich cedar leaves and animal fat to create a salve that reportedly brought quick relief when rubbed into rheumatic joints.

Cedar leaves were a cough and cold remedy, alone or blended with boiled ironwood chips. Leaf and bark teas were sweat inducers (sudorifics), and were consumed for fevers, headaches, and menstrual problems. Northern Saulteaux dried the outer and inner bark, saturated the two with fat, and applied the ointment on cuts and wounds. The Maliseet filled tooth cavities with cedar gum — it stopped the pain but unfortunately killed the tooth. Today, *Thuja occidentalis* is an active ingredient in commercial homeopathic remedies for earaches and acne.

Not much went to waste when a cedar was cut down. Cedar boughs were used for bedding, deodorizers, incense, and brooms. Leaves and inner bark were boiled into dyes. Strips of the fibrous outer bark were woven into hammocks, bags, and mats. The wood was split and bent for the ribs and frames of birch bark canoes.

Many native communities revered cedar, black ash, and white birch as sacred gifts from the spirits of nature. To express their respect and gratitude, they held ceremonies at the foot of the trees, and made offerings of tobacco.

home to the white-tailed and the yellow-bellied

Groves of cedar and hemlock are prime wintering areas for white-tailed deer. Deep snows make travel difficult, sapping their limited reserves of energy, so deer congregate where conditions are favorable. Deer yards offer shelter from the elements, reduced accumulations of snow, and nutritious and palatable food. Winter deer browsing poses no threat to taller trees, but deer, as well as snowshoe hares, cottontail rabbits, and mice can annihilate young cedar growth. An interesting feature of heavy browsing is the distinct browse line, about 2 meters (7') high, below which trees are bare of foliage.

Cedar provides excellent cover and shelter for gamebirds, songbirds, and small mammals alike. Ruffed grouse, woodcock, robins, finches, snowshoe hares, and red squirrels escape into the dense foliage to avoid predators.

The elusive yellow-bellied flycatcher, whose eastern range coincides with that of cedar, builds her nest at the base of cedars, spruce, and tamarack. The boreal or brown-capped chickadee likes to nest in a hollow cedar. The ever-friendly gray jay, or whiskey jack, lines her nest with cedar bark. Many a lumberjack's lunch has been graced with the visit of a pair of whiskey jacks, one of the tamest and prettiest of forest birds.

In autumn, cedar seeds attract pine siskins, crossbills, and finches, and, of course, the ever-present and habitually hungry red squirrel. Large, striking pileated woodpeckers feed on carpenter ants in cedar heartwood.

Basswood
(*Tilia americana*)

American linden
whitewood
lime tree

tilleul d'Amérique
bois blanc

Miami: *wikopiminsi*

Leaf
- simple, alternate; large, round, lopsided; sharply toothed; 12–16 cm (5–6″) long;
- thick, somewhat leathery texture; arranged in 2 rows along the branches;
- heart-shaped or almost flat across the base; tip pointed;
- upper side dark green; underside yellowish green, fuzzy at junctions of yellow veins;
- stem round, slender, 4–6 cm (2–3″) long;
- turn faded yellow or brown in autumn.

Flower
- small, 5-petalled, creamy yellow; fragrant; full of nectar; insect pollinated;
- in clusters dangling from mid-point of yellowish green leaf-like appendage 6–12 cm (2–4″) long; after leaves fully grown;
- appendage thin, curved, veiny, tapered at both ends; somewhat shoehorn-shaped.

Fruit
- nearly round, pea-sized, hard, woody, downy, beige gray; with tiny nipple at bottom; containing 1–2 tiny edible seeds;
- in small clusters hanging from middle of the appendage; some remain all winter;
- begin flowering at 15 years; good crop most years.

Twig
- somewhat stout, smooth, zigzag; reddish or greenish brown; often covered with gray film;
- tiny lenticels sparse;
- buds plump, rusty or rosy red, slightly pointed, lopsided, glossy.

Bark
- on younger trees, thin, smooth, greenish gray;
- on older trees, dark gray brown, deeply fissured, with flat-topped ridges.

Wood
- soft, light, weak; fine-textured; straight-grained;
- heartwood beige with faint reddish or yellowish tinge; sapwood creamy white;
- transition from sapwood to heartwood gradual and not obvious;
- annual growth rings indistinct.

Height
20–30 m (70–100′)

Diameter
60–100 cm (24–36″)

Longevity
140–180 years

fertilizer factories

Basswood is a soil enhancer. Its leaves are very rich in calcium and magnesium, and well above average in nitrogen, potassium, and phosphorus content. They are living, breathing, non-polluting fertilizer factories. Decomposed basswood leaves nourish and neutralize the soil, boosting the growth of basswoods themselves, as well as the surrounding trees and other flora. Basswood requires higher soil fertility than most of its neighbors, so it ensures its own health and growth. It flourishes on deep, well-drained loamy soils.

a prolific sprouter

Despite basswood's copious annual production of fruit, very few seeds develop into seedlings. The seeds are doubly dormant, and need very exacting conditions for germination. Many that do germinate fall prey to rabbits. Most regrowth arises from stump sprouts of trees that have been cut or killed by fire. Basswood clumps originating from sprouts are more common in our second growth forests than single stems.

a beauty in summer, a bust in the fall

Where space allows, basswood develops into a beautiful oval-crowned shade tree. Winter gives it the opportunity to show off its symmetrical branching pattern. The large round leaves and clusters of little yellow flowers are attractive from late spring until the end of summer. In autumn, basswood abdicates its aesthetic role to the colorful maples, oaks, and ashes. Leaves fade to yellow or brown, and drop off early in the season.

Basswood seeds should be gathered as soon as they ripen to grayish brown, and planted immediately, before they begin to dry. Cover lightly with 1 centimeter (½") of soil. Leave in the garden bed for two growing seasons, and transplant the following spring to an open sunny site.

For years many cities and towns have been planting basswood's European relative, littleleaf linden (*Tilia cordata*), a smaller tree suited to city conditions. It is available in several dozen cultivars from commercial nurseries. If lack of space is a factor, consider the littleleaf, or choose a smaller native tree.

the pests

By midsummer, basswood leaves are usually plagued by a host of insect blemishes. Among the pests are assorted caterpillars, leaf rollers, loopers, gall midges and mites, beetles, lacebugs, leaf miners, aphids, thrips, and the curious-looking walking stick. With the exception of the forest tent caterpillar when its population soars, the little critters are more injurious to the appearance than the health of the trees.

for the bees, not the birds

In July, basswoods are abuzz with activity. Their nectar-laden flowers are a major attraction to honeybees. The honey produced is particularly flavorful, a quality not lost on either human or black bear connoisseurs.

Other basswood beneficiaries are deer and rabbits who browse the succulent sprouts, chipmunks and squirrels who hoard the seeds, and dozens of birds and mammals, including bears, who nest and den in hollow old basswoods. The seeds hold little appeal to birds; many of the hard little nuts remain hanging throughout the winter, with nary a nibble before dropping to the ground. Enter the chipmunks.

the wood of sculptors

Our softest native hardwood has been transformed into millwork, furniture components, Venetian blinds, caskets, mobile homes, picture frames, and piano keys.

But without question, the best end use of basswood is wood carving and sculpting. The soft wood allows a skilled carver to incorporate the most minute detail. Intricate basswood scrollwork and statues adorn churches and cathedrals throughout Europe and North America. It was the wood of elaborate ships' figureheads and carnival carousel ponies. With basswood, whittling of duck decoys has ascended from a hunter's humble craft to an art form.

Iroquois carved their religious False Faces into standing live basswoods, then cut the mask out of the tree. If the tree survived the ordeal, the False Face was considered to have magical powers.

The little village of St. Jean Port Joli, on the south shore of the St. Lawrence in Quebec, is home to a community of wood carvers whose works, detailed down to the wrinkles on an old man's face, are instantly recognizable in gift shops across North America. Their choice of wood: *le tilleul*.

entwined in native life

Wherever it grew, basswood was Native people's principal source of thread, string, twine, and heavy rope. In the spring they removed the bark and soaked it in water until the fibers softened, or boiled it with wood ashes (lye) and peeled off the soft fibrous inner bark. They cut it into strips of varied widths, coiled it, and stored it for future use.

Fine single strands were used to sew moccasins, robes, pouches, birchbark baskets, and reed mats. They served as fishing line and even sutures for severe cuts. Wider strips were woven into belts, fishing nets, and occasionally snowshoe webbing. In a tradition handed down from mother to daughter, women sat together and braided the strips into twine and rope. In 1749, Swedish botanist Peter Kalm, who lived among the Indians in New York and Quebec, marveled at the quality of the rope, writing: "I could have sworn that it was fine hemp cord."

The large, round, lopsided leaves are the key to identifying basswoods in summer.

It appears that the secret of basswood's inner bark's use as cordage has been known for some time. Archeological digs have unearthed 2,000-year-old woven basswood necklaces strung with copper beads.

In Europe, the leaves of basswood's foreign counterpart were commonly steeped as a tea, the flowers dried and used as cosmetics and bath relaxants, and the flowers and nuts blended to produce a chocolate.

Here at home, the Mohawk drank a flower tea to induce sweating and relieve spasms, and a twig infusion blended with the bark of staghorn sumac as a strengthening tonic during pregnancy. The Maliseet steeped the roots or bark as a cure for worms, and Meskwakis applied bark compresses on boils. The Onondaga prescribed the boiled bark to stimulate urination, and applied poultices of boiled basswood and beech leaves to burns and scalds. In 1849, a Massachusetts doctor reported to the American Medical Association that basswood bark was the best burn remedy he had encountered.

Eastern Hemlock
(*Tsuga canadensis*)

hemlock
Canadian hemlock
hemlock spruce

pruche
prusse
tsuga du Canada
sapin du Canada
haricot

Onondaga: *o-ne-tah*

Leaf
- needles dark green and glossy above; spring needles yellowish green; 10–15 mm (⅓–⅔") long;
- underside with yellow midrib, flanked by 2 silver bands, green at edges; flat, tapered at both ends; tip rounded or notched; edges with minute prickly teeth;
- slender yellow twisted stalks spiraling around twig; appear 2-ranked in flat sprays;
- needles emanating from top of twig upside down, silver side up; often lying flat on twig.

Flower
- male small, yellow, round, stalked, scaly; in late spring;
- female pale green, erect, at end of twigs; pollinated by wind;
- male and female on same tree (monoecious), sometimes on same branch;

Fruit
- fertilized female evolves into small, 1.5–2 cm (⅔–¾") narrow oval green cone;
- in fall of same year, matures to reddish brown; hangs from branch tip on short stalk;
- tiny winged seeds released intermittently in fall and winter; dispersed by wind;
- cone scales open and release seed when dry and windy, close when wet;
- empty cones remain on branches until spring;
- begin bearing cones at age 20–40; good seed crop every 2–3 years.

Twig
- on branches not in whorls, but staggered on trunk;
- new twigs yellowish brown, slightly downy, flexible;
- stubs remain when old needles fall in 3 years, giving twig rough appearance;
- chestnut brown buds small, blunt, slightly hairy.

Bark
- on very young trees, gray and smooth, soon becoming scaly; underside of scales purple;
- on older trees, thick, reddish gray/brown; deeply furrowed with flat-topped ridges; inner bark purple.

Wood
- moderately light, hard, strong, brittle; usually knotty, coarse-textured;
- buff colored with reddish tinge; little distinction between heartwood and sapwood;
- annual growth rings distinct.

Height
18–24 m (60–80')

Diameter
60–90 cm (24–36")

Longevity
400–600 years

a tree for posterity

The recipe for growing a hemlock consists of four essential ingredients: moist fertile soil, good drainage, shelter from the elements, and plenty of patience. Hemlock is a notoriously slow grower. Although it is perfectly at home in the shade, planting in partial sunlight will stimulate its growth.

The result is worth waiting for — a tall pyramidal evergreen with wide-spreading lower limbs, slightly pendant at the tips, deep green and graceful foliage, upper branches ascending in a feathery cone, topped by a supple leader which leans away from the prevailing wind. Though symmetrical in shape, it maintains a touch of the wild. As a bonus, hundreds of tiny reddish brown cones decorate the branch tips throughout winter.

It takes more than a human lifetime for a hemlock to develop into the majestic tree it will ultimately become. Its life expectancy is four to six hundred years, or more. Future generations may well derive more benefits than the planter. It is a tree to leave to posterity.

He that plants trees loves others beside himself.
English proverb

Alternatively, closely planted hemlocks can be pruned and sheared into dense and handsome hedges.

Hemlock ranges from Nova Scotia through southern Quebec and Ontario to Minnesota, and southwards as far as northern Georgia and Alabama. A most notable hemlock found in Pennsylvania was determined to be 1,000 years old, with a diameter over 2 meters (7') and a height of 49 meters (160'). In 1931, Pennsylvania appropriately declared eastern hemlock their state tree.

the epitome of tolerance

Tolerance is the ability of a tree to grow in the shaded understory of the forest. Tolerant trees live for years suppressed under the canopy of taller trees, growing very slowly but otherwise healthy. When liberated by the departure of the trees above through natural mortality, insects or disease, windfall, or harvesting, they respond to the increased sunlight as well as the reduced competition for water and nutrients in the soil, and grow much more rapidly.

This is the forest primeval. The murmuring
  pines and the hemlocks,
Bearded with moss, and in garments green,
  indistinct in the twilight,
Stand like the Druids of eld, with voices
  sad and prophetic,
Stand like harpers hoar, with beards that
  rest on their bosoms.
Henry Wadsworth Longfellow,
"Evangeline"

Hemlocks are among the longest-living and most tolerant of our eastern trees. If left undisturbed, they can exist as small trees in the shade of the forest understory for 200 years, simply waiting for the shorter-lived trees above to die off naturally. On such sites, hemlocks ultimately dominate, and their closed canopy creates a cool microclimate below, where little else grows but a plush carpet of moss. Their needle litter is very acidic and low in nutrients. The forest reaches a climax condition, rather a rarity today in northeastern North America. Without disturbance by human or nature, the stand may remain stable for another several hundred years. But not forever.

The most impressive and accessible old-growth hemlocks in Canada are the dominant feature of Fredericton's Odell Park — massive trees that were in their youth when Samuel de Champlain came upon the St. John River four centuries ago. They are duly recognized in the Great Trees of New Brunswick collection.

old-growth forests

There are as many definitions of old-growth forests as there are types of old growth. Forest ecologists generally concur that most or all of the following elements are typically present: large diameter living trees approaching, at, or beyond their normal life expectancy; reduced growth rate, where natural mortality in the stand exceeds new growth; a more or less stable complement of tree species; standing dead trees, or snags; coarse woody debris — decaying fallen logs and branches on the ground; limited or no logging, now or in the past; occasional gaps in the forest canopy where old trees have fallen out of the pack, allowing sunlight to filter down to seedlings; and earthen mounds created by rotted stumps and roots of fallen trees.

Old-growth stands may be stable, but they are certainly not static. The forest structure is slowly and constantly evolving. Trees succumb to old age, remain standing as leafless and lifeless snags, and eventually fall to the forest floor. Wildlife tree-top nesters, tree cavity dwellers, small ground mammals, insects, and a host of other creatures down to the microscopic combine and interact to create the unique ecosystem.

its bark and its sparks

The Hemlock tree grows in every part of America in a greater or lesser degree. It is an evergreen of a very large growth, and has leaves somewhat like that of the yew; it is however quite useless, and only an encumbrance to the ground, the wood being of a very coarse grain and full of windshakes or cracks.

Jonathan Carver, 1778

There is little doubt that hemlock was once far more plentiful than it is today. The combined impacts of agricultural land clearing, forest fires, browsing by deer and snowshoe hares, and harvesting for its bark have greatly reduced its numbers.

Before the advent of synthetic chemicals, tannin extracted from tree bark was in great demand to process animal hides into leather. Hemlock, along with chestnut, was the principal source — its bark contains between 10 and 13 percent tannin.

The peeling season, when the bark separates easily from the tree, ran from the full moon in May to the full moon of August. Huge trees were cut down, their bark stripped off, cut into four-foot sections, and shipped to tanneries (for three cents a pound). At the turn of the twentieth century there were over 800 tanneries in Canada, and leather-making was an 11-million-dollar industry. In the eastern states, over one million cords of hemlock bark were harvested annually, the equivalent of a wood pile 4 feet high and 4 feet wide, stretching from Maine to Montana.

Some of the trees cut were sawn into lumber; later, some were converted to pulp and paper; but in countless cases, the denuded trees were left on the forest floor to rot. No one really knows its extent, but the waste was enormous.

Large hemlocks are renowned for having ring shake, a defect where the wood splits along the annual growth rings. Speculation is that it is a result of old age, or slow growth, or wind, or sapsucker damage. Regardless, the end result renders many hemlocks worthless for lumber, yet perfectly adequate for pulp and paper.

In the 1800s, hemlock was popular for barn construction. Many hand-hewn squared beams can still be found today in abandoned barns. Some eastern cities employed it as hexagonal paving blocks, and for wooden sidewalks. Its most common uses have been as roofing, framing, siding, subfloors, and heavy shipping crates.

Hemlock wood is buff in color, with a reddish tinge, and its pulp is difficult to bleach white. It is converted into newsprint

It's hard to believe that a potential forest giant originates from such tiny cones.

When burned as firewood, hemlock sparks a great deal, and is not recommended for open fireplaces and campfires.

sapsuckers, siskins, and liberated grosbeaks

Often the easiest way to identify an eastern hemlock is not by its needles, nor by its bark texture or cones, but by the orderly pattern of small holes riddled in its bark by the yellow-bellied sapsucker. The woodpecker feeds on the sap and bark tissues of other species such as apple and birch, but wherever it grows, hemlock is its consistent favorite. Ruby-throated hummingbirds take advantage of the sap holes for a change from their diet of flower nectar.

Since hemlock cones release their seeds intermittently from late autumn to early spring, winter-resident songbirds, particularly pine siskins, juncos, and chickadees, have the whole season to dine on the tiny morsels. Crossbills, dangling from the branch tips, crack open the cones with their unique scissor-like beaks.

In early summer, hemlock limbs become prime nesting sites for the solitary vireo, scarlet tanager, black-throated blue warbler, hermit thrush, and northern parula warbler. Rose-breasted grosbeaks line their nests with hemlock twigs, whereupon both the male and female share the duty of incubating the eggs. Gray squirrels frequently build their nests of twigs and leaves in the tops of large hemlocks.

Hemlock's broad boughs and flat sprays of foliage intercept snow before it reaches the ground, providing a sheltered habitat below for white-tailed deer. Deer also feed on the twigs and needles within reach. In some areas of New England, hemlock bark is the preferred food of porcupines. To control their populations and limit their damage, fishers, the most skilled of porky predators, have been imported into the region.

and wrapping paper, usually using the sulfite pulping process.

The wood is lightweight, fairly strong, but coarse and uneven in texture. It is hard on tools, especially the knots; many an ax has been quickly dulled limbing hemlock. It glues easily and takes paint well, but it is brittle and tends to split when nailed. It is not rot-resistant when exposed to the elements, and is difficult to impregnate with preservatives. If chemically preserved, it makes durable railway ties, piling, and culverts.

poison? quite the opposite

Mention the word "hemlock" to a scholar, and it may evoke thoughts of the poison hemlock with which Socrates committed suicide, or the potions of Macbeth's witches as they chanted: *Double, double toil and trouble; Fire burn, and cauldron bubble.*

Poison hemlock, a perennial of the parsley family, bears no relationship or resemblance to our hemlock tree. Ground hemlock, or yew, a low spreading evergreen shrub with needles similar in appearance to hemlock (hence its common name) frequently shares the same habitat.

First Nations people used the needles, bark, and roots of eastern hemlock to combat a variety of ills, from the common cold to diarrhea, from syphilis to scurvy. It is one of the conifers whose needles are rich in ascorbic acid, or vitamin C. At least seven tribes, from Wisconsin to Nova Scotia, routinely prescribed hot hemlock leaf tea for colds, coughs, bronchitis and flu. For centuries there has been speculation as to the nature of the *annedda* tree the Iroquois gave Jacques Cartier's crew to cure them of scurvy. The Onondaga Iroquois word for hemlock, *o-ne-tah,* seems to come closest.

The high tannin content of hemlock bark yields a strong astringent. The Ojibway pounded it into a powder to stop bleeding, or boiled it to form compresses to cover cuts and wounds. The Ojibway of the Great Lakes, Penobscot of Maine, and Maliseet of New Brunswick applied the powder to chafed skin, and diaper and heat rash. They also steeped a hemlock bark tea for diarrhea. Senecas boiled the needles in a pot, added a red-hot stone, covered it with a blanket, and sat on it to treat rheumatism. The Menominee and Mi'kmaq used the needles in their sweat lodges. An 1823 government report stated that the Indians of Upper Canada dried and powdered the inner bark of the roots to treat syphilis.

It was believed that hemlock possessed some property that would ward off rodents, and the Onondaga lined their root cellars and granaries with hemlock boughs. The Ojibway, Iroquois, and northeastern Algonkian all produced a mahogany dye from the inner bark.

In the nineteenth century, hemlock bark and its essential oil were listed in the *Canadian Pharmaceutical Journal,* and the pitch was listed in the *United States Pharmacopoeia* for relief of rheumatic pain. Ground hemlock, and its larger west coast cousin, the Pacific yew, are both currently showing promise as a treatment for ovarian cancer.

the luck of the hemlock

Compared with most trees, hemlocks are relatively free of life-threatening native insects. Hemlock loopers, needle-eating inchworms, occasionally can be a problem, but they have caused more mortality in balsam fir than in hemlock, particularly in Newfoundland. Hemlock borers, which usually attack trees weakened by other stresses, can expose the trunk to fungus infections.

Hemlock's shallow roots can render it susceptible to blowdown in heavy gales, as can drought if the upper layer of soil dries out. But otherwise, hemlock has been somewhat charmed — at least until the recent arrival of the hemlock woolly adelgid from Asia. The tiny aphid-like insect, which sucks the sap from young twigs, has spread northward from the Carolinas as far as Connecticut, leaving a trail of dead hemlocks in its wake.

White Elm
(*Ulmus americana*)

American elm

orme blanc
orme d'Amérique

Shawnee: *hani:pi*

Leaf
- simple, alternate; oval; thick, somewhat rough; on short stalks;
- 10–15 cm (4–6") long; in 2 rows along branch;
- base asymmetrical, tip pointed; margins double-toothed;
- veins prominent, parallel, straight; each ending in a large tooth;
- upper side dark green; underside paler, slightly hairy;
- turn yellow in autumn.

Flower
- small, inconspicuous; green and red; in tassel-like clusters;
- on individual long slender stalks;
- on previous year's twigs; before leaves emerge; wind-pollinated;
- male and female in same flower.

Fruit
- seedcase oval, flat, 8–10 mm (approx. ⅓") long; bearing 1 seed;
- in clusters on slender stalks;
- surrounded by green, spearhead-shaped, membranous wings fringed with hairs, deeply notched at tip;
- mature when leaves emerging, shed before leaves reach full size;
- dispersed by wind and water;
- begin bearing seed at age 15–20; good crop every 2–4 years.

Twig
- somewhat slender, zigzag; brownish gray; pith brown, solid, round;
- buds purplish brown; end bud angled 60° from twig;
- lateral buds pressed against twig.

Bark
- on younger trees, smooth, gray, soon cracking vertically;
- on older trees, ash gray; deeply furrowed, with wide intersecting ridges;
- often scaly.

Wood
- hard, heavy, strong, tough, flexible; odorless, tasteless; coarse-textured;
- heartwood pale yellowish or reddish brown;
- thick sapwood grayish or brownish white;
- annual growth rings distinct.

Height
25–30 m (80–100')

Diameter
90–120 cm (36–48")

Longevity
175–225 years

immune, or lucky

White elms are primarily trees of rich alluvial floodplains and bottomlands. Their wide-spreading shallow roots permeate the soil, binding it to prevent erosion, while absorbing the moisture and nutrients they require. Elms are soil improvers — their leaves, rich in iron, potassium, and calcium, decompose rapidly to replenish the soil.

While the elm population declined dramatically in the twentieth century, scattered healthy older specimens — either disease-resistant or just plain lucky — and countless young trees still remain throughout its natural range: from the Maritime provinces to eastern Saskatchewan, south to Texas and Florida, and back up to Maine.

White elm has been designated the state tree of Massachusetts.

Dutch elm disease

The load of European elm veneer logs that arrived in Ohio in 1930 was no ordinary load. It dramatically changed both the urban and rural landscape of North America, altered the ecosystem, and came close to driving to extinction one of the most beautiful trees on the continent. The bark held a secret hitchhiker — a fungus we know today as Dutch elm disease.

At that time there were 77 million elms in North American cities and towns. Today, 90 percent are gone, and the future of those that remain is uncertain. The disease has not yet completed its western migration, and in the east only the most heroic of efforts has kept precious few elms alive.

Some communities have fought hard to save their elms; most have given up in despair. Two cities noteworthy for their ongoing elm campaigns are Winnipeg and Fredericton. The commitment and expense have been worth it. Both have so far managed to preserve much of their early twentieth-century character and charm.

Dutch elm disease, so named because it was first discovered in Holland, is believed to have originated in the Himalayas. The minute sticky spores of the fungus are carried from diseased to healthy trees by two kinds of bark beetles — one native, and the other accidentally introduced from Europe in 1904.

Host trees were not hard to find. In the nineteenth century, millions of white elms had been planted in cities and towns across North America. It was the darling of tree planters — and justifiably so. It was not only beautiful, elegant and graceful, but was practical for city parks and streets — fast growing, resistant to salt and pollutants, and harmless to water and sewage lines. Its vase shape allowed good visibility for traffic and pedestrians, while casting shade over downtown streets and buildings, making life in summer more bearable for urban residents.

Urban elm monocultures were an open invitation to insects and disease — and both showed up. The disease radiated out from Ohio in all directions, borne by the flying beetles. Wounds the beetles create by boring into the bark become entry points for the disease, which quickly spreads through the tree's system. The fungus disrupts the tree's water-conducting mechanism, and within weeks, leaves wilt, turn yellow, and then brown. Some trees die within a month; others hang on for a year or two.

Efforts to save the elms have been ongoing for over half a century. Sanitation, removal of dead and dying branches or whole trees — including stumps — has slowed the rate of spread. Insecticides, including DDT for a few years in the 1960s and, later, sticky traps, were targeted at the beetles; fungicides were injected into the base of the trees. Lately, a less virulent strain of the fungus has been used to trigger the tree's defense mechanisms. And all along scientists have been working to breed naturally resistant elms. The Liberty elm, the second generation offspring of native elms with natural resistance, has so far been successful.

Leaves are asymmetrical at the base, and the veins are parallel.

How can we replace the character and charm of a streetscape lined with 150-year-old elms, whose huge limbs and crowns arch overhead, meeting to create a tunnel of natural greenery? We can't.

If the Liberty elms prove immune in the long term, we may have a solution. But not in our lifetimes.

alien invaders

Two basic lessons have been learned the hard way. First, tree monocultures are an accident waiting to happen. Magnificent as they may be, one species cannot be relied upon to beautify our cities and towns. Second, we have to maintain or increase our vigilance, to ensure that foreign insects and diseases do not arrive on our shores — or at our airports. We have had more than enough examples of deadly introductions to our continent: gypsy moth (1869), beech bark disease (1890), white pine blister rust (1900), and chestnut blight (1909), to name only a few. Foreign plants and animals can be equally destructive; purple loosestrife has invaded our wetlands, choking out native plants such as cattails, and zebra mussels are clogging our lakebeds.

In the ever-shrinking global village it is becoming increasingly difficult — but it has to be done. Foreign insects and diseases, as well as plants and animals, have no natural control mechanisms when released upon our ecosystem, and are capable of devastation unimaginable in the past.

Over 300 species of tree-feeding insects have successfully invaded North American cities and forests. Most are virtually harmless; some are deadly. They can wreak havoc within our forests, alter entire ecosystems, and have serious repercussions on our wildlife. Invasive alien species are considered second only to habitat loss as the greatest threat to biodiversity.

On the economic side of the environment/economy coin, losses due to foreign forest pests represent $4 billion a year in the United States. For example, the recent introduction of the Asian long-horned beetle in wooden crates from China has cost the cities of New York and Chicago millions to cut down infested city trees, and, without a natural predator, the beetle still has the potential to migrate to our native hardwood forests. Ten thousand spruce trees are being cut down in and around Halifax, in an attempt to stem the spread of an epidemic of brown spruce long-horned beetles — another import, this time in wood packing material at the port — into the Maritime forests. The region relies on its spruce/fir forests as the backbone of its pulp and paper industry.

room and board for birds

We naturally tend to think of white elms mainly in terms of their imposing size and majestic beauty. But they also offer room and board for many birds, in cities, villages, and in the countryside. Elm branches are a favorite spot for northern or Baltimore orioles to set up home. Females take up to a week to meticulously weave their intricate nests of plant fibers, wool, string, and hair. Warbling vireos prefer elms as well, but they work as a team — the male apparently enjoys his domestic role in helping build the nest and incubate the eggs, as he warbles all the while. Red-eyed vireos and yellow warblers prefer a less lofty site for their nests — young elms fit the bill.

Massive old white elms are often hollow or punky in the center. Woodpeckers, chickadees, and nuthatches move into the cavities to set up housekeeping. Elm's frequent waterside location proves convenient for the mallards, black ducks, and wood ducks who nest in their hollows. The seed-eating finch foursome — goldfinches, pine siskins, purple finches, and redpolls — capitalize on the early availability of elm seeds, long before those of most trees, to sustain themselves in spring. They are joined by grouse, quail, squirrels, and mice.

slippery elm

Slippery elm, or red elm (*Ulmus rubra*), has a less northerly range; in Canada it is confined to the St. Lawrence Valley to Lake Ontario, the lower Ottawa Valley, the Carolinian forest, and Manitoulin Island. Below the border, it is absent along the Atlantic coast south of Delaware. It grows best in fertile soils along streams and rivers, where its shallow spreading roots tap into an ample supply of water and nutrients.

Slippery elm has the same forking habit and ascending branches as white elm, but its branchlets do not droop at the tips, so it lacks the classic vase shape. It is also generally smaller than white elm.

In the forest, the two species could easily be confused, but there are a few distinct differences in all seasons. Slippery elm leaves are larger, with short stiff hairs on the upper side that make them feel like sandpaper. Winter buds are rounder and hairy, and the lateral buds are not pressed against the twig. In spring, the seed is hairy, but the nearly-round wing that surrounds it is hairless.

the medicinal elm

On the whole, taking into consideration this period in man's evolution, his surroundings and the disease conditions with which he had to contend, we must confess that the medical practices of the [Native peoples] were at least as sanely based as those of any other people. They were fully as much, if not more than usually successful in their application as compared to those of the white people of the same period.

Dr. Harlow Brooks, 1928,
New York Academy of Medicine

Of the elms, slippery elm was by far the most commonly used as a medicine. Over the native drugstore counter, it was prescribed as a panacea for an eclectic assortment of ailments. To relieve sore throats, Penobscot, Ojibway, and Seneca chewed the mucilaginous inner bark raw. Boiled into a decoction, the liquid was used to bathe sore eyes. The Cherokee and Mohegan drank the potion as cough syrup, the Plains tribes in the Missouri River region took it as a stomach antacid and laxative, and Onondaga used it as a treatment for kidney ailments. Meskwaki and Iroquois women drank regular doses of the bark tea during pregnancy to ensure a smooth delivery.

The Menominee inserted slivers of the inner bark into boils or infected wounds to draw out the pus, and then applied an elm-soaked compress to reduce swelling. During the American Revolutionary War, army surgeons borrowed a page from the Natives and adopted the same practice for gunshot wounds, substituting white elm bark.

Slippery elm lozenges for sore throats are available today in alternative medicine outlets and many commercial drugstores.

rock elm

The third member of the elm genus native to the east, rock elm (*Ulmus thomasii*), is far less common and much more restricted in range. In the west, Minnesota, Iowa, and Missouri are its limit; in the east, New York and a few spots in New England. It overflows into Canada only in the Carolinian forest, southeast Ontario, and the southwest corner of Quebec.

As the name implies, rock elm wood is hard, heavy, and strong — it is the hardest of the elms. It has traditionally been used for fuelwood and tool handles; the Plains tribes crafted their mortars and pestles with rock elm.

It earns its other name, cork elm, from its corky branchlets. The leaves are similar in shape to those of the other elms, but are smaller, and thick and firm. Its major difference lies in its form; rather than forking into the characteristic elm vase shape, rock elm has a straight, cylindrical trunk, with short horizontal or drooping branches. Rock elm is rarely planted as an ornamental.

In spring, the seeds are quickly cleaned up by gamebirds, songbirds, and a host of small rodents.

woe to the woodworker

All three elms are marketed simply as "elm." The wood is not in great demand by most woodworkers. Although it takes glue and nails well, the wood tends to shrink, warp, and twist when dried, and is very hard on cutting tools. It does, however, take on a handsome finish, and since it bends nicely with steam, it has found its way into chair rockers, arms, and backs.

At one time, elm was shaped into staves and hoops for dry-goods barrels, especially for containers intended to take substantial abuse, such as kegs of nails or nuts and bolts. Some elm wood was used for hockey-stick blades, pallets, crates, cheese boxes, and tool handles, but it was usually not the preferred wood.

Elm does not split easily. Most wagon wheel hubs, from those of dainty carriages and buggies, to farm vehicles, stage coaches, and the Conestoga covered wagons or prairie schooners that carried pioneers and their possessions across the continent, were crafted of elm sapwood. Since it does not deteriorate quickly underwater, wharves, piers, and docks were constructed of sturdy elm. Thin elm veneer was commonly used to make fruit baskets.

Glossary of Technical, Botanical, and Forestry Terms

alternate the arrangement of buds or leaves on a twig singly, on alternating sides of the twig (for example, ironwood, beech).

cambium the very thin living layer between the inner bark and the sapwood, whose cells divide and subdivide, creating growth in diameter.

catkins tassel-like clusters of tiny male or female flowers, usually developed in the fall on deciduous trees, which elongate and hang in the spring. Males release windborne pollen; fertilized females evolve into seed-bearing structures (for example, birches, hickories).

coarse woody debris fallen trees and branches decaying on the forest floor.

compound leaf a leaf composed of three or more leaflets on a common stalk attached to a twig; as opposed to a simple leaf (for example, walnut, hickory, Manitoba maple).

coniferous trees cone-bearing trees, with needles or scales that are retained from 2 to 13 years, thereby appearing "evergreen" (for example, pines, spruces). Tamarack is an exception. Also called softwoods or gymnosperms.

cultivar short definition for a tree or shrub variety cultivated by humans, not occurring naturally in the wild.

deciduous trees trees that shed all or most of their leaves in the fall, and regrow a new set in the spring (for example, willows, butternut). Also called broadleaf, hardwood, or angiosperm.

decoction a tea steeped from boiling water and the medicinal part of the tree (inner bark, leaf, bud, and so on).

dioecious trees or shrubs trees or shrubs that bear male flowers on some trees, and females on others. Naturally, only the females bear fruit (for example, red maple, aspens).

even-age(d) stand a forest stand in which all the trees, large and small, are roughly the same age, having originated after a disturbance (such as forest fire, clearcut, insect epidemic), natural reforestation of abandoned farmland, or a plantation.

heartwood the inner circle of wood in the trunk or branch whose tissue is no longer living, usually darker than the outer ring of sapwood.

highgrading harvesting only the larger or better quality trees in an even-aged stand, leaving the weaker, smaller, or genetically inferior trees. "Taking the best and leaving the rest."

inner bark living layer of tissues between the sapwood and the outer protective bark.

layering development of a new tree where a lower branch has contacted or is covered with soil and has taken root (for example, black spruce).

lenticels slightly raised horizontal, usually oval, pores on young, otherwise smooth bark and branches of many deciduous trees, used for gas exchange (for example, pin cherry, yellow birch).

lobed leaf a leaf with two or more indentations (for example, maples, oaks).

monoecious tree or shrub tree or shrub that bears both male and female flowers on the same plant (for example, pines, birches).

opposite the arrangement of buds or leaves in pairs on opposite sides of the twig (for example, maples, ashes).

perfect flower a flower that contains both male and female functional parts, usually insect-pollinated.

pH the measure of acidity or alkalinity, where 7 is neutral, below 7 is acid and above 7 is alkaline. In this book, the term usually applies to soils.

sapwood the outer ring of wood of the trunk or branch, composed of living tissues that transmit water and nutrients (sap) up from the roots, usually paler than the heartwood.

serotinous cone a cone that remains sealed tight when ripe, opening only when the seal is melted by extreme heat or fire (for example, jack pine).

shelterwood a harvesting system, usually undertaken in two or three stages over a period of years, whereby progressively more of the trees are cut, in order to protect or encourage natural regeneration of seedlings.

silviculture the art and science of planting, tending, and harvesting trees. Silviculture is to forestry what agriculture is to farming.

simple leaf a single undivided leaf structure attached to a twig by a stalk; as opposed to a compound leaf (for example, aspen, oak).

snag a standing dead tree, very important for many wildlife species.

stratification emulating nature by placing seeds in a moist medium, such as sand or peat, at a specific temperature and for a specific time, depending on the species, in order to break dormancy.

Bibliography

BOOKS

Books marked with an asterisk (*) are recommended reading, and would provide a good basic reference library on the subjects covered in this book.

Alden, H. A. *Hardwoods of North America*. USDA Forest Service Forest Products Laboratory General Technical Report FPL-GTR-83. Madison, WI (1995).

Anderson, H. W. et al. *A Silvicultural Guide for the Tolerant Hardwoods Working Group in Ontario*. Science and Technology Series Vol. 7. Forest Resources Group, Ontario Ministry of Natural Resources. Toronto (1990)

Assiniwi, B. *Survie en Forêt*. Les Éditions Leméac. Ottawa (1972).

Aubin, G. F. *A Proto-Algonquian Dictionary*. National Museum of Man Mercury Series, Canadian Ethnology Service Paper 29. Ottawa (1975).

Bailey, L. W. and E. Jack, *The Woods and Minerals of New Brunswick*. Fredericton, NB (1876).

Black, M. J. *Algonquin Ethnobotany: An Interpretation of Aboriginal Adaptation in Southwestern Quebec*. National Museum of Man Mercury Series, Canadian Ethnology Service Paper 65. Ottawa (1980).

Blakeslee, A. F. and C. D. Jarvis, *Northeastern Trees in Winter*. Dover. New York (1972).

* Blouin, G. *Weeds of the Woods — Small Trees and Shrubs of the Eastern Forest*. Goose Lane Editions. Fredericton, NB (1992).

*———. *Arbustes des Bois — La Flore Méconnue du Nouveau-Brunswick*. Service de Consultation Forestière, Ministère des Ressources Naturelles du Nouveau-Brunswick. Frédéricton, NB (1984).

Blouin, G. and R. Comeau, eds. *Clearcutting*. Forestry on the Hill Special Issue 2, Canadian Forestry Association. Ottawa (1991).

———. *Old Growth Forests*. Forestry on the Hill Special Issue 4, Canadian Forestry Association. Ottawa (1994).

Bond, W. K. et al. *Wetland Evaluation Guide*. North American Wetlands Conservation Council (Canada) Issues Paper 1992-1. Ottawa (1992).

Brown, H. P. and A. J. Panshin, *Commercial Timbers of the United States*. McGraw-Hill. New York (1940).

Browne, D. J. *Trees of America-Native and Foreign*. Harper & Bros. New York (1846).

Bruce, D. S. and C. J. Heeney. *A Silvicultural Guide to the Hard Maple, Yellow Birch and Hemlock Working Group in Ontario*. Ontario Ministry of Natural Resources. Toronto (1974).

Burns, G. P. and C. H. Otis, *The Trees of Vermont*. Vermont Agriculture Experiment Station Bulletin 94 (1915).

Caligiuri, E. *PFRA — 60 Years of Achievement*. Prairie Farm Rehabilitation Administration. Winnipeg (1995).

Cameron, D. A., ed. *Proceedings: White and Red Pine Symposium*. Canadian Forestry Service/ Ontario Ministry of Natural Resources O-P-6. Sault Ste. Marie, ON (1978).

Canadian Forest Service. *Proceedings: Jack Pine Symposium, Timmins, Ontario, 1983*. Canada-Ontario Joint Forestry Research Committee, O-P-12. Sault Ste. Marie, ON (1984)

Carleton, T. J. and R. W. Arnup. *Vegetation Ecology of Eastern White Pine and Red Pine Forests in Ontario*. Forest Landscape and Ecology Program Report 11. Ontario Forest Research Institute. Ontario Ministry of Natural Resources. Sault Ste. Marie, ON (1993).

Chamberlain, M. *Maliseet Vocabulary*. Harvard Cooperative Society. Cambridge, MA (1844).

Chapeskie, D. J. et al. *A Silvicultural Guide for the White Pine and Red Pine Working Groups in Ontario*. Science and Technology Series Vol. 6, Forest Resources Group, Ontario Ministry of Natural Resources. Toronto (1989).

Clément, D. *L'Ethnobotanique Montaignaise de Mingan*. Collection Nordicana, Centre d'Etudes Nordiques, Université Laval. Québec (1990).

Collingwood, G. H. and W. D. Brush. *Knowing Your Trees*. D. Butcher, rev. & ed. American Forestry Association. Washington, DC (1974).

Colton, C. *Tour of the American Lakes, and Among the Indians of the North-West Territory in 1830: Disclosing the Character and Prospects of the Indian Race*. Kennicat Press. Port Washington, NY (1972).

Conseil du Peuplier du Canada. *Le Peuplier au Service du Développement Social et Economique des Régions Rurales*. Compte Rendu de la Réunion Annuelle 1995. Québec Ministère des Ressources Naturelles. Chicoutimi, QC (1995).

Cooperative Extension Service, *Proceedings: National Northern White Cedar Conference*. Michigan State University. Escanaba, MI (1976).

Davis, C. and T. Meyer. *Field Guide to Tree Diseases of Ontario*. Canada Ontario Northern Development Agreement, Canadian Forest Service. Sault Ste. Marie, ON (1997).

DeGraaf, R. M. and G. M. Witman. *Trees, Shrubs and Vines for Attracting Birds*. University of Massachusetts Press. Amherst, MA (1979).

Densmore, F. *How Indians Use Wild Plants for Food, Medicine and Crafts*. 44th Annual Report of Bureau of American Ethnology, Washington (1926-27). Reprinted by Dover. New York (1974).

Denys, N. *Concerning the Ways of the Indians (1672)*. The Champlain Society. Toronto (1908).

* Dirr, M. A. *Manual of Woody Landscape Plants*, 5th edition, Stipes Publ. Champaign, IL (1998).

Dunster, J. and K. Dunster. *Dictionary of Natural Resources Management*. UBC Press. Vancouver (1996).

Emerson, G. B. *A Report on the Trees and Shrubs in the Forests of Massachusetts*. Vol. I & II, Little, Brown & Co. Boston (1875).

Entomological Society of Ontario. *Proceedings: White Pine Symposium*. Supplement to Vol. 116. Guelph, ON (1985).

* Erichsen-Brown, C. *Use of Plants for the Past 500 Years*. Breezy Creeks Press. Aurora, ON (1979).

* Farrar, J. L. *Trees in Canada*. Fitzhenry & Whiteside/Canadian Forest Service. Markham, ON (1995).

* Fernald, M. L. ed. *Gray's Manual of Botany*. 8th edition, American Book Co. New York (1950).

* Fernald, M. L., A. C. Kinsey and R. C. Rollins. *Edible Wild Plants of Eastern North America*. Harper & Row. New York (1958).

Flint, H. L. *Landscape Plants for Eastern North America*. John Wiley & Sons. New York (1997).

Folster, D. *The Great Trees of New Brunswick*. Canadian Forestry Association of New Brunswick (The Tree House). Fredericton, NB (1987).

Foster, S. *Forest Pharmacy — Medicinal Plants in American Forests*. Forest History Society. Durham, NC (1995).

* Fowells, H. A. *Silvics of Forest Trees of the United States*. USDA Forest Service Agriculture Handbook 271. Washington (1965).

George, M. and G. Haas. *Trees of Akwesasne*. Mohawk Council of Akwesasne (1999).

George, Chief Dan. *My Heart Soars*. Hancock House Publishers. Surrey, BC (1989).

* Gill, J. D. and W. M. Healy. *Shrubs and Vines for Northestern Wildlife*. USDA Forest Service General Technical Report NE-9. Upper Darby, PA (1974).

Gilmore, M. R. *Uses of Plants by the Indians of the Missouri River Region*. 33rd Annual Report of Bureau of American Ethnology, Washington (1919. Reprinted by University of Nebraska Press. Lincoln, NE (1991).

Graham, C. M., H. L. Farintosh and B. J. Graham, eds. *Proceedings: Larch Symposium — Potential for the Future — Toronto 1982*. Ontario Ministry of Natural Resources/University of Toronto (1983).

Grieve, M. *A Modern Herbal*. Vol I & II. Dover. New York (1971).

Gunther, R. T. ed. *The Greek Herbal of Dioscorides*. J. Goodyer, trans. Hafner Publ. New York (1959).

Hardin, J. W. and J. M. Arena. *Human Poisoning from Native and Cultivated Plants*. Duke University Press. Durham, NC (1974).

* Harlow, W. M. *Trees of the Eastern and Central United States and Canada*. Dover. New York (1957).

Harrison, H. H. *Eastern Birds' Nests*. Houghton Mifflin. Boston (1975).

Hedrick, U. P. ed. *Sturtevant's Edible Plants of the World*. Dover. New York (1972).

Heeney, C. J., J. A. Kemperman and G. Brown. *A Silvicultural Guide to the Aspen Working Group in Ontario*. Ontario Ministry of Natural Resources. Toronto (1980).

Hellson, J. C. *Ethnobotany of the Blackfoot Indians*. National Museum of Man Mercury Series, Canadian Ethnology Service Paper 19. Ottawa (1974).

Hennepin, Fr. L. *A New Discovery of a Vast Country in America (1698)*. R. G. Thwarts, ed. Coles Canadiana edition. Toronto (1974).

Henry, R. *Cayuga Thematic Dictionary*. Iroqraft. Ohsweken, ON (1988).

Herrick, J. W. *Iroquois Medical Botany*. Syracuse University Press. Syracuse, NY (1995).

Hildahl, B. and M. Benum. *Heritage Trees of Manitoba*. Manitoba Forestry Association. Winnipeg (1987).

Horton, K. W. and G. H. D. Bedell. *White and Red Pine Ecology, Silviculture and Management*. Bulletin 124, Forestry Branch, Canada Dept. Northern Affairs and National Resources. Ottawa (1960).

* Hosie, R. C. *Native Trees of Canada*. 7th edition. Canadian Forest Service. Ottawa (1969).

Howley, J. P. *The Beothuk or Red Indians*. Cambridge University Press, 1915. Facsimile edition by Coles Publishing Co. Ltd. Toronto (1980).

Hutchens, A. R. *Indian Herbalogy of North America*. Shambhala. Boston (1973).

* Johnson, D. et al. *Plants of the Western Boreal Forest & Aspen Parkland*. Lone Pine Publishing/Canadian Forest Service. Edmonton, AB (1995).

Johnson, E. P. *Flint and Feather*. The Musson Book Company Ltd., Toronto, 1912. Reprinted by Iroqrafts, Ohsweken, ON (1997).

Johnson, R. S. *Forests of Nova Scotia*. N. S. Dept. Lands and Forests/Four East Publ. Halifax, NS (1986).

Jones, G. N. *American Species of Amelanchier*. Illinois Biological Monographs, University of Illinois Press. Urbana, IL (1946).

Kimmins, H. *Balancing Act — Environmental Issues in Forestry*. UBC Press. Vancouver (1992).

Kindscher, K. *Medicinal Wild Plants of the Prairie: An Ethnobotanical Guide*. University Press of Kansas. Lawrence, KS (1992).

Krochmal, A. R., S. Walters and R. M. Doughty. *A Guide to the Medicinal Plants of Appalachia.* USDA Forest Service Research Paper NE-138. Upper Darby, PA (1969).

Lanthier, A. *Les Plantes Médicinales Canadiennes.* Éditions Paulines. Montréal (1977).

Larson, B. M. et al. *The Woodland Heritage of Southern Ontario.* Federation of Ontario Naturalists. Don Mills, ON (1999).

Larson, E. vH, ed. *Proceedings: Birch Symposium.* USDA Forest Service, Northeastern Forest Experiment Station. Upper Darby, PA (1969).

Lauriault, J. *Identification Guide to the Trees of Canada.* Fitzhenry & Whiteside. Markham, ON (1989).

LeClercq, Fr. C. *New Relations of Gaspesia, with the Customs and Religion of the Gaspesian Indians, 1691.* W. F. Ganong, trans. The Champlain Society. Toronto (1910).

Leighton, A. L. *Wild Plant Use by the Woods Cree (Nihithawak) of East-Central Saskatchewan.* National Museum of Man Mercury Series, Canadian Ethnology Service Paper 101. Ottawa (1985).

*Leopold, A. *A Sand County Almanac.* Oxford University Press, Ballantine Books edition. New York (1970).

Lewis, W. H. and M. P. F. Elvin-Lewis. *Medicinal Botany — Plants Affecting Man's Health.* John Wiley & Sons. Toronto (1977).

Lower, A. R. M. *The North American Assault on the Canadian Forest.* Ryerson Press. Toronto (1938).

* Marie-Victorin, Frère. *Flore Laurentienne,* 3rd edition, Université de Montréal Press. Montréal (1995).

Maini, J. S. and J. H. Cayford, eds. *Growth and Utilization of Poplars in Canada.* Forestry Branch, Dept. of Forestry and Rural Development Publ. 1205. Ottawa (1968).

* Martin, A. C., H. S. Zim and A. L. Nelson. *American Wildlife and Plants — A Guide to Wildlife Food Habits.* Dover. New York (1961).

McAskill, D. *Prince Edward Island Forest Wildlife Manual.* PEI Dept. Agriculture, Fisheries and Forestry. Charlottetown, PEI).

Medsger, O. P. *Edible Wild Plants.* MacMillan. New York (1940).

Meeker, J. E., J. E. Elias and J. A. Heim. *Plants Used by the Great Lakes Ojibwa.* Great Lakes Indian Fish and Wildlife Commission. Odonah, WI (1993).

Meyer, J. E. *The Herbalist.* Clarence Meyer. 1972.

Millspaugh, C. F. *American Medicinal Plants.* Dover. New York (1974).

Ministère de l'Energie et des Ressources du Québec. *Les Principaux Insectes Défoliateurs des Arbres du Québec.* Québec, QC (1979).

* Moerman, D. E. *Native American Ethnobotany.* Timber Press. Portland, OR (1998).

Muenscher, W. C. *Poisonous Plants of the United States.* MacMillan. New York (1957).

Muir, J. *The Wilderness World of John Muir.* E. W. Teale, ed. Houghton Mifflin. Boston (1954).

Muldrew, W. H. *Sylvan Ontario.* William Briggs. Toronto (1905).

Mullins, E. J. and T. S. McKnight. *Canadian Woods — Their Properties and Uses.* 3rd edition, University of Toronto Press. Toronto (1981).

Myren, D. T. ed. *Tree Diseases of Eastern Canada.* Natural Resources Canada, Canadian Forest Service, Science & Sustainable Development Directorate. Ottawa (1994).

New Brunswick Forest Research Advisory Council, *Proceedings: Larch Workshop, Fredericton, NB, 1986.* Fredericton, NB (1987).

* Peterson, R. T. *A Field Guide to the Birds East of the Rockies.* Houghton Mifflin. Boston (1980).

Polunin, N. *Botany of the Canadian Eastern Arctic — Part III: Vegetation and Ecology.* National Museum of Canada Bulletin 104, Biological Series 32. Ottawa (1948).

Rabesca, M. A. et al. *Traditional Dene Medicine.* Government of the Northwest Territories. Lac La Martre, NWT (1993-4).

Rand, S. T. *Dictionary of the Language of the Micmac Indians.* Nova Scotia Printing Co. Halifax, NS (1875).

Randall, C. E. and D. P. Edgerton, *Famous Trees.* USDA Misc. Publication 295. Washington, DC (1938).

Richardson, J. ed. *The Future of Fir.* Proceedings: Workshop on Management of Fir-Birch Forest in Newfoundland 1978. Canadian Forestry Service/Newfoundland Dept. Forestry and Agriculture. Grand Falls, NF (1979).

Robinson, F. C. *A Silvicultural Guide to the Black Spruce Working Group.* Ontario Ministry of Natural Resources, Forest Resources Group (1974).

Rogers, D. J. *Lakota Names and Traditional Uses of Native Plants by Sicangu (Brule) People in the Rosebud Area, South Dakota.* Rosebud Educational Society. St. Francis, SD (1980).

Rogers, J. E. *Trees Worth Knowing.* Doubleday, Page & Co. New York (1924).

Rose, A. H. and O. H. Lindquist. *Insects of Eastern Hardwood Trees.* Canadian Forest Service Technical Report 29. Ottawa (1982).

———. *Insects of Eastern Spruces, Fir and Hemlock.* Canadian Forest Service. Ottawa (1994).

Rose, A. H., O. H. Lindquist and K. Nystrom. *Insects of Eastern Larch, Cedar, and Juniper.* Canadian Forest Service. Ottawa (2000).

———. *Insects of Eastern Pines.* Canadian Forest Service. Ottawa (1999).

Rowe, J. S. *Forest Regions of Canada*. Dept. Fisheries and Environment, Canadian Forestry Service Publ. 1300. Ottawa (1972).

Ryan, A. G. *Native Trees and Shrubs of Newfoundland and Labrador*. Newfoundland Dept. of Tourism. St. John's, NF (1978).

* Sargent, C. S. *Manual of the Trees of North America*. (Vol. I & II). Dover. New York (1965).

Saunders, C. F. *Edible and Useful Wild Plants of the United States and Canada*. Dover. New York (1934).

Saunders, G. L. *Trees of Nova Scotia*. N. S. Dept. Lands and Forests. Halifax, NS (1970).

Scoggan, H. J. *The Flora of Canada*. (Vol I-IV), National Museum of Natural Sciences. Ottawa (1978).

Scott, J. D. *A Silvicultural Guide to the White Pine Working Group*. Ontario Ministry of Natural Resources (1983).

Selsam, M. E. *Tree Flowers*. William Morrow & Co. New York (1984).

Service Forestier du Canada, *Arbres Indigènes du Canada*. 2nd edition. Ottawa (1950).

Skinner, A. *Notes on the Eastern Cree and Northern Saulteaux*. American Museum of Natural History Anthropological Papers 9(1). New York (1911).

Smith, H. H. *Ethnobotany of the Menomini Indians*. Bulletin of the Public Museum of the City of Milwaukee 4(1). Milwaukee (1923).

———. *Ethnobotany of the Meskwaki Indians*. Bulletin of the Public Museum of the City of Milwaukee 4(2). Milwaukee (1928).

———. *Ethnobotany of the Ojibwe Indians*. Bulletin of the Public Museum of the City of Milwaukee 4(3). Milwaukee (1932).

———. *Ethnobotany of the Forest Potawatomi Indians*. Bulletin of the Public Museum of the City of Milwaukee 7(1) (1933).

* Soper, J. H. and M. L. Heimburger. *Shrubs of Ontario*. Royal Ontario Museum. Toronto (1982).

Speck, F. S. *Penobscot Man*. University of Pennsylvania Press. Philadelphia (1940).

———. *The Iroquois*. Cranbrook Institute of Science Bulletin 23. Bloomfield Hills, MI (1945).

Sternberg, G. and J. Wilson, *Landscaping with Native Trees — Northeast, Midwest, Midsouth and Southeast ed.* Chapters. Shelburne, VT (1995).

Stone, E. *Medicine Among the American Indians*. Hafner. New York (1962).

Thoreau, H. D. *Walden — and Other Writing of Henry David Thoreau*. Modern Library. New York (1937).

Tomikel, J. *Edible Wild Plants of Eastern United States and Canada*. Allegheny Press. California, PA (1976).

* Turner, N. J. and A. F. Szezawinski. *Edible Wild Fruits and Nuts of Canada*. National Museum of Natural Sciences. Ottawa (1979).

USDA. *Trees. The Yearbook of Agriculture*. Washington, DC (1949).

USDA Forest Service. *A Guide to Common Insects and Diseases of Forest Trees in the Northeastern United States*. Forest Insect and Disease Management, Northeastern Area, State and Private Forestry, NA-FR-4. Broomall, PA,1979).

———. *Wood Handbook: Wood as an Engineering Material*. Forest Products Laboratory, Agriculture Handbook 72. Washington, DC (1974).

———. *Seeds of Woody Plants in the United States*. Agriculture Handbook 450. Washington, DC (1974).

* Van Dersal, W. R. *Native Woody Plants of the United States — Their Erosion Control and Wildlife Values*. USDA Misc. Publication 303. Washington, DC (1939).

* Vogel, V. *American Indian Medicine*. University of Oklahoma Press. Norman, OK (1970).

Volney, W. J. A. et al. *Proceedings, Jack Pine Budworm Symposium: Jack Pine Budworm Biology and Management — Winnipeg, 1995*. Canadian Forest Service, North Central Info Report NOR-X-342 (1995).

Waldron, G. E. *The Tree Book*. Project Green. Windsor, ON (1997).

Walker, L. C. *Trees — An Introduction to Trees and Forest Ecology for the Amateur Naturalist*. Prentice-Hall. Englewood Cliffs, NJ (1984).

Wallis, W. D. and R. S. Wallis. *The Micmac Indians of Eastern Canada*. University of Minnesota Press. Minneapolis (1955).

Waugh, F. W. *Iroquois Foods and Food Preparation*. Canada Dept. Mines Mem. 86, Anthropological Series 12, 1916. Reprinted by Iroqraft. Ohsweken, ON (1991).

White, J. ed. *Handbook of Indians of Canada*. Geographic Board of Canada. C. H. Parmalee. Ottawa, 1913. Coles Canadiana edition (1971).

Wilson, B. F. *The Growing Tree*. University of Massachusetts Press. Amherst (1970).

Wilson, E. H. *Aristocrats of the Trees*. Stratford Co. Boston, 1930. Reprinted by Dover. New York (1974).

Wilson, R. W. Jr, and A. F. Hough, *A Selected and Annotated Bibliography of Eastern White Pine (Pinus strobus L.), 1890-1954*. USDA Forest Service Research Paper NE-44. Northeastern Forest Experiment Station (1966).

Wood, H. C. et al. *The Dispensatory of the United States of America*, 21st edition. J. P. Lippincott Co. Philadelphia (1926).

Yiesla, S. A. and F. A. Giles, *Shade Trees for the Central and Northern United States and Canada*. Stipes Publ. Champaign, IL (1992).

* Young, J. A. and C. G. Young, *Seeds of Woody Plants of North America*. Dioscorides Press. Portland, OR (1992).

PERIODICALS

For readers who wish to pursue further a particular aspect of the content of this book, following is a list of scientific and technical journal articles, federal, provincial and state reports, university publications, and papers presented at conferences.

Abou-Zaid, M. M., R. J. Marles and J. T. Arnason. Use of Historical Knowledge of Medicinal Plants Used by Northern Ontario First Nations People as a Guide to the Identification of New Bioactive Natural Products. Canadian Forest Service, Great Lakes Forestry Centre. (unpublished)

Adams, J. *Medicinal Plants and their Cultivation in Canada*. Dept. of Agriculture, Dominion Experimental Farms Bulletin 23 (1915).

Adney, E. T. "The Malecite Indian's Names for Native Berries and Fruits, and their Meanings." *Acadian Naturalist* 1 (3) (1944): 103–110.

Aird, P. L. *In Praise of Pine*. Canadian Forestry Service, National Forest Institute Info Report PI-X-52 (1985).

American Forests. *National Register of Big Trees 1998–99*. 104 (1) (1998): 24–45.

American Forests. *The National Register of Big Trees 2000*.

Archambault, S. and Y. Bergeron, "An 802-Year Tree-Ring Chronology from the Quebec Boreal Forest." *Canadian Journal of Forest Research* 22 (1992): 674–682.

Arnason, T., R. J. Hebda and T. Johns. "Use of Plants for Food and Medicine by Native peoples of Eastern Canada." *Canadian Journal of Botany* 59 (1981): 2189–2295.

Barnes, B. V. "The Clonal Growth Habit of American Aspens." *Ecology* 47 (3) (1966): 439–447.

Basham, J. T. *Trembling Aspen Quality in Northern Ontario: Various Aspects of Decay and Stain Studies and their Management Implications*. Forestry Canada, Great Lakes Forestry Centre Info Report O-X-21 (1993).

Baskerville, G. L. and W. C. Colvert. *An Exceptional Black Spruce Stand*. Canada Dept. Forestry and Rural Development, Maritimes Region Info Report M-X-13 (1967).

Beauchamp, W. M. "Onondaga Plant Names." *Journal of American Folk-lore* 15 (62) (1902): 91–103.

Bedard, J., M. Crête and E. Audy. "Short-Term Influence of Moose upon Woody Plants of an Early Seral Wintering Site in Gaspé Peninsula, Quebec." *Canadian Journal of Forest Research* 8 (1978): 407–415.

Behr, E. *How Durable is Northern White Cedar?* Cooperative Extension Service. Michigan State Univ. Extension Bulletin E-929 (1977).

Bender, F. *Canada Balsam: Its Preparation and Uses*. Canada Dept. Forestry and Rural Development, Forestry Branch Publication 1182 (1967).

Benedict, L. and R.. David. *Handbook for Black Ash Preservation Reforestation/Regeneration*. Mohawk Council of Akwesasne Dept. of Environment (2000).

Bergeron, Y. and D. Gagnon, "Age Structure of Red Pine (*Pinus resinosa* Ait.) at its Northern Limit in Quebec." *Canadian Journal of Forest Research* 17 (1987): 129–137.

Berry, E. W. "Notes on the History of the Willows and Poplars." *Plant World* 20 (1917): 16–28.

Blais, J. R. "Recurrence of Spruce Budworm Outbreaks for Two Hundred Years in Western Quebec." *Forestry Chronicle* 57 (Dec. 1981): 273–275.

Blouin, G. *Manitoba Maple: An Untapped Resource*. Canada-Saskatchewan Partnership Agreement in Forestry (1992).

Bowers, W. W. and A. Hopkin. *ARNEWS and North American Maple Project (NAMP)*. Canadian Forest Service Info Report ST-X-14, Natural Resources Canada (1997).

Bragg, D. C. et al. "Relationship Between "Birdseye" Sugar Maple (*Acer saccharum*) Occurrence and Its Environment." *Canadian Journal of Forest Research* 27 (1997): 1182–1191.

Bragg, D. C. "The Birdseye Figured Grain in Sugar Maple (*Acer saccharum*): Literature Review, Nomenclature, and Structural Characteristics." *Canadian Journal of Forest Research* 29 (1999): 1637–1648.

Bragg, D. C. and D. D. Stokke. *Field Identification of Birdseye In Sugar Maple*. USDA Forest Service, North Central Forest Experiment Station Research Paper NC-317 (1994).

Brooks, H. "The Medicine of the American Indian." *Bulletin of New York Academy of Medicine* 2 (5) (1929): 509–537.

Brown, C. P. "Food of Maine Ruffed Grouse by Seasons and Cover Types." *Journal of Wildlife Management* 10 (1) (1946): 17–28.

Burns, B. S. and D. R. Houston. "Managing Beech Bark Disease: Evaluating Defects and Reducing Losses." *Northern Journal of Applied Forestry* 4 (1987): 28–33.

Canadian Wildlife Service. *Hinterland Who's Who* series. Environment Canada.

Cantin, M. *Machining Properties of 16 Eastern Canadian Woods*. Canada Dept. Forestry Publication 1111 (1965).

Carmody, C., ed. *Alien Forest Pests*. Canadian Forest Service, Natural Resources Canada (1999).

Carr, L. G. and C. Westez. "Surviving Folktales and Herbal Lore Among the Shinnecook Indians of Long Island." *Journal of American Folk-lore* 58 (1945): 117–123.

Cayford, J. H. *Influence of the Aspen Overstory on White Spruce Growth in Saskatchewan*. Canada Dept. of Northern Affairs and National Resources Forestry Branch, Forest Research Division Technical Note 58 (1957).

Chamberlain, L.S. "Plants Used by the Indians of Eastern North America." *American Naturalist* 35 (409) (1901): 1–10.

Chandler, R. F., L. Freeman, and S. N. Hooper. "Herbal Remedies of the Maritime Indians." *Journal of Ethnopharmacology* 1 (1979): 49–68.

Christian, D. P. et al. "Bird and Small Mammal Use of Short-Rotation Hybrid Poplar Plantations." *Journal of Wildlife Management* 61 (1) (1997): 171–182.

Cook, D. B. and F. C. Edminster. "Survival and Growth of Shrubs Planted for Wildlife in New York." *Journal of Wildlife Management* 8 (1944): 185–191.

COSEWIC. *Canadian Species at Risk*. Committee on the Status of Endangered Wildlife in Canada, (1999).

Cowardin, L. M., G. F. Cummings, and P. B. Reed. "Stump and Tree Nesting by Mallards and Black Ducks." *Journal of Wildlife Management* 31 (2) (1967): 229–237.

Crichton, V. "Autumn and Winter Foods of the Spruce Grouse in Central Ontario." *Journal of Wildlife Management* 27 (1963): 597.

Curtis, J. D. "Northern White Cedar on Upland Soils in Maine." *Journal of Forestry* 42 (1944): 756–759.

Curtis, J. D. "Preliminary Observations on Northern White Cedar in Maine." *Ecology* 27 (1) (1946): 23–34.

Davidson, W. H. *Results of Tree and Shrub Plantings on Low pH Strip-Mine Banks*. USDA Forest Service Research Note NE-285 (1979).

Day, G. M. "The Indian as an Ecological Factor in the Northeastern Forest." *Ecology* 34 (2) (1953): 329–346.

DeGraaf, R. M. and A. L. Shigo. *Managing Cavity Trees for Wildlife in the Northeast*. USDA Forest Service General Technical Report NE-108 (1986).

DeWolf, G. "Shad Bush." *Horticulture* (May 1982): 22–23.

Dendron Resource Surveys Inc. *Distribution and Abundance of Pitch Pine in Ontario*. Ontario Ministry of Natural Resources, Southern Ontario Science & Technology Unit Info Report IR-005 (1995).

Doucet, R. *La Culture de la Tremblaie*. Québec Ministère de l'Énergie et des Ressources ERI-4401-2C (1981).

Drinkwater, M. H. *Field Spruce in Nova Scotia*. Canada Dept. Northern Affairs and National Resources, Forestry Branch, Forest Research Division Technical Note 65 (1957).

Edlund, S. A. and P.A. Egginton. "Morphology and Description of an Outlier Population of Tree-Sized Willows on Western Victoria Island, District of Franklin." In *Current Research, Part A, Geological Survey of Canada* Paper 84-1A (1984): 274–285.

Fayle, D. C. F. "Sugar Maple, Black Spruce and Tamarack Do Not Reproduce Vegetatively from Roots." *Forestry Chronicle* 72 (8) (1996): 283–285.

Fenton, W. F. *Contacts Between Iroquois Herbalism and Colonial Medicine*. Annual Report, Smithsonian Institution (1941): 503–526, Facsimile Reproduction, Shorey Book Store, Seattle, WA (1971).

Fernald, M. L. "Lithological Factors Limiting the Ranges of *Pinus banksiana* and *Thuja occidentalis*." *Rhodora* 21 (243) (1919): 41–67.

Fitzgerald, C. H., R. P. Belanger, and W. W. Lester. "Characteristics and Growth of Natural Green Ash Stands." *Journal of Forestry* 73 (8) (1975): 486–488.

Fowler, D. P. and D. T. Lester. *The Genetics of Red Pine*. USDA Forest Service Research Paper WO-8 (1970).

Fox, K. and M. George. *Traditional Medicines*. Mohawk Council of Akwesasne (undated).

Freedman, B. "Environmental Impacts of Hardwood Forest Management in Atlantic Canada." In Canadian Forest Service Info Report M-X-138 (1982).

Frothingham, E. H. *White Pine Under Forest Management*. USDA Forest Service Bulletin 13 (1914).

Gatschet, A. S. "Micmac Fans and Games." *Bulletin of the Museum of Science and Art* 2 (3) (1900): 1–5.

Goldsmith, F. B. and J. C. Lees. "Regeneration and Management of White Ash in Nova Scotia and New Brunswick." *Forestry Chronicle* 58 (Feb. 1982): 35–39.

Goodell, E. "Walnuts for the Northeast." *Arnoldia* 44 (1984): 1–19.

Gross, H. L. "Crown Deterioration and Reduced Growth Associated with Excessive Seed Production in Birch." *Canadian Journal of Botany* 50 (1972): 2431–2437.

Hadlock, W. S. "The Significance of Certain Textiles Found at Redbank, New Brunswick, in Relation to the History of the Culture Area." *Acadian Naturalist* 2 (8) (1947): 49–62.

Halliday, W. E. D. and A. W. A. Brown. "The Distribution of Some Important Forest Trees in Canada." *Ecology* 24 (3) (1943): 353–373.

Hamilton, W. J. Jr. "Notes on Food of Red Foxes in New York and New England." *Journal of Mammalogy* 16 (1935): 16–21.

———. "Seasonal Food of Skunks in New York." *Journal of Mammalogy* 17 (1936): 240–246.

Hart, A. C. *Silvical Characteristics of Red Spruce (Picea rubens).* USDA Forest Service, Northeastern Forest Experiment Station Paper 124 (1959).

Hawboldt, L. S. "History of Spread of the Beech Scale, *Cryptococcus fagi (Baeren sprung)*, An Insect Introduced into the Maritime Provinces." *Acadian Naturalist* 1 (4) (1944): 137–146.

Hay, G. U. "A Glance at Forest Conditions in New Brunswick." *Canadian Forestry Journal,* Canadian Forestry Association (Jan. 1905): 23–27.

Heimburger, C. "The Evolution of Black Spruce." In Proceedings, 19th Meeting, Canadian Tree Improvement Association (1983): 163–166.

Henkel, A. *American Medicinal Barks.* USDA Bureau of Plant Industry Bulletin 139 (1909).

———. *American Medicinal Flowers, Fruits, and Seeds.* USDA Bureau of Plant Industry Bulletin 26 (1913).

———. *Wild Medicinal Plants of the United States.* USDA Bureau of Plant Industry Bulletin 89 (1906).

Henry, D. G. *Foliar Nutrient Concentrations of Some Minnesota Forest Species.* Minnesota Forestry Research Note 241. University of Minnesota (1973).

Hirth, H. F. "Small Mammals in Old Field Succession." *Ecology* 40 (3) (1959): 417–425.

Hoffman, W. J. *The Mide'wiwin or "Grand Medicine Society" of the Ojibway.* 7th Annual Report, Bureau of Ethnology, Smithsonian Institution (1891): 149–300.

Hosley, N. W. and R. K. Ziebarth. "Some Winter Relations of the White-Tailed Deer in the Forests of North Central Massachusetts." *Ecology* 16 (4) (1935): 535–553.

Hough, A. F. *Silvical Characteristics of Black Cherry (Prunus serotina).* USDA Forest Service, Northeastern Forest Experiment Station Paper 139 (1960).

———. *Silvical Characteristics of Eastern Hemlock (Tsuga canadensis).* USDA Forest Service, Northeastern Forest Experiment Station Paper 132, 1960.

Howard, C. D. "Prussic Acid in Wild Cherry Leaves." *New Hampshire Agricultural Experiment Station Bulletin* 56 (1898): 112–123.

Hsu, W. E. "Products Made with Poplar Wood and Future Trends." *Le Peuplier au Service du Developpement Social et Economique des Regions Rurales.* Comtes Rendus de la Reunion Annuelle du Conseil du Peuplier du Canada (1995): 25–31.

Hubbes, M. "The American Elm and Dutch Elm Disease." *Forestry Chronicle* 75 (2) (1999): 265–273.

Hunter, M. L. Jr. "What Constitutes an Old-Growth Stand?" *Journal of Forestry* 87 (8) (1989): 33–35.

Hutnik, R. J. and F. E. Cunningham. *Silvical Characteristics of Paper Birch (Betula papyrifera).* USDA Forest Service, Northeastern Forest Experiment Station Paper 141 (1961).

Hyvarinen, M. J. *Paper Birch: Its Characteristics, Properties, and Uses.* USDA Forest Service Research Paper NC-22 (1968).

Irland, L. C. "White Pine: The Case for Optimism." In Proceedings, *Eastern White Pine: Today and Tomorrow.* USDA Forest Service General Technical Report WO-51 (1986): 1–6.

Iverson, H. J. *Short Rotation Hybrid Poplar Production.* Paper presented at First Biomass Conference of the Americas. Burlington, VT (1993).

Jenkins, C. F. "Hemlock: Queen of the Conifers." *Arnoldia* 6 (1946): 49–60.

Jones, J. R. and D. C. Markstrom. *Aspen... An American Wood.* USDA Forest Service FS-217 (1973).

Kalcounis, M. C. and R. M. Brigham. "Secondary Use of Aspen Cavities by Tree-Roosting Big Brown Bats." *Journal of Wildlife Management* 62 (2): 603–611.

Kallio, E. and R. M. Godman. *American Basswood...An American Wood.* USDA Forest Service FS-219, (1973).

Kallio, E. and C. H. Tubbs. *Sugar Maple... An American Wood.* USDA Forest Service FS-246 (1980).

Kelly, P. E., E. R. Cook and D. W. Larson. "A 1397-Year Tree-Ring Chronology of *Thuja occidentalis* from Cliff Faces of the Niagara Escarpment, Southern Ontario, Canada." *Canadian Journal of Forest Research* 24 (1994): 1049–1057.

Kenney, W. A. "The Role of *Salicaceae* Species in Windbreaks." *Forestry Chronicle* 68 (2) (1992): 209–213.

Kerr, R. "A Report of the Trees, Shrubs, and Plants Used by the Indians of Upper Canada as Medicine, and for the Purpose of Dying, etc.: With Their Indian Names." Art. VII (1823): 200–205.

Kidd, R. P. and M. R. Koelling. *Aspen Management in Michigan.* Michigan State University Cooperative Extension Service Bulletin E-1552 (1981).

King, R. T. "Ruffed Grouse Management." *Journal of Forestry* 35 (1937): 523–532.

Korstian, C. F. "The Indicator Significance of Native Vegetation in the Determination of Forest Sites." *Plant World* 20 (9) (1917): 267–287.

Kort, J. and P. Michiels. "Maple Syrup From Manitoba Maple (*Acer negundo L.*) on the Canadian Prairies." *Forestry Chronicle* 73 (3) (1997): 327–330.

Krefting, L. W. and E. I. Roe. "The Role of Some Birds and Mammals in Seed Germination." *Ecological Monographs* 19 (3) (1949): 271–286.

Kristensen, D. *An Assessment of the Songbird Habitat Quality Provided by Red Pine Plantations in Eastern Ontario.* Eastern Ontario Model Forest Info Report 25 (1996).

Lachance, D. et al. *Health of Sugar Maple in Canada.* Canadian Forest Service Info Report ST-X-10 (1995).

Laflamme, G. *Scleroderris Canker on Pine.* Forestry Canada, Quebec Region, Info Leaflet LFC-3 (1991).

Lamb, G. N. *Willows: Their Growth, Use, and Importance.* USDA Forest Service Bulletin 316 (1915).

Lancaster, K. F. and W. B. Leak. *A Silvicultural Guide for White Pine in the Northeast.* USDA Forest Service, Northeastern Forest Experiment Station Technical Report NE-41 (1978).

Lanteigne, L. J. "Cutover Response of a Fir-Spruce Stand in Central New Brunswick." In Proceedings, 67th Annual Meeting Woodlands Section, Canadian Pulp & Paper Association. Montréal (1986): 17–20.

Larson, D. W. and P. E. Kelly. "The Extent of Old-Growth *Thuja occidentalis* on Cliffs of the Niagara Escarpment." *Canadian Journal of Botany* 69 (1991): 1628–1636.

Larson, D. W., U. Matthes, and P. E. Kelly. "Cliffs as Natural Refuges." *American Scientist* (Sept./Oct. 1999): 411–417.

Lavallée, A. *La Maladie Corticale du Hêtre: Dix Ans d'Existence au Québec.* Can. Centre Rech. For. Laurentides. Rapp. Inf. LAU-X-21 (1976).

Lavallée, R., G. Bonneau, and C. Coulombe. *Mechanical and Biological Control of the White Pine Weevil.* Natural Resources Canada, Canadian Forest Service, Laurentian Forestry Centre, Info Leaflet LFC 28 (1997).

Lees, J. C. "Adding Value to Woodlot Products: Maritime Maple." *Forestry Chronicle* 70 (3) (1994): 268–272.

Lees, J. C., ed. *Fuel or Fibre.* Canadian Forest Service Info Report M-X-138 (1982).

Longnecker, G. W. and R. Ellarson. *Landscape Plants that Attract Birds.* University of Wisconsin (1960).

MacLean, D. A. and P. Ebert. "The Impact of Hemlock Looper (*Lambdina fiscellaria (Guen.)*) on Balsam Fir and Spruce in New Brunswick, Canada." Forest Ecology and Management 120 (1999): 77–87.

Magasi, L. P. and W. R. Newell. "The Status of Beech Bark Disease in the Maritime Provinces of Canada." In Proceedings, IUFRO Beech Bark Disease Working Party Conference. USDA Forest Service, Northeastern Forest Experiment Station (1983): 13–17.

Magasi, L. P. et al. *Three Decades of Dutch Elm Disease in Fredericton, NB: 1961–1990.* Natural Resources Canada Info Report M-X-185 E (1993).

Maini, J. S. "Silvics and Ecology of Populus in Canada." In Proceedings, *Growth and Utilization of Poplars in Canada.* Dept. of Forestry and Rural Development Forestry Branch Publ. 1205 (1968): 20–69.

Manley, S. A. M. *Identification of Red, Black, and Hybrid Spruces.* Canadian Forestry Service Publication 1301 (1971).

Marks, P. L. "The Role of Pin Cherry (*Prunus pensylvanica L.*) in the Maintenance of Stability in Northern Hardwood Ecosystems." *Biological Monographs* 44 (1974): 73–78.

Matheson, J. D. and D. W. Larson. "Influence of Cliffs on Bird Community Diversity." *Canadian Journal of Zoology* 76 (2) (1998): 278–287.

Mautz, W. W. et al. "Digestibility and Related Nutritional Data for Seven Northern Deer Browse Species." *Journal of Wildlife Management* 40 (4) (1976): 630–637.

Maxwell, H. *Uses of Commercial Woods of the United States: Beech, Birches, and Maples.* USDA Bulletin 12 (1913).

McAtee, W. L. *Groups of Plants Valuable for Wildlife Utilization and Erosion Control.* USDA Circular 412 (1936).

———. *How to Attract Birds in Northeastern United States.* USDA Farmers' Bulletin 621 (1914).

McKay, S. M. "A Biosystematic Study of the Genus Amelanchier in Ontario." Masters thesis. University of Toronto, 1973.

Mechling, W. H. "Malecite Indians, with Notes on the Micmacs." *Anthropologica* 8 (1959): 239–274.

Megill, W. S. "Potash in Canada's Past and Saskatchewan's Present." *Canadian Geographic Journal* 68 (6) (1964): 178–187.

Miles, M. L. and E. C. Smith. "A Study of the Origin of Hemlock Forests in Southwestern Nova Scotia." *Forestry Chronicle* 36 (Dec. 1960): 375–392.

Mills, A. A. "Canada Balsam." *Annals of Science* 48 (1991): 173–185.

Moore, M. I. "Eastern White Pine and Eastern White Cedar." *Forestry Chronicle* 54 (Aug. 1978): 222–223.

Morley, P. M. "Management and Use of Aspen Poplar in North America." *Forestry Chronicle* 62 (April 1986): 104–107.

Morley, P. M. and J. J. Blatinecz. *Trends and Prospects in Poplar Utilization in Canada.* Poplar Council of Canada (1991).

Morton, J. F. "Principal Wild Food Plants of the United States." *Economic Botany* 17 (1962): 319–330.

Naylor, B. J. "Managing Wildlife Habitat in Red Pine and White Pine Forests of Central Ontario." *Forestry Chronicle* 70 (4) (1994): 411–419.

Nealis, V.G. "Population Dynamics of the White Pine Weevil, *Pissodes strobi*, Infecting Jack Pine, *Pinus banksiana*, in Ontario, Canada." *Ecological Entomology* 23 (1998): 305–313.

Ostry, M. E., M. E. Mielke and D. D. Skilling. *Butternut: Strategies for Managing a Threatened Tree.* USDA Forest Service, North Central Forest Experiment Station General Technical Report NC-165 (1994).

Palmer, E. "Plants Used by the Indians of the United States." *American Naturalist* 12 (1878): 593–606, 646–655.

Paquet, Bruno. "Les Frênes." *Forêt Conservation* (July/Aug. 1989): 8–9.

Park, B. C. "The Yield and Persistence of Wildlife Food Plants." *Journal of Wildlife Management* 6 (2) (1942): 118–121.

Pease, J. L., R. H. Vowles and L. B. Keith. "Interaction of Snowshoe Hares and Woody Vegetation." *Journal of Wildlife Management* 43 (1) (1979): 43–60.

Piene, H. "Spruce Budworm Defoliation: Foliage Production: Difference Between White Spruce and Balsam Fir." In Proceedings, *Population Dynamics, Impacts, and Integrated Management of Forest Defoliating Insects.* Banska Stiavnica, Slovak Republic (1996). USDA Forest Service General Technical Report NE-247 (1998): 247–252.

Powell, G. R. "'Fall' in the Forest." *UNB Forestry Focus* 5(4) (1980).

Powell, G. R.. "Seedfall Studies in Red Spruce." *Forestry Chronicle* 51 (2) (1975): 55–58.

Randall, C. E. and D. P. Edgerton. *Famous Trees.* USDA Miscellaneous Publication 295 (1938).

Read, R. A. and L. C. Walker. "Influence of Eastern Red Cedar on Soil in Connecticut Pine Plantations." *Journal of Forestry* 48(8) (1950): 337–339.

Reagan, A. B. "Some Chippewa Medicinal Receipts." *American Anthropologist* 23 (1921): 246–249.

Reiners, W. A. and N. M. Reiners. "Energy and Nutrient Dynamics of Forest Floors in Three Minnesota Forests." *Journal of Ecology* 58 (1970): 497–579.

Remphrey, W. R.. "Use of Woody Plants in the Prairie Landscape: A History." *Prairie Landscape* (Aug./Sept. 1999): 6–8.

Rogers, R. S. "Forests Dominated by Hemlock (*Tsuga canadensis*): Distribution as Related to Site and Postsettlement History." *Canadian Journal of Botany* 56 (1978): 843–854.

Safford, L. O. *Silvicultural Guide for Paper Birch in the Northeast.* USDA Forest Service, Northeastern Forest Experiment Station Research Paper NE-535 (1983).

Saint-Laurent, F. "Bois Précieux." *Géographica* (Sept./Oct. 1998): 14–17.

Schroeder, J. G. *Butternut...An American Wood.* USDA Forest Service FS-223 (1972).

Schulman, E. "Bristlecone Pine, Oldest Known Living Thing." *National Geographic* 113 (1958): 355–368.

Scott, M. and P. G. Murphy. "Regeneration Patterns of Northern White Cedar, an Old-Growth Forest Dominant." *American Midland Naturalist* 117 (1) (1987): 10–16.

Seigler, D. S. "Plants of the Northeastern United States that Produce Cyanogenic Compounds." *Economic Botany* 30 (1975): 395–407.

Sievers, A. F. *American Medicinal Plants of Commercial Importance.* USDA Misc. Publication 77 (1930).

Sinclair, S. A. and R. L. Govett. "Production and Distribution of Balsam Fir Lumber in Eastern North America." *Forestry Chronicle* 59 (June 1983): 128–131.

Skinner, W. R. "Spring, Summer and Fall Foods of the White-Tailed Deer." Masters thesis. Univ. of New Brunswick, 1968.

Spalding, V. M. and B. E. Fernow. *The White Pine* (Pinus strobus Linnaeus). USDA Division of Forestry Bulletin 22 (1899).

Speck, F. G. "Medicine Practices of the Northeastern Algonquians." XIX International Congress of Americanists. University of Pennsylvania (1917): 303–321.

Speck, F. G. and R. W. Dexter. "Utilization of Animals and Plants by the Micmac Indians of New Brunswick." *Journal of Washington Academy of Sciences* 41 (8) (1951): 250–259.

———. "Utilization of Animals and Plants by the Malecite Indians of New Brunswick." *Journal of Washington Academy of Sciences* 42 (1) (1952): 1–7.

Steill, W. M. "Silviculture of Eastern White Pine." In Proceedings, Entomological Society of Ontario 116 (1985): 95-107.

Steneker, G. A. "Factors Affecting the Suckering of Trembling Aspen." *Forestry Chronicle* 50 (Feb. 1974): 32–34.

———. *Guide to the Silvicultural Management of Trembling Aspen in the Prairie Provinces.* Environment Canada Forestry Service, Northern Forest Research Centre Info Report NOR-X-164 (1976).

Sutton, R. F. *Silvics of White Spruce.* Canada Dept. Fisheries and Forestry, Forestry Branch Publication 1250 (1969).

Svoboda, F. J. and G. W. Gullion. "Preferential Use of Aspen by Ruffed Grouse in Northern Minnesota." *Journal of Wildlife Management* 36 (4) (1972): 1167–1179.

Syme, P. D. *Red Pine and the European Pine Shoot Moth in Ontario.* Environment Canada, Canadian Forestry Service Report O-X-244 (1976).

Tantaquidgeon, G. "Notes on the Origin and Uses of Plants of the Lake St. John Montagnais." *Journal of American Folk-lore* 45 (1932): 265–267.

Treichler, R., R. W. Stow, and A. L. Nelson. "Nutrient Content of Some Winter Foods of Ruffed Grouse." *Journal of Wildlife Management* 10 (1) (1946): 12–17.

Truscott, J. H. L. et al. *A Survey of the Ascorbic Acid Content of Fruits, Vegetables, and Some Native Plants Grown in Ontario, Canada.* Dept. of National Health and Welfare (undated).

Tubbs, C. H. et al. *Guide to Wildlife Tree Management in New England Northern Hardwoods.* USDA Forest Service General Technical Report NE-118 (1987).

Tyrell, L. E. and T. R. Crow. "Structural Characteristics of Old-Growth Hemlock — Hardwood Forests in Relation to Age." *Ecology* 75 (2) (1994): 370–386.

USDA. *Slippery Elm.* USDA Forest Service Circular 85 (April 1907).

———. *What's Known About Managing Eastern White Pine.* USDA Forest Service Station Paper 121, Northeastern Forest Experiment Station (1959).

———. *White Ash (*Fraxinus americana*).* USDA Forest Service Circular 84 (1907).

Van Wart, A. F. "The Indians of the Maritime Provinces, Their Diseases and Native Cures." *Canadian Medical Association Journal* 59 (1948): 573–577.

Vincent, A. B. *Black Spruce: A Review of its Silvics, Ecology, and Silviculture.* Canada Dept. Forestry Publication 1100 (1965).

Wainio, W. and E. B. Forbes. "The Chemical Composition of Forest Fruits and Nuts from Pennsylvania." *Journal of Agricultural Research* 62 (10) (1941): 627–635.

Wall, R. E. "Effects of Black Knot Disease on Pin Cherry." *Canadian Journal of Plant Pathology* 8 (1986): 71–77.

Wallis, W. D. "Medicines Used by the Micmac Indians." *American Anthropologist* 24 (1922): 24–30.

Wallis, W. D. and R. S. Wallis. *The Malecite Indians of New Brunswick.* National Museum of Canada Bulletin 148 Anthropological Series 40 (1957): 27–54.

Waugh, F. W. "Wild Plants as Food." *The Ottawa Naturalist* (April 1918): 2–5.

Webb, F. E. and H. J. Irving. "My Fir Lady: The New Brunswick Production with its Facts and Fancies." *Forestry Chronicle* 59 (June 1983): 118–122.

Wellwood, R. W. "The Utilization of Spruce in Canada." *Forestry Chronicle* 36 (June 1960): 126–135.

Wentling, J. P. *Woods Used for Packing Boxes in New England.* USDA Forest Service Circular 78 (1907).

Westveld, M. "Ecology and Silviculture of the Spruce-Fir Forests of Eastern North America." *Journal of Forestry* 51 (1953).

Wiegand, K. M. "The Genus *Amelanchier* in Eastern North America." *Rhodora* 14 (1912): 117–161.

———. "Additional Notes on *Amelanchier.*" *Rhodora* 22 (1920): 146–151.

Wight, W. F. *Native American Species of Prunus.* USDA Bureau of Plant Industry Bulletin 179 (1915).

Wilde, S. A. "Soil-Fertility Standards for Game Food Plants." *Journal of Wildlife Management* 10 (2) (1946): 77–81.

Wilson, R. W. Jr. and W. E. McQuilkin. *Silvical Characteristics of Eastern White Pine (*Pinus strobus*).* USDA Forest Service, Northeastern Forest Experiment Station Research Paper NE-13 (1963).

Winget, C. H. "Species Composition and Development of Small-Growth Hardwood Stands in Québec." *Forestry Chronicle* 44 (6) (1968): 31–35.

Witzke, C. *Pitch Pine (*Pinus rigida *Miller): Genetics, Reproduction, and Silvicultural Management.* Eastern Ontario Model Forest Info Report 31 (1996).

Woodcock, J. et al. "Indirect Effects of Conifer Release Alternatives on Songbird Populations in Northwestern Ontario." *Forestry Chronicle* 73 (1) (1997): 107–112.

Wright, J. W. *Silvical Characteristics of Green Ash.* USDA Forest Service, Northeastern Forest Experiment Station Paper 126 (1959).

———. *Silvical Characteristics of White Ash.* USDA Forest Service, Northeastern Forest Experiment Station Paper 123 (1959).

Yang, R. C. "Growth of White Spruce Following Release from Aspen Competition: 35 Year Results." *Forestry Chronicle* 67 (6) (1991): 706–711.

Yanovsky, E. *Food Plants of the North American Indian.* USDA Miscellaneous Bulletin 237 (1936).

Youngken, H. W. "The Drugs of the North American Indian." *American Journal of Pharmacy & the Sciences Supporting Public Health* 96 (1924): 485–502.

Youngken, H. W. "The Drugs of the North American Indians." *American Journal of Pharmacy & the Sciences Supporting Public Health* 97 (1925): 158–267, 257–271.

Zarnovican, R. *Precommercial Thinning in a Young Sugar Maple-Yellow Birch Stand: Results after 10 Years.* Natural Resources Canada, Laurentian Forestry Centre Info Report LAU-X-123E (1998):